Basics *of* Hebrew Discourse

A Guide to Working with Biblical Hebrew Prose and Poetry

Matthew H. Patton
Frederic Clarke Putnam
Edited by
Miles V. Van Pelt

ZONDERVAN ACADEMIC

ZONDERVAN ACADEMIC

Basics of Hebrew Discourse

ISBN 978-0-310-53576-8 (softcover)

Requests for information should be addressed to:
Zondervan, *3900 Sparks Dr. SE, Grand Rapids, Michigan 49546*

Cover design: Joel Shoemacher
Interior design: Kait Lamphere

Printed in the United States of America

HB 01.24.2024

To Howard Marblestone,
Hebrew teacher, beloved friend, and a true philologist

צְרוּפָה אִמְרָתְךָ מְאֹד וְעַבְדְּךָ אֲהֵבָהּ׃

PSALM 119:140

To Emilie

רַבּוֹת בָּנוֹת עָשׂוּ חָיִל וְאַתְּ עָלִית עַל־כֻּלָּנָה׃

PROVERBS 31:29

וִיהִי נֹעַם אֲדֹנָי אֱלֹהֵינוּ עָלֵינוּ וּמַעֲשֵׂה יָדֵינוּ כּוֹנְנָה עָלֵינוּ
וּמַעֲשֵׂה יָדֵינוּ כּוֹנְנֵהוּ׃

"And may the favor of the Lord our God be upon us;
and the work of our hands establish for us;
and the work of our hands, establish it."

PSALM 90:17

Contents

Acknowledgments

Matthew thanks Gerry Wheaton for inviting him to teach on Hebrew discourse analysis in Costa Rica. His invitation and the curiosity of his students set Matthew on the trajectory that culminated in this book. His doctoral advisor, Dan Block, showed how vital this topic is for exegesis, and Bob Cohn, Shawn Goodwin, Richard Schultz, Charlie Trimm, and Carmen Imes all offered many valuable suggestions on this work. Matthew's wife, Trina, and the elders at Covenant Presbyterian Church in Vandalia, OH, have been so supportive in the long process of publication. Matthew is grateful for Nancy Erickson's unfailing encouragement in this project and for Miles graciously including him in it. It is an honor to work with Fred, who was one of his first Hebrew teachers. With fond memory of many hours reading biblical languages together he dedicates this book to the memory of his first Hebrew teacher, Howard Marblestone.

Fred thanks Dr. Jonathan Yonan, former dean of the Templeton Honors College at Eastern University, the Agora Institute for Civic Virtue and the Common Good, and Dr. Robert Schuettinger, founder and president of the Oxford Studies Abroad Programme (OSAP), whose generosity jointly made possible the study leave that contributed much to this work. He also thanks the library staff at Biblical Seminary in Hatfield, PA, for allowing him a private space for study, his students Emmalee Moffitt and Micah Skinner for their thoughtful comments, and Meredith Castor for her editorial help. He is especially grateful to his collaborators, Miles and Matthew, for their patience, helpful comments, and corrections, although he alone is accountable for his errors. As always, his greatest thanks are to his wife, Emilie, for putting up with his physical and mental absence and for her unflagging support, encouragement, and prayers. Without her he could not.

Introduction

Basics of Hebrew Discourse has been constructed and designed in order to provide students of the Hebrew Bible with a functional introduction to the use and application of discourse analysis as a necessary component to textual analysis and the exegetical process. Beginning Hebrew courses rightly focus on morphology and basic clause syntax, while courses in Hebrew exegesis tend to focus on word studies, textual criticism, historical backgrounds, and other necessary components of study. Even so-called intermediate or advanced Hebrew courses tend to focus on vocabulary acquisition and the various uses of individual words or grammatical constructions that appear regularly *within individual clauses*, such as the use of the definite article or the variety of nuances expressed by the construct state in Biblical Hebrew. We have also observed, however, that very little attention has been devoted to either classroom instruction or the production of introductory resources designed to help students develop skills in discourse analysis. But this raises the question, what is discourse analysis?

There is no officially recognized or standard definition for what is called discourse analysis, but we can certainly describe what it is. When we study a language like Biblical Hebrew, we are studying the meaningful relationships between sounds (phonology), sound units (morphology), and words (syntax). Discourse analysis is simply the next logical progression on the language continuum. Sounds create sound units and sounds units create words that appear together in individual clauses, and these clauses also relate to each other in meaningful ways. Discourse analysis is, therefore, the study of the meaningful relationships that exist between individual clauses in the production of a textual unit, from individual paragraphs to larger discourse units and even whole books. Discourse analysis works to identify and understand the ways in which texts are ordered and connected to express meaning and logical progression.

As you will soon discover, the conventions of English discourse are not always the same as those employed in Biblical Hebrew, and so we must become attentive to these differences in order to better understand the structure and meaning of any given Hebrew text. If we want to understand what the author of a biblical text intended to communicate to us, then we must study the Hebrew alphabet (phonology), the inflectional endings of the Perfect conjugation (morphology), the relationship between a verb and all of the other words in its clause (syntax), *and* the conventions used to connect and relate these clauses into meaningful textual units, that is, *discourse analysis*. In this book, the authors have bravely set out to introduce students of the Hebrew Bible to this exciting and fruitful course of study.

Students should also understand that the formal study of discourse analysis as a discipline of linguistic description is relatively new with regard to its application to Biblical Hebrew. This reality creates two basic problems for most students—the problem of nomenclature and the problem of methodology. As newer fields of study emerge and grow, so do the number of academic professionals who work to advance our understanding of the discipline. These professionals come from a variety of academic backgrounds who then employ a variety of theoretical frameworks in order to solve problems and advance knowledge. As a whole, this eclectic force of academic effort often lacks basic organization or systematic models for presentation, and this has resulted in the rapid development of names, labels, and terms used to describe the various features of the discipline. So, for example, some practitioners of what we are calling discourse analysis may prefer the designations "macro-syntax" or "text linguistics," each of which contain slightly different nuances that may or may not be apparent in their analysis of the text and the methodology employed in that analysis. Fear not, however! This book is not designed to enter into those debates, though its authors are acutely aware of these challenges as the following bibliography demonstrates. Rather, this resource is designed to help students of the Hebrew

Bible engage the text in a way that allows the text itself to set the agenda, and this is one of the primary benefits of discourse analysis.

In this book, the study and application of discourse analysis is divided into two main parts: (1) discourse analysis for *prose* by Patton and (2) discourse analysis for *poetry* by Putnam. The reason for this division is the fact that different discourse features are employed in each of these two genres. Even the beginning student will "feel" the difference between prose and poetry when reading the text. The language is the same (Hebrew), but many of the basic ways the text is put together will differ. Additionally, the authors of this book understand that there are a number of different models and methods for engaging discourse analysis and they do not claim to have provided the final or definitive word on the matter. On the contrary, it is hoped that the construction and use of a practical introduction for the beginning student will advance, refine, and strengthen the field of study, especially as it is applied to our understanding of the biblical text.

When using this book, either on your own or in a classroom environment, it will help to begin by studying and applying only one or two discourse features at a time. For example, if you are working with narrative, perhaps begin with the analysis of verbal sequences or the use of the conjunction *waw*. Once you understand how something works, then move onto the next discourse feature. When it comes to poetry, work incrementally through the different features described by Putnam—glossing, parsing, lineation, etc. It is best to master one feature before moving on to the next one. This system of incremental learning, or process abstraction, will prevent you from becoming overwhelmed as you develop your skills with discourse analysis. Also, when using *BHD*, you will want to keep your Hebrew Bible close at hand. One of the great things about this resource is that it helps us to handle the biblical text with more care and attention to detail. Note that in places where Hebrew versification and English differ, the English is provided in brackets.

Finally, this editor expresses his admiration and esteem for the two men who have labored to provide this resource for students of the Hebrew Bible. Their work is both academically rigorous and thoughtfully practical. One of the many strengths of this work is that these two authors are actual practitioners of the discipline. They are outstanding scholars, gifted teachers, and faithful servants in the kingdom. By the grace of the one who has redeemed us from sin and death, may the dedicatory prayer of this book from Psalm 90:17 ring true, "And may the favor of the Lord our God be upon us; and the work of our hands establish for us; and the work of our hands, establish it."

Miles V. Van Pelt, editor
May 2019

Abbreviations

ApOTC	Apollos Old Testament Commentary
BH	Biblical Hebrew
BHS	*Biblia Hebraica Stuttgartensia*
BibInt	Biblical Interpretation Series
CTL	Cambridge Textbooks in Linguistics
GBHS	*A Guide to Biblical Hebrew Syntax*. Bill T. Arnold and John H. Choi. Cambridge: Cambridge University Press, 2003
GKC	*Gesenius' Hebrew Grammar*. Edited by Emil Kautzsch. Translated by Arthur E. Cowley. 2nd ed. Oxford: Clarendon, 1910
HS	*Hebrew Studies*
HSM	Harvard Semitic Monographs
HSS	Harvard Semitic Studies
IBHS	*An Introduction to Biblical Hebrew Syntax*. Bruce K. Waltke and Michael O'Connor. Winona Lake, IN: Eisenbrauns, 1990
imv	imperative
JBL	*Journal of Biblical Literature*
JBLMS	Journal of Biblical Literature Monograph Series
JBS	Jerusalem Biblical Studies
Joüon	Joüon, Paul. *A Grammar of Biblical Hebrew*. Translated and revised by T. Muraoka. 2 vols. Rome: Pontifical Biblical Institute, 1991
JSOTSup	Journal for the Study of the Old Testament Supplement Series
JSS	*Journal of Semitic Studies*
JOTT	*Journal of Translation and Textlinguistics*
LSAWS	Linguistic Studies in Ancient West Semitic
LXX	Septuagint
MT	Masoretic Text

OTM	Oxford Theological Monographs
ptc	participle
SSLL	Studies in Semitic Languages and Linguistics
SSN	Studia Semitica Neerlandica
STDJ	Studies on the Texts of the Desert of Judah
TynBul	*Tyndale Bulletin*
VTSup	Supplements to Vetus Testamentum
ZECOT	Zondervan Exegetical Commentary on the Old Testament

Table of Grammatical Terms

For the sake of consistency and convenience, it was decided to employ transliteration nomenclature when referring to the basic finite verbal forms in Biblical Hebrew. The following chart correlates these terms with other standard terms that appear in a variety of Hebrew resources—introductory, intermediate, and advanced.

Transliterated Designations	Alternative Designations
qatal	Perfect, Suffix Conjugation
weqatal	Perfect with *Waw* Consecutive, Consecutive Perfect, Converted Perfect
yiqtol	Imperfect, Prefix Conjugation
wayyiqtol	Imperfect with *Waw* Consecutive, Consecutive Imperfect, Preterite

Bibliography

Andersen, Francis I. *The Hebrew Verbless Clause in the Pentateuch*. JBLMS 14. Nashville: Abingdon, 1970.

———. *The Sentence in Biblical Hebrew*. Janua Linguarum 231. The Hague: Mouton, 1974.

Bandstra, Barry L. "Word Order and Emphasis in Biblical Hebrew Narrative: Syntactic Observations on Genesis 22 from a Discourse Perspective." Pages 109–23 in *Linguistics and Biblical Hebrew*. Edited by Walter R. Bodine. Winona Lake, IN: Eisenbrauns, 1992.

Block, Daniel I. *Ruth: A Discourse Analysis of the Hebrew Bible*. ZECOT. Grand Rapids: Zondervan, 2015.

Brown, Gillian, and George Yule. *Discourse Analysis*. CTL. Cambridge: Cambridge University Press, 1983.

Buth, Randall. "Functional Grammar, Hebrew and Aramaic: An Integrated, Textlinguistic Approach to Syntax." Pages 77–102 in *Discourse Analysis of Biblical Literature: What It Is and What It Offers*. Edited by Walter R. Bodine. Semeia Studies. Atlanta: Scholars Press, 1995.

———. "The Hebrew Verb in Current Discussions." *JOTT* 5 (1992): 91–105.

Collins, C. John. "The Wayyiqtol as 'Pluperfect': When and Why." *TynBul* 46 (1995): 117–40.

Conklin, Blane. *Oath Formulas in Biblical Hebrew*. LSAWS 5. Winona Lake, IN: Eisenbrauns, 2011.

Cook, John A. "The Semantics of Verbal Pragmatics: Clarifying the Roles of *Wayyiqtol* and *Weqatal* in Biblical Hebrew Prose." *JSS* 49 (2004): 247–73.

———. *Time and the Biblical Hebrew Verb: The Expression of Tense, Aspect, and Modality in Biblical Hebrew*. LSAWS 7. Winona Lake, IN: Eisenbrauns, 2012.

Dawson, David Allan. *Text-Linguistics and Biblical Hebrew*. Sheffield: Sheffield Academic, 1994.

Dempster, Stephen G. "Linguistic Features of Hebrew Narrative: A Discourse Analysis of Narrative from the Classical Period." PhD diss., University of Toronto, 1985.

DeRouchie, Jason S. *A Call to Covenant Love: Text Grammar and Literary Structure in Deuteronomy 5–11*. Gorgias Dissertations 30. Piscataway, NJ: Gorgias, 2007.

Endo, Yoshinobu. *The Verbal System of Classical Hebrew in the Joseph Story: An Approach from Discourse Analysis*. SSN. Assen: Van Gorcum, 1996.

Eskhult, M. "Verbal Syntax in Late Biblical Hebrew." Pages 84–93 in *Diggers at the Well: Proceedings of a Third International Symposium on the Hebrew of the Dead Sea Scrolls and Ben Sira*. Edited by T. Muraoka and John F. Elwolde. STDJ 36. Leiden: Brill, 2000.

Fraser, Bruce. "What Are Discourse Markers?" *Journal of Pragmatics* 31 (1999): 931–52.

Garrett, Duane A., and Jason S. DeRouchie. *A Modern Grammar for Biblical Hebrew*. Nashville, TN: B&H Academic, 2009.

Goldfajn, Tal. *Word Order and Time in Biblical Hebrew Narrative*. OTM. Oxford: Clarendon, 1998.

Heimerdinger, Jean-Marc. *Topic, Focus and Foreground in Ancient Hebrew Narratives*. JSOTSup 295. Sheffield: Bloomsbury, 1999.

Heller, Roy L. *Narrative Structure and Discourse Constellations: An Analysis of Clause Function in Biblical Hebrew Prose*. HSS 55. Winona Lake, IN: Eisenbrauns, 2004.

Holmstedt, Robert D. *The Relative Clause in Biblical Hebrew*. LSAWS 10. Winona Lake, IN: Eisenbrauns, 2016.

Hornkohl, Aaron D. *Ancient Hebrew Periodization and the Language of the Book of Jeremiah: The Case for a Sixth-Century Date of Composition*. SSLL 74. Leiden: Brill, 2014.

Joosten, Jan. *The Verbal System of Biblical Hebrew: A New Synthesis Elaborated on the Basis of Classical Prose*. JBS 10. Jerusalem: Simor, 2012.

Long, Gary A. *Grammatical Concepts 101 for Biblical Hebrew*. 2nd ed. Grand Rapids: Baker Academic, 2001.

Longacre, Robert E. "Discourse Peak as Zone of Turbulence." Pages 81–92 in *Beyond the Sentence: Discourse and Sentential Form*. Edited by J. R. Wirth. Ann Arbor, MI: Karoma, 1985.

———. "Discourse Perspective on the Hebrew Verb: Affirmation and Restatement." Pages 177–89 in *Linguistics and Biblical Hebrew*. Edited by Walter R. Bodine. Winona Lake, IN: Eisenbrauns, 1992.

———. *Joseph: A Story of Divine Providence : A Text Theoretical and Textlinguistic Analysis of Genesis 37 and 39–48*. 2nd ed. Winona Lake, IN: Eisenbrauns, 2003.

———. *The Grammar of Discourse*. 2nd ed. Topics in Language and Linguistics. New York: Plenum, 1996.

———. "*Weqatal* Forms in Biblical Hebrew Prose: A Discourse-Modular Approach." Pages 50–98 in *Biblical Hebrew and Discourse Linguistics*. Edited by Robert D. Bergen. Dallas, TX: Summer Institute of Linguistics, 1994.

Longacre, Robert E., and Andrew C. Bowling. *Understanding Biblical Hebrew Verb Forms: Distribution and Function across Genres*. Dallas: SIL International, 2015.

Longacre, Robert E., and Shin Ja J. Hwang. *Holistic Discourse Analysis*. 2nd ed. Dallas: SIL International, 2012.

McConville, J. G. *Deuteronomy*. ApOTC 5. Leicester, UK: Apollos, 2002.

McFall, Leslie. *The Enigma of the Hebrew Verbal System*. Historic Texts and Interpreters in Biblical Scholarship 2. Sheffield: Almond, 1982.

Miller, Cynthia L. "Introducing Direct Discourse in Biblical Hebrew Narrative." Pages 199–241 in *Biblical Hebrew and Discourse Linguistics*. Edited by Robert D. Bergen. Dallas, TX: Summer Institute of Linguistics, 1994.

———. *The Representation of Speech in Biblical Hebrew Narrative: A Linguistic Analysis*. HSM 55. Atlanta: Scholars Press, 2003.

Moshavi, Adina. *Word Order in the Biblical Hebrew Finite Clause: A Syntactic and Pragmatic Analysis of Preposing*. LSAWS 4. Winona Lake, IN: Eisenbrauns, 2010.

Niccacci, Alviero. "On the Hebrew Verbal System." Pages 117–37 in *Biblical Hebrew and Discourse Linguistics*. Edited by Robert D. Bergen. Dallas, TX: Summer Institute of Linguistics, 1994.

O'Connor, M. "Discourse Linguistics and the Study of Biblical Hebrew." Pages 17–42 in *Congress Volume: Basel 2001*. Edited by A. Lemaire. VTSup 92. Leiden: Brill, 2001.

Paltridge, Brian. *Discourse Analysis: An Introduction*. 2nd ed. Bloomsbury Discourse Series. London: Bloomsbury Academic, 2012.

Pike, Kenneth L. "Beyond the Sentence." *College Composition and Communication* 15 (1964): 129–35.

Putnam, Frederic Clarke. *A New Grammar of Biblical Hebrew*. Sheffield: Sheffield Phoenix, 2010.

Robar, Elizabeth. *The Verb and the Paragraph in Biblical Hebrew: A Cognitive-Linguistic Approach*. SSLL 78. Leiden: Brill, 2015.

Rocine, B. M. *Learning Biblical Hebrew: A New Approach Using Discourse Analysis*. Macon, GA: Smith & Helwys, 2000.

Sáenz-Badillos, Ángel. *A History of the Hebrew Language*. Cambridge: Cambridge University Press, 1993.

Schiffrin, Deborah. *Approaches to Discourse*. Blackwell Textbooks in Linguistics. Oxford: Wiley-Blackwell, 1994.

Schneider, Wolfgang. *Grammatik Des Biblischen Hebräisch: Ein Lehrbuch*. Munich: Claudius, 1974.

Schreiner, Thomas R. *Interpreting the Pauline Epistles*. Guides to New Testament Exegesis 5. Grand Rapids: Baker Academic, 2011.

Shimasaki, Katsuomi. *Focus Structure in Biblical Hebrew: A Study of Word Order and Information Structure*. Bethesda, MD: CDL, 2002.

Steiner, Richard C. "Does the Biblical Hebrew Conjunction-W Have Many Meanings, One Meaning, or No Meaning at All?" *JBL* 119 (2000): 249–67.

van der Merwe, Christo H. J., Jackie A. Naudé, and Jan H. Kroeze. *A Biblical Hebrew Reference Grammar*. 2nd ed. London: Bloomsbury, 2017.

———. "A Critical Analysis of Narrative Syntactic Approaches, with Special Attention to Their Relationship to Discourse Analysis." Pages 133–56 in *Narrative Syntax and the Hebrew Bible: Papers of the Tilburg Conference 1996*. Edited by Ellen van Wolde. BibInt 29. Leiden: Brill, 1997.

———. "An Overview of Hebrew Narrative Syntax." Pages 1–20 in *Narrative Syntax and the Hebrew Bible: Papers of the Tilburg Conference 1996*. Edited by Ellen van Wolde. BibInt 29. Leiden: Brill, 1997.

———. "The Elusive Biblical Hebrew Term WYHY: A Perspective in Terms of Its Syntax, Semantics, and Pragmatics in 1 Samuel." *HS* 40 (1999): 83–114.

van Wolde, Ellen. "The Verbless Clause and Its Textual Function." Pages 321–36 in *The Verbless Clause in Biblical Hebrew: Linguistic Approaches*. LSAWS 1. Winona Lake, IN: Eisenbrauns, 1999.

Wallace, Daniel B. *Greek Grammar Beyond the Basics: An Exegetical Syntax of the New Testament*. Grand Rapids: Zondervan, 1996.

Waltke, Bruce K., and M. O'Connor. *An Introduction to Biblical Hebrew Syntax*. Winona Lake, IN: Eisenbrauns, 1990.

Yule, George. *The Study of Language*. 6th ed. Cambridge: Cambridge University Press, 2017.

Zewi, Tamar. *Parenthesis in Biblical Hebrew*. SSLL 50. Leiden: Brill, 2007.

PART 1

Working with Biblical Hebrew Prose

Matthew H. Patton

Expanded Table of Contents

Chapter 1

Introduction

A text's meaning crystallizes only when we can trace the flow of thought from start to finish. In-depth knowledge of individual words, phrases, and clauses is of little value if we cannot *relate* each of these parts together in the text. Many different kinds of relationships exist in a text. In the case of clauses and sentences, the relationships often are either temporal (e.g., one event following another) or logical (e.g., a conclusion on the basis of foregoing reasons). Moving up from these low-level relationships, we can then speak of the relationship between larger units (paragraphs) and much larger units (sections or chapters or even books in a multi-volume work). We have identified the flow of a text when we can describe how each part relates to the other parts in the text, and this description of a text's flow of thought is the goal of discourse analysis.[1]

All languages provide cues for allowing readers and listeners to identify the relationships between parts of a discourse. In English, we use linking words like "therefore" or "meanwhile" as one way to signal clausal relationships. To conclude a longer discourse we might begin with, "To sum up." But in many cases, sentences are simply laid next to each other with no linking words, and the reader or listener must grasp the relationship between the sentences using other contextual cues.

Each language has its own conventions for communicating discourse relationships, and therefore different tools of discourse analysis are needed for each language. As we will see, Biblical Hebrew (BH) often

1. This text-oriented definition of discourse analysis contrasts with the sociocultural focus of discourse analysis for some linguists such as Paltridge (*Discourse Analysis: An Introduction*, 2nd ed., Bloomsbury Discourse Series [London: Bloomsbury Academic, 2012], 1–12). However, as Paltridge himself observes, textual and sociocularal approaches are not mutually exlusive. In chapter 7 we discuss the relevance of sociocultural contexts for discourse analysis.

relies on chains of *wayyiqtol*[2] verbs to communicate a story.[3] A chain of *weqatal* verbs is a conventional way to provide instructions for a process, like making a sacrifice. Word order is also important in BH (especially, which word occupies the first slot in a clause). An attempt to understand a BH prose text that does not attend to chains of verbs or to the kinds of words that occupy the first slot in a clause will fail to attend to some of the most salient ways in which BH writers marked discourse relationships in narrative.

To introduce the analysis of BH prose, this first half is further divided into nine chapters:

- In chapter 1, we introduce the idea of discourse analysis, demonstrate its usefulness, and summarize the scholarly discussion on the discourse analysis of Biblical Hebrew prose.
- In chapter 2, we survey common discourse relationships that arise in prose texts. These discourse relationships are communicable in any language. Since identifying these relationships properly is the goal of discourse analysis, this chapter enriches our understanding of what we are seeking through our analysis.
- In chapters 3–6, we survey the tools in the BH prose writer's toolkit for signaling the discourse relationships in chapter 2. For BH prose, there are three main kinds of communicative conventions: discourse markers, verbal sequences, and word order. Understanding the specifics of how BH prose operates will prepare us for analysis. *Note: there is a lot of detail in these four chapters. To avoid being bogged down in the details, we recommend you read through them in a cursory manner the first time and then refer back to them as you begin to do discourse analysis.*
- In chapter 7, we provide a process for analyzing BH prose texts using our knowledge of the communicative signals in chapters 3–6.
- In chapter 8, we conclude with several examples where we enact the process described in chapter 7.
- In chapter 9, we provide a summary chart of discourse analysis.

---

2. See p. 17 for a table where we correlate our terms for Hebrew verbal forms with those used in other textbooks.

3. Our corpus for this textbook is limited to the Biblical Hebrew canon.

I. DISCOURSE ANALYSIS AS FOUNDATION FOR FURTHER STUDY

One reason why discourse analysis is so important is that it provides the stimulus and foundation for further literary, historical, and theological study. Consider the following example from the speech of the people on the plains of Shinar in Gen 11:4. This short example in English assumes a close analysis of the original Hebrew text and shows the results of discourse analysis:

Genesis 11:4

	Text	Discourse Analysis
4b[4]	Come, let us build for ourselves a city and a tower,	Self-mandate to build a city and a tower
4c	and let its top be in the heavens,	Expansion on the tower in 4b: its top in the heavens
4d	and let us make a name for ourselves,	Positive purpose for building in 4b–c: to make a name
4e	so that we are not dispersed over the face of the whole earth.	Negative purpose for building 4b–c: to avoid being dispersed

This discourse analysis identifies the self-mandate to build in verse 4b as the central idea: all the other clauses relate to it and qualify it. A qualifying statement in verse 4c expands one aspect of that central idea, the specifications of the tower. The last two phrases identify positive and negative purposes for the building: they are urging each other to build so that they can make a name for themselves and avoid being dispersed.[5]

This analysis shows the usefulness of discourse analysis for an exegete with literary, historical, and theological concerns. A casual reading may miss the purpose relationships between verses 4b–c on the one hand, and verse 4d and verse 4e on the other. Recognizing this

4. We opt for enumerating subsections of Hebrew verses by clause (each clause in the verse receives a letter) and not by the Masoretic accents. This approach provides a straightforward way for the student to diagram the text that is more conducive to the clause-by-clause kind of analysis we are advocating.

5. The decision to understand vv. 4d–e as purpose clauses is assumed here for the sake of argument but could be defended using the analytical approach given in this book.

relationship invites further reflection: why do the speakers believe that building a city and tower will make their name great? How do the city and tower prevent the people from being dispersed?

The next step is to relate this text to the larger discourse: how does this speech relate to the first speech made in verse 3? How does it set the stage for the next dramatic events in verses 5–9? At a higher level, how does Genesis 11:1–9 relate to the other sections in the larger unit in which it is found (Gen 1–11)? And how does the tower of Babel text help us understand even larger relationships, like Genesis 1–11 as a prologue to Genesis 12–50? Do these reflections enrich our understanding of Genesis within the Pentateuch or the Primary History (Genesis–2 Kings)?[6]

As important as these larger reflections are, our goal in this book will be on the more modest (but still quite complex!) level of individual clauses (in this example, not stopping until we have elucidated each clause in Gen 11:1–9). We are seeking a rigorous approach to BH prose texts that will ask: how does each clause relate to those that precede it and those that follow it? Such an analysis provides the foundation for broader considerations.

II. DISCOURSE ANALYSIS HELPS RESOLVE EXEGETICAL DEBATES

The previous example shows how discourse analysis helps to slow the reader down and ask purposefully about the relationships that exist between clauses, paragraphs, and higher units of discourse. The results of discourse analysis elicit new questions that are useful for scholars with broader literary, historical, and theological interests. But discourse analysis is also essential for understanding a small textual unit. The following example from Deut 30:1–6 shows how important it is that we conduct our discourse analysis in the original language.

Scholars have debated how to understand YHWH's promise to circumcise Israel's heart in Deut 30:6. On the one hand, Paul A. Barker contends

6. For the sake of asking these high-level questions, we rely on previous scholarly results regarding the structure of Genesis and its relationship to other books. However, as we will see below, discourse analysis helps to evaluate these structural proposals and also to suggest new ones.

that this promise is an absolute statement, not conditioned by any action on Israel's part: YHWH will circumcise Israel's heart.[7] Others like J. G. McConville understand the promise to be conditioned on the repentance of Israel envisioned in Deut 30:1–2: when Israel returns to YHWH, *then* YHWH will circumcise their heart.[8] Major theological issues, including the question of whether it is possible for Israel to repent without YHWH's prior gracious initiative, are at stake in this exegetical question.

Discourse analysis is extremely helpful in resolving the question of whether YHWH's promise to circumcise Israel's heart is conditional or not. The following table shows the text in English (with some relative clauses and parenthetical comments removed for clarity), along with the Hebrew construction for each clause.

Deuteronomy 30:1–6

	Text (adapted from ESV)	Hebrew Construction
1a	And when all these things come upon you, the blessing and the curse, . . .	*wehayah* + *ki* + *yiqtol* (וְהָיָה כִי־יָבֹאוּ)
1c	and you call them to mind among all the nations . . .	*weqatal* (וַהֲשֵׁבֹתָ)
2a	and return to the LORD your God, . . .	*weqatal* (וְשַׁבְתָּ)
2b	and obey his voice . . .	*weqatal* (וְשָׁמַעְתָּ)
3a	then the LORD your God will restore your fortunes	*weqatal* (וְשָׁב יְהוָה)
3b	and have compassion on you,	*weqatal* (וְרִחֲמֶךָ)
3c	and he will gather you again from all the peoples . . .	*weqatal* (וְשָׁב וְקִבֶּצְךָ)[9]
5a	and the LORD your God will bring you into the land . . .	*weqatal* (וֶהֱבִיאֲךָ)[10]
5c	that you may possess it.	*weqatal* (וִירִשְׁתָּהּ)

(cont.)

7. Paul A. Barker, *The Triumph of Grace in Deuteronomy: Faithless Israel, Faithful Yahweh in Deuteronomy* (Carlisle, Cumbria: Paternoster, 2004), 219.

8. J. G. McConville, *Deuteronomy*, ApOTC 5 (Leicester, UK: Apollos, 2002), 424.

9. Recall that when the root שׁוב is closely accompanied by another verb, the root שׁוב can mean that the other verb is done again.

10. Verse 4 is parenthetical and therefore omitted. It can be recognized as a parenthesis both from its content, which simply emphasizes and expands on what is said in vv. 3c–d,

	Text (adapted from ESV)	Hebrew Construction
5d	And he will make you more prosperous	*weqatal* (וְהֵיטִבְךָ)
5e	and numerous than your fathers.	*weqatal* (וְהִרְבְּךָ)
6a	And the Lord your God will circumcise your heart and the heart of your offspring	*weqatal* (וּמָל)

Notice that after the introductory clause (v. 1a), every clause thereafter is the same construction: *weqatal*.[11] The כִּי at the beginning is temporal: "when." It therefore introduces a protasis (a "when" or "if" clause) that must be completed by a corresponding "then" clause (called the "apodosis"). The first question is: when does the apodosis (the "then" clause) begin? The shift of subject from "you" (Israel) in verses 1–2 to YHWH in verses 3–6 supports the decision of the ESV and other versions to introduce the apodosis at verse 3a (as we will see below, apodoses often begin with a simple *weqatal*). This decision is supported by the content of the text, which on this interpretation yields a simple action and response structure: Israel repents, and YHWH restores (for a similar structure in a similar theological context, see Lev 26:40–42; Zech 1:3; Mal 3:7).

Now we can return to the important question raised earlier: how does this analysis help us understand verse 6a, whether it is unconditional or conditional? In our discussion of *weqatal* below, we will show that *weqatal* can certainly begin new units, and so it is impossible to rule out Barker's interpretation completely (i.e., that verse 6a begins a new unit). However, from the perspective of discourse analysis, there is nothing in this text to suggest that any kind of shift has taken place in the discourse between verse 5e and verse 6a. There is no shift of sentence form, no new conjuction, and no discourse marker of any kind.[12] The content of verse 6a is also similar to the foregoing: it is a promise similar to those found in verses 3–5. Instead of anything new that would indicate a new beginning, verse 6a simply continues the *weqatal* chain, suggesting that it continues the apodosis begun in verse 3a. On this analysis, verses

and from its construction (a conditional sentence prefaced by אִם, which departs from the *weqatal* pattern of the surrounding verses).

11. With the exception of v. 4; see the previous footnote.

12. There is a brief shift in v. 5c to the second person to explain the result of v. 5a, but this does not interrupt the apodosis begun in v. 3, which marches on in vv. 5d–e.

3–6 conjoin one restoration benefit to another in a beautiful collage of redemptive promises. And, since verse 3 begins the apodosis to the condition set in verses 1–2, we conclude that YHWH's promise to circumcise Israel's heart, as with all the promises in verses 3–5, are conditioned on Israel's repentance (vv. 1–2). To paraphrase: "When you return (vv. 1–2), then I will restore (v. 3a) and have compassion (v. 3b) and gather (v. 3c) . . . and circumcise (v. 6a)." Israel should not expect to have their hearts circumcised until they have repented with all their heart and all their soul.[13]

Discourse analysis provides powerful resources for evaluating difficult exegetical problems like the relationship of Deut 30:6 to the preceding clauses.

III. SURVEY OF SCHOLARSHIP

A significant challenge in producing a textbook on this topic is the relatively recent and unsettled nature of the scholarly discussion regarding BH discourse analysis.[14] Older grammarians recognized that BH had distinctive ways of communicating certain kinds of discourse relationships. For example, Gesenius details how conditional clauses (like those beginning with "if" or "when" in English) can be achieved with particles like אִם (GKC §159.3), but also without particles, simply by the juxtaposition of certain verbal forms (GKC §159.2). But these discussions are grouped under the larger heading "Special Kinds of *Sentences*" (emphasis mine). Theoretically, the grammarian's work stopped at the level of sentence syntax. Beyond sentence syntax, the relationship between sentences was the province of the literary critic, even though due diligence required

13. This conclusion then raises the question: how could Israel ever repent with all their heart and all their soul without first having their hearts circumcised? We cannot address this question here, but we believe that this understanding of Deut 30:1–10 does not contravene the emphasis found elsewhere on the need for God's unilateral gracious action to produce genuine repentance (Jer 31:33; 32:40).

14. For summaries of literature, see David Allan Dawson, *Text-Linguistics and Biblical Hebrew* (Sheffield: Sheffield Academic, 1994); Jason S. DeRouchie, *A Call to Covenant Love: Text Grammar and Literary Structure in Deuteronomy 5–11*, Gorgias Dissertations 30 (Piscataway, NJ: Gorgias, 2007), 25–35; Roy L. Heller, *Narrative Structure and Discourse Constellations: An Analysis of Clause Function in Biblical Hebrew Prose*, HSS 55 (Winona Lake, IN: Eisenbrauns, 2004), 3–24; Christo H. J. van der Merwe, "An Overview of Hebrew Narrative Syntax," in *Narrative Syntax and the Hebrew Bible: Papers of the Tilburg Conference 1996*, ed. Ellen van Wolde, BibInt 29 (Leiden: Brill, 1997), 1–20.

grammarians to discuss some complex multi-clause sentences like "if-then" sentences.

This classic approach to language, grammar, and syntax was surpassed in the twentieth century when linguists began to attend more rigorously to structures beyond the sentence. Kenneth L. Pike argued that "*beyond the sentence* lie grammatical structures available to linguistic analysis, describable by technical procedures, and usable by the author for the generation of literary works through which he reports to us his observations."[15] This quote highlights a fundamental insight that lies behind discourse analysis: namely, that a grammarian can inquire not only into how a language forms sentences (sentence syntax) but also into how a language forms larger discourse units like paragraphs (discourse syntax).[16] As we will see, some features of BH like וַיְהִי clauses, or interruptions of *wayyiqtol* chains, or particles like הִנֵּה primarily operate at the discourse level, marking discourse relationships between clauses.

This insight provoked new questions in BH studies.[17] In order to summarize the complicated jungle of contemporary scholarship on the discourse analysis of BH, we will list some of these important new questions:

1. How do the forms of sentences (e.g., a *wayyiqtol* sentence vs. *waw* + a noun + *qatal*) relate to their discourse function? An early study by Francis I. Andersen, building on Pike, showed how many sentence structures are closely correlated to their purpose in the discourse.[18] More recently, Roy L. Heller's work,[19] building on Robert E. Longacre, notes that certain sentence forms are often found together, depending on what type of text is in view. In hortatory discourse

15. Kenneth L. Pike, "Beyond the Sentence," *College Composition and Communication* 15 (1964): 129 (emphasis original).

16. For surveys and approaches to discourse analysis in general linguistics from a variety of perspectives, see Gillian Brown and George Yule, *Discourse Analysis*, CTL (Cambridge: Cambridge University Press, 1983); Robert E. Longacre and Shin Ja J. Hwang, *Holistic Discourse Analysis*, 2nd ed. (Dallas: SIL International, 2012); Paltridge, *Discourse Analysis*; Deborah Schiffrin, *Approaches to Discourse*, Blackwell Textbooks in Linguistics (Oxford: Wiley-Blackwell, 1994), 45–334.

17. For more reasons on why BH grammarians have turned to a discourse approach, see van der Merwe, "An Overview of Hebrew Narrative Syntax," 3–5.

18. Francis I. Andersen, *The Sentence in Biblical Hebrew*, Janua Linguarum 231 (The Hague: Mouton, 1974).

19. Heller, *Narrative Structure*.

(when the speaker is exhorting the audience to some action), the primary verb forms are imperatives (after all, the speaker is telling them to do something!). And these primary verbs are accompanied by *qatal*, *yiqtol*, and other non-imperatives, which provide explanatory material. In narrative discourse one finds a different constellation of verb forms dominated by *wayyiqtol*. In short, the way a sentence is formed (e.g., using *waw* + subject + *qatal* instead of *wayyiqtol* + subject) is often influenced by how that form functions in discourses.

2. Closely related to the previous question is: are certain verb forms (especially *wayyiqtol* and *weqatal*) primarily functioning on a discourse level, marking the relationship between clauses? To what extent do they continue to express the basic verbal ideas of tense, aspect, or mood? To take one example, Longacre identified *wayyiqtol* and *weqatal* as primarily discourse-oriented forms,[20] a point disputed by John A. Cook, who believes that, even apart from their discourse function (which he grants), these forms have a default semantic weight relating to tense, aspect, and mood.[21] For example, in his view, *wayyiqtol* (apart from its role in the larger discourse) suggests a simple past tense, and *weqatal* suggests unreal mood (counterfactual ideas like "he would have gone").[22] These defaults can be overridden by the larger context, but for Cook they are still part of what these verb forms convey.
3. Given that many verbal forms have a discourse function, what exactly is the function of each? In the case of *wayyiqtol*, many initial studies considered it to mark temporal succession or foreground (i.e., the main storyline) in narrative, but Robar has argued that *wayyiqtol* is simply a continuative form, continuing whatever flow of thought has already been initiated.[23] If a background com-

20. Robert E. Longacre, "*Weqatal* Forms in Biblical Hebrew Prose: A Discourse-Modular Approach," in *Biblical Hebrew and Discourse Linguistics*, ed. Robert D. Bergen (Dallas, TX: Summer Institute of Linguistics, 1994), 95.

21. John A. Cook, "The Semantics of Verbal Pragmatics: Clarifying the Roles of *Wayyiqtol* and *Weqatal* in Biblical Hebrew Prose," *JSS* 49 (2004): 247–73; John A. Cook, *Time and the Biblical Hebrew Verb: The Expression of Tense, Aspect, and Modality in Biblical Hebrew*, LSAWS 7 (Winona Lake, IN: Eisenbrauns, 2012), 249–65. See also Randall Buth, "The Hebrew Verb in Current Discussions," *JOTT* 5 (1992): 96–100.

22. Cook, *Time and the Biblical Hebrew Verb*, 427.

23. Elizabeth Robar, *The Verb and the Paragraph in Biblical Hebrew: A Cognitive-Linguistic Approach*, SSLL 78 (Leiden: Brill, 2015), 77.

ment is in view, *wayyiqtol* continues that background comment. If the main storyline (foreground) is in view, *wayyiqtol* continues that storyline. The discourse functions of other verbal forms are also debated (especially *weqatal*).

Another important observation is that the discourse function of a verb is dependent not only on its form, but on the context in the discourse where it is found.[24] Hence *weqatal* in the midst of a *wayyiqtol* sequence in narrative should be understood differently from *weqatal* in the midst of a *weqatal* sequence in direct speech. We will return to this important observation in subsequent chapters.

4. How does the order of words in a sentence serve larger discourse roles? As we will see, וַיֵּרֶד יוֹנָה ("and Jonah went down") should be analyzed differently from וְיוֹנָה יָרַד, even though on a sentence level their semantics are quite similar. Many scholars have noted that the second instance, when the noun is put before the verb, serves important discourse roles, such as the introduction of a new topic or the beginning of a background comment.[25] Thus, not only are verb forms and sequences of verbs important for structuring BH discourses but so is the *order of words* in a sentence.
5. For all of the questions above, to what extent is the concept of a "text type" relevant for explaining how BH discourses operate? We have already mentioned two major kinds of texts: prose and poetry. In BH prose, Longacre enumerated four main text types: (1) narrative, (2) predictive, (3) expository, and (4) hortatory discourse.[26] For Longacre, each text type has its own function

24. Andersen particularly emphasized this point.

25. For discussions of BH word order from a discourse perspective, see: Barry L. Bandstra, "Word Order and Emphasis in Biblical Hebrew Narrative: Syntactic Observations on Genesis 22 from a Discourse Perspective," in *Linguistics and Biblical Hebrew*, ed. Walter R. Bodine (Winona Lake, IN: Eisenbrauns, 1992), 109–23; Stephen G. Dempster, "Linguistic Features of Hebrew Narrative: A Discourse Analysis of Narrative from the Classical Period" (PhD diss., University of Toronto, 1985), 53–105; Tal Goldfajn, *Word Order and Time in Biblical Hebrew Narrative*, OTM (Oxford: Clarendon, 1998); Jean-Marc Heimerdinger, *Topic, Focus and Foreground in Ancient Hebrew Narratives*, JSOTSup 295 (Sheffield, UK: Bloomsbury, 1999); Adina Moshavi, *Word Order in the Biblical Hebrew Finite Clause: A Syntactic and Pragmatic Analysis of Preposing*, LSAWS 4 (Winona Lake, IN: Eisenbrauns, 2010); Katsuomi Shimasaki, *Focus Structure in Biblical Hebrew: A Study of Word Order and Information Structure* (Bethesda, MD: CDL, 2002).

26. Robert E. Longacre, "Discourse Perspective on the Hebrew Verb: Affirmation and Restatement," in *Linguistics and Biblical Hebrew*, ed. Walter R. Bodine (Winona Lake, IN:

(reporting past events, predicting future events, etc.), and—quite important!—each communicates using its own distinctive set of sentence types and verb forms. Scholars have debated whether it is valid to distinguish between text types, and if so, how to enumerate them.[27] Since predictive, expository, and hortatory discourse operate so similarly, in our discussion below we gather them together into one type—non-narrative, which we set against the other type, narrative.[28]

6. Many studies have used an awareness of discourse concerns to ask fresh questions about the way in which BH achieves things like parenthesis (Zewi),[29] direct speech (Miller),[30] and so on. As the foregoing questions indicate, hardly any aspect of BH syntax and semantics is untouched by discourse considerations. How verbs communicate tense, aspect, and mood; how words are ordered in a sentence; how particles like כִּי and הִנֵּה operate—all of these phenomena must reckon with the larger discourse.
7. Finally, to what extent does the historical evolution of BH affect discourse analysis? BH is not static; scholars have observed development in the language over time.[31] Therefore we must ask, for example: to what extent the discourse function of *wayyiqtol* changes over time?[32] These kinds of questions are vexed by the difficult issue of how to date the texts of the Hebrew Bible, a complex matter where scholars often struggle to reach a consensus.

Eisenbrauns, 1992), 177–89; Robert E. Longacre, *Joseph: A Story of Divine Providence: A Text Theoretical and Textlinguistic Analysis of Genesis 37 and 39–48*, 2nd ed. (Winona Lake, IN: Eisenbrauns, 2003), 57, 79. For Longacre on discourse types in general, see Longacre and Hwang, *Holistic Discourse Analysis*, 35–44.

27. See, for example, DeRouchie, *Covenant Love*, 82–87; Alviero Niccacci, "On the Hebrew Verbal System," in *Biblical Hebrew and Discourse Linguistics*, ed. Robert D. Bergen (Dallas, TX: Summer Institute of Linguistics, 1994), 118; Robar, *The Verb and the Paragraph*, 68–72, 148–49.

28. See Cook, *Time and the Biblical Hebrew Verb*, 171–72; Niccacci, "On the Hebrew Verbal System," 118–19.

29. Tamar Zewi, *Parenthesis in Biblical Hebrew*, SSLL 50 (Leiden: Brill, 2007).

30. Cynthia L. Miller, *The Representation of Speech in Biblical Hebrew Narrative: A Linguistic Analysis*, HSM 55 (Atlanta: Scholars Press, 2003).

31. See the classic study by Ángel Sáenz-Badillos, *A History of the Hebrew Language* (Cambridge: Cambridge University Press, 1993). For a recent survey of the diachronic study of ancient Hebrew, see Aaron D. Hornkohl, *Ancient Hebrew Periodization and the Language of the Book of Jeremiah: The Case for a Sixth-Century Date of Composition*, SSLL 74 (Leiden: Brill, 2014), 8–16.

32. This is an especially interesting example because *wayyiqtol* falls into disuse after the biblical period.

While many consider BH discourse studies to be still in their infancy,[33] some encouraging trends suggest otherwise. For example, early studies tended to make a simple one-to-one correspondence between a discourse feature and its use (e.g., "*wayyiqtol* marks foreground in narrative"), while recent studies acknowledge the flexibility of different discourse features (e.g., Robar[34]). A key concern in the chapters below is to avoid oversimplification.

Recent grammars (e.g., *Williams' Hebrew Syntax*[35]) have been slow to adopt discourse considerations and prefer to stop at the level of the sentence, which is understandable given its newness.[36] On the other hand, some grammars have integrated discourse analytical insights in substantial ways (see Garrett and DeRouchie;[37] Long;[38] Putnam;[39] Rocine;[40] Schneider;[41] and van der Merwe, Naudé, and Kroeze[42]). However, we have yet to see a definitive and scholarly account of BH discourse that comprehensively treats the foregoing questions and provides a complete analytical approach and taxonomy for BH text types, discourse markers,

---

33. One indication of this is the variety of terms used for the object of study. European scholars prefer the term "textual linguistics" (German *Textlinguistik*). One also sees "narrative syntax," "text grammar," and "discourse grammar." See discussion in Christo H. J. van der Merwe, "A Critical Analysis of Narrative Syntactic Approaches, with Special Attention to Their Relationship to Discourse Analysis," in *Narrative Syntax and the Hebrew Bible: Papers of the Tilburg Conference 1996*, ed. Ellen van Wolde, BibInt 29 (Leiden: Brill, 1997), 134–35.

34. Robar, *The Verb and the Paragraph*. An extreme example is Robert E. Longacre and Andrew C. Bowling, *Understanding Biblical Hebrew Verb Forms: Distribution and Function across Genres* (Dallas: SIL International, 2015), which details many different discourse functions of BH verb forms, but with little synthesis to guide the interpreter in using this information.

35. Ronald J. Williams, *Williams' Hebrew Syntax*, 3rd ed. (Toronto: University of Toronto, 2007).

36. See O'Connor's discussion of discourse analysis, which provides a rationale for his and Waltke's approach in their grammar: M. O'Connor, "Discourse Linguistics and the Study of Biblical Hebrew," in *Congress Volume: Basel 2001*, ed. A. Lemaire, VTSup 92 (Leiden: Brill, 2001), 17–42.

37. Duane A. Garrett and Jason S. DeRouchie, *A Modern Grammar for Biblical Hebrew* (Nashville, TN: B&H Academic, 2009), 283–335.

38. Gary A. Long, *Grammatical Concepts 101 for Biblical Hebrew*, 2nd ed. (Grand Rapids: Baker Academic, 2001), 173–97.

39. Frederic Clarke Putnam, *A New Grammar of Biblical Hebrew* (Sheffield: Sheffield Phoenix, 2010).

40. B. M. Rocine, *Learning Biblical Hebrew: A New Approach Using Discourse Analysis* (Macon, GA: Smith & Helwys, 2000).

41. Wolfgang Schneider, *Grammatik des Biblischen Hebräisch: Ein Lehrbuch* (Munich: Claudius, 1974), 223–64.

42. Christo H. J. Van der Merwe, Jackie A. Naudé, and Jan H. Kroeze, *A Biblical Hebrew Reference Grammar*, 2nd ed. (London: Bloomsbury, 2017), 188–99, 497–510.

and discourse relationships over the entire corpus of BH prose (nor does the present work claim to achieve these goals).

Even though there is much yet to learn about BH discourse grammar, a testimony to the present usefulness of discourse analysis for BH can be seen in the burgeoning list of exegetical studies that utilize discourse analysis to understand specific texts.[43] The new Zondervan Exegetical Commentary of the Old Testament uses discourse analysis as a core element of its approach to each text.[44] We believe that the discourse analysis of BH has matured to the place where it can be usefully taught and that its insights are urgently needed by exegetes of BH.

43. The Joseph story has been especially popular: Dempster, "Linguistic Features of Hebrew Narrative"; Yoshinobu Endo, *The Verbal System of Classical Hebrew in the Joseph Story: An Approach from Discourse Analysis*, SSN (Assen: Van Gorcum, 1996); Longacre, *Joseph*. On Deuteronomy 5–11, see DeRouchie, *Covenant Love*.

44. See, for example, Daniel I. Block, *Ruth: A Discourse Analysis of the Hebrew Bible*, ZECOT (Grand Rapids: Zondervan, 2015).

Chapter 2

Discourse Relationships

This chapter describes the kinds of discourse relationships that can exist between clauses in any language. Understanding how BH communicates these relationships is the goal of this book.

I. BASIC DEFINITIONS

The following discussion will employ some terms commonly used in discourse analysis:

- **Clauses**. Every text is composed of a series of clauses, where clauses have a subject (usually a noun) and a predicate (usually a verb). A sentence is made up of one or more clauses.[1] Two important distinctions can be made regarding clauses. First, clauses can be *independent* and stand by themselves ("He ate") or *dependent* and be governed by another clause ("While he was running . . ."). Second, clauses can be *syndetic* (with a conjunction or particle at the beginning to connect it to the preceding clause) or *asyndetic* (without a conjunction at the beginning).

1. Sometimes we will treat verbals (infinitive phrases and participial phrases) as separate clauses when they convey an idea that is distinct enough from the main verb to merit its own line in the discourse. For example, in this sentence, "He ate to be strong for his journey," the infinitive phrase "to be strong for his journey" can be analyzed separately as the *purpose* of "He ate." However, when the verbal is used as a noun ("Being strong is important for the journey"), or when the verbal is the complement of the main verb ("I want to be strong"), then the verbal is not treated as a separate clause in the discourse.

- **Discourse Relationships**. The goal of discourse analysis is to describe how one unit of text relates to another. Units of text can include: clauses, sentences, paragraphs, on up to larger sections of text. When we speak of the "relationship" between two units of text, we are attempting to describe the conceptual link between the two units, whether logical, temporal, or some other concept. In the text "He feasted and was satisfied," one could say that the relationship between (A) "he feasted" and (B) "and was satisfied" is that A is *the cause* of B: because he feasted, he was satisfied. In this small example, we have provided a conceptual description of the relationship between two clauses.

- **Foreground/Background**. Foreground describes the main flow of thought in a text. Background describes any peripheral information that does not move the main flow of thought forward. If the text is a narrative, then the foreground is the main storyline.[2] The foreground can be paused to give background information, such as a flashback, a visual description, etc. If the text is a procedure in non-narrative (e.g., how to do a sacrifice), the foreground comprises the primary steps of the procedure, while the background gives qualifications and side comments. Gen 31:33–34 yields an example of foreground and background in narrative.

2. Defining foreground in narrative as "the main storyline" does not mean that we equate "foreground" with a bounded succession of events (i.e., one event followed by another, followed by another). (For refutations of this proposal, see DeRouchie, *Covenant Love*, 133–42; Ellen van Wolde, "The Verbless Clause and Its Textual Function," in *The Verbless Clause in Biblical Hebrew: Linguistic Approaches*, LSAWS 1 [Winona Lake, IN: Eisenbrauns, 1999], 324–25). As we will see in our discussion of *wayyiqtol* below, an event can be simultaneous with the preceding event and still on the foreground.

Cook points out that foreground is not so much a question of temporal succession as it is a matter of saliency (importance, prominence), which is "a psycholinguistic feature of our production and perception of discourse" ("The Semantics of Verbal Pragmatics," 257). For this reason we define foreground as being about the "main flow of thought."

For recent overviews of the scholarship regarding foreground and background, along with critique, see Moshavi, *Word Order*, 27–31; Robar, *The Verb and the Paragraph*, 63–67, 149–51.

Genesis 31:33–34

	Text (ESV)	Discourse Mode
33a	So Laban went into Jacob's tent and into Leah's tent and into the tent of the two female servants,	Foreground
33b	but he did not find them.	Foreground
33c	And he went out of Leah's tent	Foreground
33d	and entered Rachel's.	Foreground
34a	Now Rachel had taken the household gods	*Background*
34b	and put them in the camel's saddle	*Background*
34c	and sat on them.	*Background*
34d	Laban felt all about the tent,	Foreground
34e	but did not find them.	Foreground

- **Discourse Mode**. Whether the discourse is currently in "foreground" or "background." Both types of discourse (narrative and non-narrative; defined below) can operate in either discourse mode.

- **Discourse Type**. In BH prose, we distinguish between two main types of discourse:
  i. *Narrative*: when a speaker tells a story, whether fictional or in the past.
  ii. *Non-Narrative*: when a speaker addresses an audience for any purpose besides telling a story, whether to exhort, to predict, to instruct, or any other purpose.

II. SOME BASIC DISCOURSE RELATIONSHIPS

We list below some common discourse relationships that occur in texts. This list helps give a name to relationships between clauses. Because this list is not exhaustive, there will be times when you must give your own name to discourse relationships.[3]

3. For extensive lists, see Robert E. Longacre, *The Grammar of Discourse*, 2nd ed., Topics in Language and Linguistics (New York: Plenum, 1996), 51–122, esp. 101–22. See also Thomas

For simplicity and clarity, examples are provided in English. For all these examples, "B" is the *current* clause being examined, and "A" is the clause just prior to it. In the text, we would have:

A
B
. . .

Some discourse relationships happen between more than two clauses. In these cases, "A" or "B" can be a set of clauses, not just one.

A. NARRATIVE RELATIONSHIPS

Note: The relationships listed below are divided into two lists, narrative and non-narrative. However, these relationships are not exclusively constrained to one discourse type or the other. For example, "contrast" frequently occurs in both narrative and non-narrative.

1. Coordinate Relationships in Narrative

Coordinate relationships are on the same "level" with each other, in contrast to subordinate relationships, where a clause depends conceptually upon and in some way supports a clause at a higher level. Note that this concept of "coordinate" vs. "subordinate" is on the level of concepts; it is not a question of subordination at the level of sentence syntax. One could have two syntactically coordinate clauses: "YHWH brought calamity upon them and destroyed their cities" (from the example under Expansion below). Yet the second clause is considered "subordinate" in the sense that it explains the broader concept given first, that YHWH brought calamity. The distinction between coordinate and subordinate is fluid. For example, sometimes "result" can be analyzed as subordinate (see below), and other times it makes sense to analyze it as coordinate, at the same level as the clause that preceded it.

R. Schreiner, *Interpreting the Pauline Epistles*, Guides to New Testament Exegesis 5 (Grand Rapids: Baker Academic, 2011), 99–113.

A. Next Event

Definition: B happens after A in a narrative sequence.

Example:

A. The woman put the child in the basket
B. and set it among the reeds.

Clarification:

- Sometimes B not only follows A, but B is in contrast to A. In this case, use "contrast" to define the next event.
- Sometimes B not only follows A, but A causes B. In this case, use "result."

B. Contrast

Definition: Either (1) B and A are events, where B follows after A and differs from it; or (2) B and A are states, where B differs from A.

Example 1 (contrasting events):

A. The Assyrians boasted of victory,
B. but God defeated them.

Example 2 (contrasting states):

A. The poor were satisfied,
B. but the rich were hungry.

Clarification:

- Sometimes the contrast is between two events happening simultaneously. In this case, still use "contrast" to define the relationship.
- In narrative, contrasts often appear between two different expectations. In Example 1, the Assyrians expect to win, but the actual outcome is different from that expectation: they are defeated.

C. Simultaneous Action

Definition: B happens at the same time as A in a narrative sequence.

Example:

A. He ate
B. and drank.

Clarification:

- Simultaneous action is not as descriptive as other relationships and should be resorted to only when these other descriptors do not apply:
  - Sometimes B is the same event as A and gives greater detail about it. In this case, use "expansion" to define the relationship.
  - Sometimes A is a larger event that gives the setting for B. In this case, use "circumstance."
  - Sometimes B is in contrast to A. In this case, use "contrast."
  - Sometimes B is similar to A. In this case, use "addition."

D. Summary

Definition: B summarizes A (A could be any number of clauses).

Example:

A[1]. Ahaz made an altar like the one in Damascus
A[2]. and set it in the temple.
B. Thus he sinned against God.

E. New Episode

Definition: B begins a new episode. (A either does not exist [e.g., at the beginning of a book], or it is the last clause of the previous episode).

Example:

A. Abram journeyed on to the Negev. (Bringing the previous narrative to a close.)
B. Now there was a famine in the land.

F. Initiate Background

Definition: B initiates a side comment that does not move the story forward. (See the definition of "background" on p. 43).

Example:

A. Abram went forth as God had told him.
B. Now Abram was seventy-five years old when he left Haran.

2. Subordinate Relationships in Narrative

A. Result

Definition: B is the result of A in a narrative sequence. A is the cause of B, or at least the circumstance that precipitates B.

Example:

A. The dream disturbed Pharaoh,
B. so he sent for his advisors.

B. Expansion

Definition: B is the same event as A (or a part of it). B gives greater detail about A, sometimes explaining the manner in which A happens.

Example 1 (providing more detail):

A. YHWH brought calamity upon them,
B. and destroyed their cities.

Example 2 (explaining the manner in which something happens):

A. David played beautifully,
B. strumming lightly on the strings.

C. Circumstance

Definition: B describes a broader event or situation that is happening when A happens.

Example:

A. Ahab erected an altar for Baal
B. when he was ruling over Israel.

Clarification:

- Sometimes B is the same event as A and gives greater detail about it. In this case, use "expansion" to define the relationship.
- Sometimes B and A happen at the same time and are events of similar scope. In this case, use "simultaneous action."

B. NON-NARRATIVE RELATIONSHIPS

Some of the relationships listed above under "narrative" can also occur in non-narrative (e.g., contrast, result, expansion, etc.). They are not repeated here.

1. Coordinate Relationships in Non-Narrative

a. Next Step

Definition: B is the next action after A in a temporal sequence of some kind (e.g., a series of instructions).

Example:

A. You shall take the animal from the offerer
B. and sacrifice it.

b. Inference ("Therefore")

Definition: B is the logical conclusion from A. (Remember, A could be a series of clauses.)

Example:

A. Achan sinned.
B. Therefore God was angry with Israel.

c. Reason

Definition: B gives the logical ground for A. The "reason" relationship is the inverse of "inference."

Example:

A. Give thanks to YHWH
B. for he is good.

d. Answer

Definition: B is the answer to a question, A.

Example:

A. Why do you stand there?
B. We fear the Philistines.

e. Addition ("What Is More," "Moreover," "In Addition")

Definition: B is true as well as A, where the thing predicated in both cases is similar, or where B builds upon A.

Example 1 (similar cases):

A. Break down the altars,
B. and burn the graven images.

Example 2 (B builds on A):

A. I will go down with you to Egypt,
B. and I will also bring you up.

2. *Subordinate Relationships in Non-Narrative*

A. Purpose

Definition: B is the goal for A. The goal can be positive ("so that") or negative ("so that not").

Example:

A. Obey YHWH's commands
B. so that you may live.

B. Comparison ("As," "Like")

Definition: B is like A. This is the opposite of the "contrast" relationship.

Example:

A. YHWH spoke with Moses
B. as a man speaks to his friend.

C. Condition ("If . . . Then")

Definition: If B is true, then A is true.

Example:

A. I will not destroy the city
B. if I find fifty righteous people there.

D. Concession ("Even Though")

Definition: B is true despite A being true. B is in tension with A.

Example:

A. You will stumble over each other in alarm
B. even though no one is pursuing you.

Chapter 3

Element #1 of Biblical Hebrew Prose

Discourse Markers

Understanding discourse relationships is the primary goal of discourse analysis. Chapter 2 surveyed some discourse relationships that can be conveyed in any language. Now we begin to get specific about how Biblical Hebrew conveys discourse relationships. What are the basic means for communicating discourse relationships in BH prose?

One of the clearest ways to control the flow of a text is with discourse markers.

> **Definition**: Discourse markers are any nonverbal words that identify the function of a clause in the discourse, usually by relating two or more clauses together.

Discourse markers include a wide range of particles and expressions, including the following:

A. Conjunctions (e.g., אִם; כִּי; לְמַעַן; פֶּן)
B. Relatives (e.g., אֲשֶׁר; זוּ; שֶׁ)
C. Interrogatives (e.g., אֵי; אֵיפֹה; הֲ-)
D. Adverbs (e.g., אַךְ; רַק)
E. Interjections (e.g., אוֹי; הִנֵּה)
F. Special expressions (e.g., וְהִנֵּה; וְעַתָּה; לֵאמֹר)

All of these markers often appear at the beginning of a clause to signal that clause's function in the whole discourse.

One may object that some of these markers do not seem to relate clauses to one another.[1] For example, interrogatives identify the clause as a question. These are often followed by an answer. But other times, as in the case of rhetorical questions, they are not. In these cases, we can still recognize that these words operate at the discourse level, identifying the kind of sentence in view and suggesting its role in the larger discourse. Likewise, the interjection אוֹי ("woe") suggests that the purpose of the sentence will be to threaten or lament, without suggesting a relationship with the preceding clauses.

Many discourse markers have a single basic meaning (e.g., יַעַן; פֶּן), and so we can say they make the connection between clauses *explicit.* However, some discourse markers have a variety of uses (e.g., וְעַתָּה; וְהִנֵּה). Since many discourse markers are amply discussed in lexicons and advanced grammars, only a few examples of discourse markers are provided below. For discussions in reference grammars, see:

Bill T. Arnold and John H. Choi, *A Guide to Biblical Hebrew Syntax* (Cambridge: Cambridge University Press, 2003), 95–161.

Christo H. J. van der Merwe, Jackie A. Naudé, and Jan H. Kroeze, *A Biblical Hebrew Reference Grammar,* 2nd ed. (London: Bloomsbury, 2017), §§39–42, 44.

P. Joüon and T. Muraoka, *A Grammar of Biblical Hebrew,* 2nd ed. (Roma: Gregorian & Biblical, 2006), §§158, 160–75.

Finally, a reminder about what we are doing in this chapter and chapters 4–6: these chapters provide lists of the ways in which discourse

1. Bruce Fraser argues that the term "discourse marker" should be reserved for words that indicate the *relationship* between clauses, since otherwise the category becomes unwieldy and unspecified, conflating discourse-related uses of words with non-discourse-related uses ("What Are Discourse Markers?," *Journal of Pragmatics* 31 [1999]: 931–52). However, we believe that we can expand the category to include not only words that specify relationships between clauses but also words that indicate what kind of speech act is in view (as in the examples of rhetorical questions and the interjection אוֹי given here). What unifies these words as a category is that they can be used to indicate a clause's function in the discourse.

markers, verbal sequences, and other phenomena are commonly used to communicate discourse relationships. These lists are not meant to be exhaustive, nor do they provide much guidance for how you would recognize that one usage is at work in a given text as opposed to another possible usage. Discerning which discourse function is being actualized in a given text is the goal of analysis, which is discussed in chapter 7. But for our analysis to succeed, we need a working knowledge of the primary ways BH texts communicate discourse relationships, and therefore the student must be familiar with these lists (a summary table is provided in chapter 9).

I. EXAMPLES OF DISCOURSE MARKERS

EXAMPLE DISCOURSE MARKER #1: פֶּן

This marker usually follows commands or plans and gives a negative purpose for them (i.e., something to be avoided).

Note: For all tables in chapters 3–6, the right-most column contains a translation, not a discourse analysis of the Hebrew text. However, it is a translation informed by discourse analysis.

Deuteronomy 6:12

12a	הִשָּׁמֶר לְךָ	Watch yourself
12b	פֶּן־תִּשְׁכַּח אֶת־יְהוָה אֲשֶׁר הוֹצִיאֲךָ מֵאֶרֶץ מִצְרַיִם מִבֵּית עֲבָדִים׃	***so that you do not*** forget YHWH who brought you out from the land of Egypt, from the house of slaves.

Moses commands the Israelites to be careful so that they do not forget YHWH. This purpose relationship is communicated through the discourse marker פֶּן. (See also: Gen 11:4; Exod 1:10; Deut 4:9, 16, 19, 23; 6:14–15; Ruth 4:6.)

EXAMPLE DISCOURSE MARKER #2: יַעַן

This marker often initiates a dependent clause. The dependent clause is the cause or reason for the main clause on which it depends.

1 Samuel 15:23c–d

23c	יַעַן מָאַסְתָּ אֶת־דְּבַר יְהוָה	*Because* you have rejected the word of YHWH
23d	וַיִּמְאָסְךָ מִמֶּלֶךְ׃	he has rejected you from being king.

The יַעַן clause in verse 23c gives the reason for God rejecting Saul in verse 23d. (See also: Num 20:12; 1 Sam 30:22; 1 Kgs 14:13.)

EXAMPLE DISCOURSE MARKER #3: אֲשֶׁר

The primary purpose of אֲשֶׁר is to initiate a relative clause, but it can also serve other purposes.

Common Discourse Functions:

Note: Because of the complexity of this discourse marker and the ready availability of more extended treatments in lexicons and advanced grammars (see list above), this section is abbreviated.[2]

1. **Expansion** ("which," "who," etc.): the noun to which the אֲשֶׁר refers is clarified, explained, or in some way made more precise (by far the most common). "Expansions" include both limiting relative clauses (which distinguish the substantive from others like it; e.g., "the waters which were under the firmament" vs. those that are not [Gen 1:7]) and non-limiting relative clauses (a parenthetical comment about the substantive without constrasting it with others; e.g., "Now you are cursed from the ground, which has opened its mouth to receive your brother's blood" [Gen 4:11]).[3]
2. **Cause** ("because"): the אֲשֶׁר clause gives the situation that gave rise to the preceding clause (Gen 30:18; 34:13; 1 Sam 20:42).
3. **Result** ("such that"): the אֲשֶׁר clause explains the outcome (real or envisioned) of the preceding clause (Gen 11:7; 13:16; 22:14).
4. **Condition** ("if"): the אֲשֶׁר clause introduces a conditional clause (Lev 4:22; Deut 11:27).

---

2. See the full discussion in Robert D. Holmstedt, *The Relative Clause in Biblical Hebrew*, LSAWS 10 (Winona Lake, IN: Eisenbrauns, 2016), 57–101.

3. See Joüon §158a*.

Note: אֲשֶׁר *is not always used as a discourse marker. In the expression* וְשָׁכַח אֵת אֲשֶׁר־עָשִׂיתָ לוֹ *("And he will forget what you have done to him"; Gen 27:45),* אֲשֶׁר *is used with* אֵת *in a substantive way to form a noun phrase.*

EXAMPLE DISCOURSE MARKER #4: כִּי

The primary purposes of כִּי are to indicate: cause ("for"), temporal circumstances ("when"), and the complement of verbs of knowing and seeing ("that").

Common Discourse Functions:

Note: Because of the complexity of this discourse marker and the ready availability of more extended treatments in lexicons and advanced grammars (see list above), this section is abbreviated.

1. **Cause** ("for," "because"): the כִּי clause gives the situation that gave rise to the preceding clause (Gen 12:10; 43:18).
2. **Circumstance** ("when"): the כִּי clause (which often follows וַיְהִי or וְהָיָה) gives the situation when a following clause is true or when a command should be acted upon (Gen 12:12; Exod 7:9).
3. **Condition** ("if"): much like "circumstance" above, but the כִּי clause is used in a future or legal context where the incident is hypothetical (Exod 21:18).
4. **Expansion** ("that"): as a complement to a verb of seeing or knowing, the כִּי clause fills out what was said or seen or known (Gen 1:10; 12:11).
5. **Contrast** ("but instead"): the כִּי clause states what is true instead of the previous clause (Gen 17:15).

EXAMPLE DISCOURSE MARKER #5: וְעַתָּה

This marker highlights a new direction in the discourse, often a logical conclusion or a shift from the speaker's past to the speaker's present time.

Common Discourse Functions:

1. **Inference**: in light of foregoing reasons, וְעַתָּה introduces a logical conclusion, often summoning the audience to some action.

1 Samuel 26:18b–19a

18b	לָ֤מָּה זֶּה֙ אֲדֹנִ֔י רֹדֵ֖ף אַחֲרֵ֣י עַבְדּ֑וֹ	Why does my lord pursue after his servant?
18c	כִּ֚י מֶ֣ה עָשִׂ֔יתִי	For what have I done?
18d	וּמַה־בְּיָדִ֖י רָעָֽה׃	What evil is on my hands?
19a	וְעַתָּ֗ה יִֽשְׁמַֽע־נָא֙ אֲדֹנִ֣י הַמֶּ֔לֶךְ אֵ֖ת דִּבְרֵ֣י עַבְדּ֑וֹ	***Now therefore***, please let my lord the king listen to the words of his servant.

In verses 18b–d David protests his innocence with a series of rhetorical questions. Verse 19a introduces an important transition using וְעַתָּה, where David, in light of his innocence, asks Saul to listen to his plea. (See also: Num 22:6; 1 Sam 25:17; 2 Sam 17:16; 1 Kgs 1:12; 8:25; 2 Kgs 5:15.)

2. **Shifts time reference to the present**: in contrast to past events, וְעַתָּה shifts the focus to the present.

Deuteronomy 10:22

22a	בְּשִׁבְעִ֣ים נֶ֔פֶשׁ יָרְד֥וּ אֲבֹתֶ֖יךָ מִצְרָ֑יְמָה	Your fathers went down to Egypt seventy persons,
22b	וְעַתָּ֗ה שָֽׂמְךָ֙ יְהוָ֣ה אֱלֹהֶ֔יךָ כְּכוֹכְבֵ֥י הַשָּׁמַ֖יִם לָרֹֽב׃	*and now* YHWH your God has made you as numerous as the stars of heaven.

Verse 22b contrasts the present situation with the past situation described in verse 22a. (See also: Judg 6:13; Ruth 3:11; 1 Kgs 12:11.)

EXAMPLE DISCOURSE MARKER #6: וְהִנֵּה

This marker introduces something new and important to both narrative and non-narrative speech. The new thing can be a point of view, something newly perceived, or a new character or idea. It is similar in function to הִנֵּה, but different enough to be treated on its own.

Common Discourse Functions:

1. **New point of view**: וְהִנֵּה can shift the point of view of a story, often giving the perspective of a character in the story.

Ruth 2:3b–4b

3b	וַתָּבוֹא	So she [Ruth] came
3c	וַתְּלַקֵּט בַּשָּׂדֶה אַחֲרֵי הַקֹּצְרִים	and gleaned in the field after the reapers.
3d	וַיִּקֶר מִקְרֶהָ חֶלְקַת הַשָּׂדֶה לְבֹעַז אֲשֶׁר מִמִּשְׁפַּחַת אֱלִימֶלֶךְ׃	And she happened to be in the portion of the field belonging to Boaz, who was of the family of Elimelech.
4a	וְהִנֵּה־בֹעַז בָּא מִבֵּית לֶחֶם	***And look***, Boaz was coming from Bethelehem,
4b	וַיֹּאמֶר לַקּוֹצְרִים	and he said to the reapers . . .

Verse 3 focuses on Ruth and her activities, but verse 4 shifts the point of view to Boaz, as perceived by Ruth and the other reapers. The marker וְהִנֵּה signals this shift. Note that in terms of the discourse relationships listed above, verse 4a would be "next event" after verse 3d, but the added nuance of a new point of view should also be noted. (See also: Gen 15:17; 24:15; Judg 11:34; 2 Sam 16:1; 1 Kgs 13:1.)

2. **Imperative to consider a new topic**: this usage is similar to (1) above, except it is found in non-narrative. The speaker seeks to draw the listener's attention from the previous topic to a new topic, often one of great importance. The new topic can be something concrete, capable of being seen with the eyes (e.g., Gen 29:6), or it can be an idea (e.g., Gen 27:36).

1 Samuel 10:2d–f

2d	נִמְצְאוּ הָאֲתֹנוֹת אֲשֶׁר הָלַכְתָּ לְבַקֵּשׁ	The donkeys are found which you went to seek.
2e	וְהִנֵּה נָטַשׁ אָבִיךָ אֶת־דִּבְרֵי הָאֲתֹנוֹת	***Now look***, your father has ceased to care about the donkeys
2f	וְדָאַג לָכֶם	and is worried about you.

The speech begins with a report about Saul's donkeys being found (v. 2d) but shifts immediately to a new situation that demands Saul's attention: that his father is now anxious about him (vv. 2e–f). The imperative to consider this new topic is conveyed by וְהִנֵּה. (See also: Gen 18:10; 27:36; 28:15; 29:6; 1 Sam 12:13.)

3. **Results of looking**: new information gained by looking can be introduced with וְהִנֵּה. Often the new information is shocking or momentous (e.g., Gen 29:25; 1 Sam 3:11).

   This usage involves some complexity:

   - Sometimes the looking is assumed (e.g., Gen 8:11); other times it is explicit (e.g., Gen 8:13).
   - This usage occasionally overlaps with (1) above, where the result of looking leads to a new point of view for the story.

2 Kings 6:17e–g

17e	וַיִּפְקַח יְהוָה אֶת־עֵינֵי הַנַּעַר	And YHWH opened the eyes of the young man
17f	וַיַּרְא	and he saw,
17g	וְהִנֵּה הָהָר מָלֵא סוּסִים וְרֶכֶב אֵשׁ סְבִיבֹת אֱלִישָׁע׃	***and behold***, the mountain was full of horses and chariots of fire all around Elisha.

When the servant's eyes are opened, he is shocked to see the mountain full of horses and chariots. Because of the awesome nature of this supernatural event, it is appropriate to use the archaic "behold." (See also: Gen 1:31; 6:12; 22:13; Judg 3:24; 1 Sam 5:3; 14:17.)

4. **Inference**: sometimes when a speaker draws attention to a new idea, this new idea is the logical conclusion of the foregoing discourse.

2 Samuel 19:21[20]

21a	כִּי יָדַע עַבְדְּךָ	For your servant knows
21b	כִּי אֲנִי חָטָאתִי	that I [Shimei] have sinned.
21c	וְהִנֵּה־בָאתִי הַיּוֹם רִאשׁוֹן לְכָל־בֵּית יוֹסֵף לָרֶדֶת לִקְרַאת אֲדֹנִי הַמֶּלֶךְ׃	***Therefore*** I have come today, the first of all the house of Joseph to come down to meet my lord the king.

Shimei pleads with David. The knowledge of his sin (v. 21a) led him to conclude that he must come down to meet the king (v. 21b), and this logical conclusion is marked with וְהִנֵּה. (See also: Gen 15:3; 2 Sam 3:12.)

EXAMPLE DISCOURSE MARKER #7: לֵאמֹר

This expression almost always introduces direct speech.[4]

Genesis 1:22a–d

22a	וַיְבָרֶךְ אֹתָם אֱלֹהִים	And God blessed them,
22b	לֵאמֹר	saying,
22c	פְּרוּ	"Be fruitful
22d	וּרְבוּ	and multiply . . ."

The לֵאמֹר construction marks or introduces the content (in directly spoken words) of the blessing in verse 22a. Sometimes, as in the case of 1 Kings 1:5, this expression can introduce not so much words that are spoken but thoughts that a character says to himself/herself. (See also: Exod 1:22.)

II. *WAW* AS A DISCOURSE MARKER?

Should *waw* be considered a discourse marker? On the one hand, *waw* can conjoin noun phrases or prepositional phrases (אֵת הַשָּׁמַיִם וְאֵת הָאָרֶץ; Gen 1:1), but this is not relevant to our discussion about discourse markers, since it is not conjoining clauses. But *waw* can also conjoin two clauses, like many of the discourse markers above. This clause-connecting use of *waw* breaks down into three scenarios:

4. This expression rarely functions as a standard *l* + infinitive construct; see Gen 26:7. See the fuller discussion in Miller, *Representation of Speech*. For Miller, לֵאמֹר is "an infinitive that has become grammaticalized as a complementizer introducing the complement of direct speech" ("Introducing Direct Discourse in Biblical Hebrew Narrative," in *Biblical Hebrew and Discourse Linguistics*, ed. Robert D. Bergen [Dallas, TX: Summer Institute of Linguistics, 1994], 209).

1. The *waw* could head a verbal form (*wayyiqtol, weqatal, waw* + imperative, etc.). When it does so, the *waw*'s significance is primarily its contribution to the verbal form, and so our focus in discourse analysis will be on the verbal form (see chapters 4–5 below).
2. The *waw* could head a non-verb phrase (a noun phrase or prepositional phrase or some other adverbial phrase) that is followed by a verb (e.g., וְאַבְרָהָם שָׁב). In this case, the word order shift is more salient than the *waw* conjunction, so we treat it in chapter 6 below (on word order).
3. Finally, the *waw* could head a verbless clause. In this case, its discourse function will be similar to that of (2) above, so we will also treat it in chapter 6.

In short, the seemingly endless functions of *waw* are actually not so much functions of *waw* alone but of the larger clausal and supra-clausal structures of which *waw* is a part.[5] Therefore we do not treat *waw* as a discourse marker unto itself like those listed above.

5. For a survey of *waw*'s polysemy and proposals to address it (including a proposal quite different from what we offer here), see Richard C. Steiner, "Does the Biblical Hebrew Conjunction-W Have Many Meanings, One Meaning, or No Meaning at All?," *JBL* 119 (2000): 249–67.

—— *Chapter 4* ——

Element #2 of Biblical Hebrew Prose (Part 1 of 2)

Verbal Sequences in Narrative

I. INTRODUCTION

In addition to discourse markers, BH uses sequences of verbs to communicate discourse relationships. For example, a *waw* + *yiqtol* after an imperative usually communicates purpose ("so that"):

Judges 1:3b–c

3b	עֲלֵה אִתִּי בְגוֹרָלִי	Come up with me into my allotment
3c	וְנִלָּחֲמָה בַּכְּנַעֲנִי	***so that*** we might fight against the Canaanites.

The discourse relationship of purpose is communicated simply *by the verbs being in certain forms and in a certain order.* In this example there is no discourse marker meaning "so that" in verse 3c, but the idea of "purpose" is still communicated *by this sequence of verbs.* Although verbal sequences may seem unintuitive to us, these simple structures sometimes have the same explicit clarity as the markers in chapter 3 above.

II. TWO LEVELS OF MEANING FOR HEBREW VERBS

Before we can discuss how verbal sequences convey specific discourse relationships, we need to understand that Hebrew verbs can convey meaning on two distinct levels:

Level 1: Tense, Aspect, and Mood: the first level is what people often mean when they speak of "verbal semantics." Every verbal form (*wayyiqtol*, *weqatal*, etc.) communicates something about how the verbal action or state relates to time (tense and aspect) and reality (mood). This level focuses on the action or state that the verb represents *as a single unit*.

Level 2: Discourse Relationships: in addition to the verbal semantics in Level 1, verbal forms can also communicate something about how a clause relates to the others around it. This level, the way verbal forms communicate discourse relationships, is the focus of this chapter and the next.

To see how a verbal form operates on both levels, consider the *wayyiqtol* form. The *wayyiqtol* usually communicates past tense, perfective aspect, and indicative mood (Level 1). But this form also has a discourse function, usually continuing the narrative flow that is already in motion (Level 2).

THE BASICS OF TENSE, ASPECT, AND MOOD

Classic verbal semantics (tense, aspect, and mood; Level 1 above) are not technically under the heading of discourse analysis, but since many students are unfamiliar with these concepts and they will come up repeatedly below, we provide a simple primer here.

1. *Tense* refers to the location of a situation in time.[1] This location is relative to some other reference point (usually the speaker's present). The most common locations are: before, overlapping with, or after the reference point. Example tenses in English:
    - Past ("he went")
    - Present ("he goes")
    - Future ("he will go")

1. This definition and the definitions for aspect and mood are adapted from Cook, *Time and the Biblical Hebrew Verb*, 70, 191. The definition of mood also incorporates insights from Daniel B. Wallace, *Greek Grammar Beyond the Basics: An Exegetical Syntax of the New Testament* (Grand Rapids: Zondervan, 1996), 444–45. For a fuller discussion of tense, aspect, and mood, see Cook, *Time and the Biblical Hebrew Verb*, 1–76.

In English, there is a specific verb form for each tense idea. For example, the past tense form of a verb conveys the past tense idea. In BH, there is no past tense verb form. Instead, BH conveys tense using a combination of signals, including both verb forms and contextual factors, as we discuss below.

2. *Aspect* refers to the structure of a situation in time. There are many different kinds of aspect, but the two most relevant for BH are perfective and imperfective aspect, which operate from a viewpoint perspective.
   - *Perfective aspect* views a situation as an undifferentiated whole ("he ran to the store"). Like a wide-angle camera lens, it captures an entire situation, but from a distant perspective.
   - *Imperfective aspect* has the temporal progression of a situation in view ("he was running to the store"). It views the situation like a close-up, where the beginning and end are cropped and the action is seen as being in progress.

Note that perfective and imperfective aspect can occur in different tenses, as the table below shows in English.

	Past Tense	Future Tense
Perfective aspect	He went	He will go
Imperfective aspect	He was going	He will be going

3. *Mood* refers to how a speaker portrays a situation with respect to its reality. The two most basic kinds of mood are the real and unreal mood. The real is the most common and is the default in BH. The unreal mood is marked in several ways and has many variations.
   - *Real mood* (referred to in the rest of this book as "indicative") portrays a situation as a certain reality ("he ran").
   - *Unreal mood* involves some kind of uncertainty. Some common kinds include:
     a. Volitional ("run!"): a speaker commands something to be real.

b. Permissive ("you may run"): a speaker grants that something is allowed to happen.
c. Purpose ("so that I might run"): a speaker expresses intention (whether of himself/herself or others).
d. Contingent ("he would run"): a speaker expresses that a situation is true if/when other situations are true.
e. Interrogative ("will you run?"): a speaker asks a question.

How BH expresses tense, aspect, and mood is one of the most challenging questions in the study of BH.[2] For the purpose of this book, we will build on the conclusion argued by John A. Cook that *each verbal form (qatal, yiqtol, etc.) has its own "default" meaning in terms of tense, aspect, and mood, but that these defaults can be overridden based on discourse considerations.* A chart of the default meanings for each verbal form (adapted from Cook's work on the verb) is below.[3]

Default Verbal Semantics

Form	Default Semantics		
	Tense	Aspect	Mood
wayyiqtol	Past	Perfective	Indicative
qatal	Past	Perfective	Indicative
weqatal	*Unspecified*	*Unspecified*	Unreal (conditional, imperative, etc.)
yiqtol	Future	Imperfective	Indicative
Participle	Present	Imperfective	Indicative
Imperative	*Unspecified*	*Unspecified*	Imperative
Verbless clauses (nominal sentences)	Present	Stative[4]	Indicative

2. The question has provoked titles like Leslie McFall's *The Enigma of the Hebrew Verbal System*, Historic Texts and Interpreters in Biblical Scholarship 2 (Sheffield: Almond, 1982). For a recent survey of scholarship on the Hebrew verb and how Hebrew expresses tense, aspect and mood, see Cook, *Time and the Biblical Hebrew Verb*.

3. Cook, *Time and the Biblical Hebrew Verb*, 176–271. For an extensive taxonomy of the various uses of each verbal form, see Jan Joosten, *The Verbal System of Biblical Hebrew: A New Synthesis Elaborated on the Basis of Classical Prose*, JBS 10 (Jerusalem: Simor, 2012). However, Joosten's conclusions about default verbal semantics differ from the chart provided here.

4. Stative aspect refers to a state of being, rather than an action. For example: "he was tired."

Note that this chart simply provides the *default* semantics of the verb—that is, the semantics that each form suggests when considered alone. As we will see, these defaults are often overridden by contextual considerations.[5] For example, although *qatal* usually evokes a past tense idea (עָשִׂיתָ in Gen 4:10), it can also express present tense (יָעַצְתִּי in 2 Sam 17:11) and future tense (לָקַחְתִּי in 1 Sam 2:16), depending on context.

Such examples do not mean that the BH verbal system is arbitrary or unintelligible. As we will see, discourse analysis helps the interpreter decide about tense, aspect, and mood in a well-informed and rigorous manner. But since context often overrides these defaults, we can make a vital observation: BH conveys tense, aspect, and mood not simply through the forms of verbs (as is usually the case in English), but through *the forms of verbs in their discourse context*. Our examples in Chapter 8 demonstrate repeatedly how context informs our understanding of the tense, aspect, and mood of a given verbal form.

III. CONTINUATIVE FORMS

In addition to conveying ideas about tense, aspect, and mood (level 1), each BH verbal form communicates discourse relationships (level 2). The most fundamental discourse relationship is that of *continuation*, where a continuative verb form prolongs the ideas of the previous clause, which may have been set in motion much earlier in the discourse. These pre-existing ideas include:

- Verbal semantics (i.e., whatever tense, aspect, or mood happens to be active). If a biblical author has initiated past tense, progressive aspect, and indicative mood, we expect that the continuative verb form will continue these verbal semantics.
- Discourse mode (i.e., whether the text is in foreground or background). If a text is narrating an event in the foreground, we expect

5. For an overview of how these defaults can be overriden by contextual factors, see Joosten, *The Verbal System*, 79–123.

that a continuative form will continue to relate that event rather than introducing a background comment.

- Other discourse scenarios. For example, a clause may continue a protasis (the "if" or "when" clause of a conditional statement), or the condition of an oath, or the content of a blessing, or the complement of a verb of perception.[6] Once these discourse scenarios have been initiated, they may be continued.

Each discourse type has its own continuative verb form:

- Narrative's continuative form is *wayyiqtol*.[7]
- Non-narrative's continuative form is *weqatal*.

A continuative form assumes that certain discourse modes and verbal semantics are established earlier in the immediate context. The continuative forms then continue these ideas "automatically." For example:

Deuteronomy 8:1

1a	כָּל־הַמִּצְוָה . . . תִּשְׁמְרוּן לַעֲשׂוֹת	All the commandments you shall be careful to keep
1b	לְמַעַן תִּחְיוּן	so that you might live
1c	וּרְבִיתֶם	***and multiply***
1d	וּבָאתֶם	***and enter***
1e	וִירִשְׁתֶּם אֶת־הָאָרֶץ אֲשֶׁר־נִשְׁבַּע יְהוָה לַאֲבֹתֵיכֶם׃	***and possess*** the land which YHWH swore to your fathers.

The verb תִּחְיוּן in verse 1b has a subjunctive mood, as indicated by the לְמַעַן conjunction. The three *weqatal* forms in verses 1c–e continue that purpose idea. We could render them woodenly: e.g., "and *so that you might* multiply."

6. For the last example, consider how *wayyiqtol* is used in Gen 28:6–7.
7. On *wayyiqtol*'s primary function as a continuative form, see Robar, *The Verb and the Paragraph*, 101–111.

Weqatal can also continue:

- Imperative mood: e.g., Gen 6:14; Exod 7:15; Lev 1:2; Ruth 2:9.
- Volitional mood: e.g., Gen 12:13; Deut 4:1; 5:33.
- Hypothetical scenarios: e.g., Exod 1:16; Deut 4:25; Ruth 1:11.
- Predictions/promises: e.g., Gen 6:18; 7:4; Deut 4:22; 1 Kgs 13:2.
- And many other scenarios: customs (Ruth 4:7), blessings (Ruth 4:15), etc.

Much like *weqatal, wayyiqtol* can also continue a wide variety of verbal ideas, as well as both discourse modes (background and foreground). In the following example *wayyiqtol* continues background as well as a pluperfect tense idea:

Genesis 31:33d–34e

33d	וַיָּבֹ֖א בְּאֹ֥הֶל רָחֵֽל׃	And he [Laban] entered Rachel's tent.
34a[8]	וְרָחֵ֞ל לָקְחָ֣ה אֶת־הַתְּרָפִ֗ים	Now Rachel had taken the household gods
34b	וַתְּשִׂמֵ֛ם בְּכַ֥ר הַגָּמָ֖ל	***and had put them*** in the camel's saddle,
34c	וַתֵּ֣שֶׁב עֲלֵיהֶ֑ם	***and had sat*** on them.
34d	וַיְמַשֵּׁ֥שׁ לָבָ֛ן אֶת־כָּל־הָאֹ֖הֶל	So Laban felt through all the tent,
34e	וְלֹ֥א מָצָֽא׃	but he did not find them.

The foreground sequence of Laban's search in verse 33 is interrupted by an aside about Rachel's previous activity in hiding the idols (vv. 34a–34c). This aside is initiated by a *waw* + x + *qatal* (v. 34a), which has a pluperfect meaning ("had taken"). The two *wayyiqtol* verbs in verses 34b–c continue the background narrative once it has been initiated in verse 34a. In particular, they continue both the pluperfect tense and the background discourse mode.[9] Then the foreground resumes in verse 34d.[10]

8. The "x" slot can be filled by a subject, an object, or an adverbial (such as a prepositional phrase).

9. This example shows that it is a mistake to assume that *wayyiqtol* inherently means foreground, as is sometimes claimed.

10. For a similar situation, see the flashback in 2 Kgs 13:14–20b: a *waw* + x + *qatal* heads the flashback in v. 14a and establishes the pluperfect context (confirmed by the mention of Joash in v. 14c, who was dead and buried in v. 13). A series of *wayyiqtol* verbs continues a

Wayyiqtol can also continue iterative aspect (the idea of a habitual action): in 2 Sam 15:2–4 a daily routine is introduced using *weqatal* (vv. 2a–b), and then *wayyiqtol* continues the iterative aspect in verses 2c–4.

IV. IMPORTANT VERBAL SEQUENCES IN NARRATIVE

Verbal sequences can convey many other discourse relationships besides continuation. In the rest of this chapter, we survey the most important verbal sequences in narrative. In the next chapter, we survey the most important verbal sequences in non-narrative.

1. *WAYYIQTOL*

Wayyiqtol is the continuative form in narrative discourse. Several of the discourse functions below are specific kinds of continuation (e.g., "next event," "contrast,"[11] "result"), but one is disjunctive ("new episode"), showing the flexibility of this form.

Note: One special instance of wayyiqtol is וַיְהִי, *which is discussed separately below* *(pp. 71–73).*

Common Discourse Functions:

1. **Next Event**: the event in view takes place after the previous one.

1 Kings 17:19c–d, f

19c	וַיִּקָּחֵהוּ מֵחֵיקָהּ	Then he [Elijah] took him [the widow's son] from her bosom,
19d	וַיַּעֲלֵהוּ אֶל־הָעֲלִיָּה	***and he brought him*** to the upper chamber
19f	וַיַּשְׁכִּבֵהוּ עַל־מִטָּתוֹ׃	***and laid him*** on his bed.

These three clauses narrate three distinct events, each one following the other. Elijah (1) takes the boy, (2) brings him up (a relative clause is omitted), and (3) lays him on the bed. (See also: Gen 22:3; Judg 9:45; 1 Sam 17:31.)

lengthy flashback story that sets the stage for the narrative in vv. 20c–21. See also Judg 4:11; 11:1; 1 Sam 28:3; 1 Kgs 18:3–4; 2 Kgs 5:2; Jon 1:5.

11. We can still say that the contrast relationship is continuative in that it continues the tense, aspect, and mood of the preceding clauses, as well as the discourse mode.

2. **Contrast** ("but"): this is an added nuance to the previous discourse function, "next event." Sometimes the next event is noticeably surprising: it is in spite of, or in contrast to, the previous chain of events.

Genesis 37:35a–b

35a	וַיָּקֻמוּ כָל־בָּנָיו וְכָל־בְּנֹתָיו לְנַחֲמוֹ	And all his [Jacob's] sons and all his daughters arose to comfort him,
35b	וַיְמָאֵן לְהִתְנַחֵם	***but he refused*** to be comforted.

In contrast with the attempt to comfort Jacob (v. 35a), he refuses to be comforted (v. 35b). (See also: Gen 12:17; 29:8; 1 Kgs 13:22.)

3. **Result** ("and so"): this is an added nuance to the first discourse function, "next event." Sometimes the next event is caused by the previous events.

Genesis 37:28a–d

28a	וַיַּעַבְרוּ אֲנָשִׁים מִדְיָנִים סֹחֲרִים	Then some Midianite traders passed by,
28b	וַיִּמְשְׁכוּ	***so they dragged***
28c	וַיַּעֲלוּ אֶת־יוֹסֵף מִן־הַבּוֹר	and lifted up Joseph from the pit
28d	וַיִּמְכְּרוּ אֶת־יוֹסֵף לַיִּשְׁמְעֵאלִים בְּעֶשְׂרִים כָּסֶף	and sold Joseph to the Ishmaelites for 20 pieces of silver.

The Midianite traders (v. 28a) triggered the selling of Joseph into slavery (v. 28b–d). (See also: Gen 8:11; Exod 1:7; 1 Sam 22:11.)

4. **Simultaneous** ("and at the same time"): the event conveyed by *wayyiqtol* happens at the same time as the event marked by the previous *wayyiqtol*.

Genesis 24:54a–b

54a	וַיֹּאכְלוּ	And they ate
54b	וַיִּשְׁתּוּ	***and they drank***

In all likelihood, the eating and drinking are happening at basically the same time, as two aspects of one event (the dinner at Bethuel's house). (See also: Gen 45:2; Josh 2:4; Judg 7:20.)

5. **Expansion** ("and what's more"): this is an added nuance to the previous discourse function, "simultaneous event." Sometimes the event marked by *wayyiqtol* not only happens at the same time as the previous *wayyiqtol* event, but the second *wayyiqtol* gives additional information about the first.

1 Samuel 4:2c–d

2c	וַיִּנָּגֶף יִשְׂרָאֵל לִפְנֵי פְלִשְׁתִּים	And Israel was defeated before the Philistines,
2d	וַיַּכּוּ בַמַּעֲרָכָה בַּשָּׂדֶה כְּאַרְבַּעַת אֲלָפִים אִישׁ׃	*who killed* in the field about four thousand men from the army.

The defeat in verse 2c is further detailed in verse 2d, which provides information regarding how many men the Philistines killed. Sometimes a *wayyiqtol* that expands on a previous one can be translated as a relative clause (beginning with "who" or "which"). (See also: Gen 24:50; Exod 2:10 [וַתֹּאמֶר].)

6. **New episode** ("Now . . ."): the event narrated by the *wayyiqtol* begins a new unit in the narrative or even a new book (e.g., Lev 1:1). In these situations, *wayyiqtol* initiates a new foreground sequence.

Genesis 11:32a–12:1a

11:32a	וַיִּהְיוּ יְמֵי־תֶרַח חָמֵשׁ שָׁנִים וּמָאתַיִם שָׁנָה	Now the days of Terah were two hundred and five years,
11:32b	וַיָּמָת תֶּרַח בְּחָרָן׃	and Terah died in Haran.
12:1a	וַיֹּאמֶר יְהוָה אֶל־אַבְרָם	*Now* YHWH *said* to Abram, . . .

The narrative about Terah comes to an end, and a new episode begins with 12:1a, narrated by a simple *wayyiqtol* (וַיֹּאמֶר). (See also: Lev 1:1; Num 1:1; 2 Sam 9:1.)

2. וַיְהִי

The special *wayyiqtol* verb form וַיְהִי has unique syntax and discourse functions. The first two uses occur when וַיְהִי is followed immediately by a temporal phrase.[12]

Common Discourse Functions:

1. **New Unit**: וַיְהִי can introduce a temporal phrase that gives the setting for the narrative that follows. The new unit can be a paragraph, a story, or even a book.

Genesis 38:1a–b

1a	וַיְהִי֙ בָּעֵ֣ת הַהִ֔וא	At that time
1b	וַיֵּ֥רֶד יְהוּדָ֖ה מֵאֵ֣ת אֶחָ֑יו	Judah went down from his brothers.

The וַיְהִי here signals a new episode in Genesis. The temporal phrase (בָּעֵת הַהִוא; "at that time") gives the circumstances for Judah's action in verse 1b. Although older translations render וַיְהִי as something like "and it came to pass," it does not need to be translated. The phrase "at that time" can be made in English to directly modify the following clause, thus making one clause in English out of two clauses in Hebrew. (See also: Gen 6:1; 40:1; Josh 1:1; 1 Sam 28:1; 2 Kgs 25:27.)

2. **Shift in Time**: this usage is similar to the previous one, only it occurs in the midst of units. The וַיְהִי allows the narrator to move the narrative timeframe to a new point in time. As with usage (1), the temporal phrase immediately after וַיְהִי gives the circumstances (and often the *cause*) of the next clause. Sometimes the new point in time is something that just happened, allowing the narrator to talk about things happening simultaneously (see Num 16:31; 1 Sam 4:18; 13:10).

---

12. For fuller discussion from a discourse perspective, see Christo H. J. van der Merwe, "The Elusive Biblical Hebrew Term WYHY: A Perspective in Terms of Its Syntax, Semantics, and Pragmatics in 1 Samuel," *HS* 40 (1999): 83–114.

1 Kings 16:17a–18b

17a	וַיַּעֲלֶה עָמְרִי וְכָל־יִשְׂרָאֵל עִמּוֹ מִגִּבְּתוֹן	And Omri went up from Gibbethon, and all Israel with him,
17b	וַיָּצֻרוּ עַל־תִּרְצָה׃	and they beseiged Tirzah.
18a	וַיְהִי כִּרְאוֹת זִמְרִי כִּי־נִלְכְּדָה הָעִיר	*Now* when Zimri saw that the city had been captured,
18b	וַיָּבֹא אֶל־אַרְמוֹן בֵּית־הַמֶּלֶךְ	he went into the citadel of the king's house.

Verses 17a–b narrate the advance of Omri and his army on Tirzah. In verse 18a, the narrative shifts forward in time to the capture of the city and Zimri's response. This shift is signaled with וַיְהִי. (See also: Judg 19:5; 2 Sam 17:27; 1 Kgs 13:23.)

3. **Result**: the וַיְהִי reports the results of the previous *wayyiqtol* chain. Usually the result is a state of being or a piece of information, not an event.

Joshua 8:24c–25a

24c	וַיָּשֻׁבוּ כָל־יִשְׂרָאֵל הָעַי	Then all Israel returned to Ai,
24d	וַיַּכּוּ אֹתָהּ לְפִי־חָרֶב׃	and they struck it with the edge of the sword.
25a	וַיְהִי כָל־הַנֹּפְלִים בַּיּוֹם הַהוּא מֵאִישׁ וְעַד־אִשָּׁה שְׁנֵים עָשָׂר אֶלֶף	All those who fell that day, both man and woman, were 12,000.

The previous *wayyiqtol* verbs narrate the fall of Ai. The וַיְהִי reports a statistic resulting from the battle. (See also: Gen 47:28; 50:9; Exod 1:5; 34:28; Num 31:52; Josh 6:27; 8:25; 21:40; Judg 6:40; 7:6.)

4. **Standard *wayyiqtol***: in addition to the special uses above, וַיְהִי can also function as a typical *wayyiqtol* verb with the usual meaning of היה in the *qal* ("to be" or "to happen" or "to become"). This situation is sometimes called a "non-discourse" usage of וַיְהִי. In this case it is capable of all the standard uses of *wayyiqtol* listed above (see pp. 68–70).

Note: One clue to identifying this usage is that it will sometimes be followed by a subject noun that agrees in gender and number (masc. and sg.).

Exodus 7:10c–d

10c	וַיַּשְׁלֵ֨ךְ אַהֲרֹ֜ן אֶת־מַטֵּ֗הוּ לִפְנֵ֥י פַרְעֹ֖ה וְלִפְנֵ֣י עֲבָדָ֑יו	Then Aaron threw down his staff before Pharaoh and before his servants,
10d	וַיְהִ֥י לְתַנִּֽין׃	***and it became*** a serpent.

Here the וַיְהִי functions as a standard *wayyiqtol* verb. Verse 10d is the next event after verse 10c. (See also: Exod 2:10; 1 Sam 14:25; 28:16.)

3. *WAW* + X + *QATAL* IN A *WAYYIQTOL* SEQUENCE

Definition: In the sequence above, the "x" slot can be filled by a subject, an object, or an adverbial (such as a prepositional phrase). Examples of this pattern:

וְאַחֲרֵי־כֵן֩ קָבַ֨ר אַבְרָהָ֜ם	"And after this, Abraham buried . . ." (Gen 23:19) A prepositional phrase at the beginning
וְיִשְׂרָאֵ֗ל אָהַ֤ב אֶת־יוֹסֵף֙	"Now Israel loved Joseph . . ." (Gen 37:3) A subject at the beginning

Since narrative is carried forward by the continuative form *wayyiqtol*, any departure from *wayyiqtol* merits close attention. In a *wayyiqtol* chain, a clause in the form of *waw* + x + *qatal* can indicate a number of different discourse relationships. These relationships are treated below in chapter 6, where we treat in one place the situations (in both narrative and non-narrative) where subjects, objects and adverbials precede a verb.

4. *WEQATAL* IN A *WAYYIQTOL* SEQUENCE

In addition to *waw* + x + *qatal*, another important departure from *wayyiqtol* in narrative is *weqatal*.[13] Although *weqatal* is common in non-narrative, it is unusual in narrative.[14]

13. On the question of whether we must distinguish *weqatal* (*waw* consecutive) from *waw* + *qatal* (*waw* conjunctive), see p. 77.

14. Scholars note that *wayyiqtol* eventually became obsolete in post-classical Hebrew,

Common Discourse Functions:

1. **Mark a Foreground Event as Climactic or Final**: sometimes the *weqatal* is an event in the foreground that is noticeably important. Often this event comes at the end of a narrative as the momentous consequences of what has preceded.

2 Kings 24:12b–14a

12b	וַיִּקַּח אֹתוֹ מֶלֶךְ בָּבֶל בִּשְׁנַת שְׁמֹנֶה לְמָלְכוֹ׃	So the king of Babylon took him [Jehoiachin] in the eighth year of his reign,
13a	וַיּוֹצֵא מִשָּׁם אֶת־כָּל־אוֹצְרוֹת בֵּית יְהוָה	and he brought out from there all the treasures of the house of YHWH
14a	וְהִגְלָה אֶת־כָּל־יְרוּשָׁלַםִ	***and thus he exiled*** all Jerusalem.

Judah's history draws to a close with the capture of Jerusalem and its king. The series of actions Nebuchadnezzar carried out to capture and plunder the city come to a close (and a climax) with the exiling of all Jerusalem in verse 14a. The following verses (vv. 15–16) then give a summary of his actions using *wayyiqtol*. (See also: Gen 15:6; Judg 3:23.)

2. **Initiate a Background *weqatal* Sequence, Conveying Habitual Information**: sometimes a *weqatal* in the midst of a narrative is the beginning of a *weqatal* sequence, where *weqatal* functions as it does in non-narrative (discussed below; see pp. 77–81). In this case, the *weqatal* sequence conveys background information while the foreground is halted.

---

being replaced by *weqatal* and *waw* + x + *qatal*. Even in late BH, we begin to see this change: e.g., Eccl 9:14–15. See M. Eskhult, "Verbal Syntax in Late Biblical Hebrew," in *Diggers at the Well: Proceedings of a Third International Symposium on the Hebrew of the Dead Sea Scrolls and Ben Sira*, ed. T. Muraoka and John F. Elwolde, STDJ 36 (Leiden: Brill, 2000), 84–93; Joüon §119za; Joosten, *The Verbal System*, 224–25.

Genesis 29:2–3

2a	וַיַּרְא	And he looked,
2b	וְהִנֵּה בְאֵר בַּשָּׂדֶה	and he saw a well in the field.
3a	וְנֶאֶסְפוּ־שָׁמָּה כָל־הָעֲדָרִים	***When*** all the flocks ***would gather*** there,
3b	וְגָלֲלוּ אֶת־הָאֶבֶן מֵעַל פִּי הַבְּאֵר	they would roll the stone from the mouth of the well,
3c	וְהִשְׁקוּ אֶת־הַצֹּאן	and would water the flock.
3d	וְהֵשִׁיבוּ אֶת־הָאֶבֶן עַל־פִּי הַבְּאֵר לִמְקֹמָהּ׃	Then they would put the stone back on the mouth of the well in its place.

The narrative about Jacob's flight from Esau is halted in verse 2, and a short *weqatal* sequence occurs in verse 3 that explains how the well was used by the shepherds. Then the narrative resumes in verse 4. Verse 3 is thus a background comment in which *weqatal* has a variety of uses: in verse 3a it forms a protasis ("when"), which then has a two-part apodosis ("then") in verse 3b–c. Verse 3d then describes a subsequent step after the watering in verse 3c. (See also: Exod 18:25; 33:7–11; Num 21:9; Judg 6:3.)

3. **Indistiguishable from *wayyiqtol***: sometimes *weqatal* is used when *wayyiqtol* is expected, but there is no apparent reason for the shift in form. Isolated explanations can be found for these variations but no compelling patterns.[15] These anomalies reflect our incomplete knowledge of BH.

1 Samuel 17:38

38a	וַיַּלְבֵּשׁ שָׁאוּל אֶת־דָּוִד מַדָּיו	So Saul clothed David with his garments,
38b	וְנָתַן קוֹבַע נְחֹשֶׁת עַל־רֹאשׁוֹ	and put a helmet of bronze on his head,
38c	וַיַּלְבֵּשׁ אֹתוֹ שִׁרְיוֹן׃	and clothed him with armor.

15. For example, Longacre sees the introduction of *weqatal* in 2 Kgs 25:29 as signaling a shift from narrative discourse to procedural discourse. Even though the first *weqatal* is not frequentative (he did not have to keep on changing his clothes), instead it is "his initial step in his new life as pensioner of the king of Babylon" ("*Weqatal* Forms," 59). However, if this were true, we would expect the second *weqatal* (וְאָכַל) to begin the procedural discourse not the *weqatal* at the beginning of the verse (וְשִׁנָּא), which probably conveys a once-for-all action

The *weqatal* form in verse 38b falls in a *wayyiqtol* sequence with no clear reason for the variation in form. (See also: Gen 28:6; Num 10:21–22, 25; 1 Sam 5:7; 1 Kgs 13:3; 2 Kgs 25:29.)

5. וְהָיָה

When וְהָיָה appears in narrative, it often introduces a background comment about a habitual action or event ("whenever" is usually a good rendering).

1 Samuel 16:22a–23c

22a	וַיִּשְׁלַח שָׁאוּל אֶל־יִשַׁי לֵאמֹר	And Saul sent to Jesse, saying,
22b	יַעֲמָד־נָא דָוִד לְפָנַי	"Let David stand before me,
22c	כִּי־מָצָא חֵן בְּעֵינָי׃	for he has found favor in my eyes."
23a	וְהָיָה בִּהְיוֹת רוּחַ־אֱלֹהִים אֶל־שָׁאוּל	***And whenever*** the harmful spirit from God was upon Saul,
23b	וְלָקַח דָּוִד אֶת־הַכִּנּוֹר	David would take his lyre
23c	וְנִגֵּן בְּיָדוֹ	play it with his hand.

The specific events of verse 22 give way to a description of David's habitual actions when Saul was afflicted. (See also: Exod 33:9; Judg 6:3; 12:5; 2 Sam 15:5.)

V. CONCLUSION

The most basic verbal sequence in narrative is a *wayyiqtol* chain. The verbal constructions *waw* + x + *qatal* and *weqatal* have special significance in narrative because they mark a departure from this default storytelling form. For this reason, we cannot treat *waw* + x + *qatal* and *weqatal* alone, apart from their context. Precisely because they interrupt a *wayyiqtol* chain, they take on special discourse functions in narrative. This is why we speak of verbal *sequences* as crucial for understanding BH discourse. In the next chapter, we will see how *weqatal* has a different set of discourse functions when it occurs in the context of non-narrative.

(changing the clothes). The changing of the clothes is much like the other unique actions in v. 28, all expressed with *wayyiqtol*, and therefore its usage here is anomalous. For more on this question, see Robar, *The Verb and the Paragraph*, 152–59.

— *Chapter 5* —

Element #2 of Biblical Hebrew Prose (Part 2 of 2)

Verbal Sequences in Non-Narrative

Biblical Hebrew non-narrative has its own set of verbal constructions for conveying discourse relationships, distinct from those used in BH narrative. Many kinds of discourse are grouped together here under the label "non-narrative," including law, prediction, instruction, and reports. Although there are many differences between these kinds of discourse, they all tend to use the same verbal sequences in similar ways.

I. IMPORTANT VERBAL SEQUENCES IN NON-NARRATIVE

1. *WEQATAL*

Like *wayyiqtol* in narrative, *weqatal* is the most important form for non-narrative.[1] Both are continuative forms in their respective discourse

1. Many grammarians draw a distinction between *weqatal* and a simple *waw* conjunction + *qatal* (a distinction sometimes called *waw* relative vs. *waw* copulative, or *waw* consecutive vs. *waw* conjunctive). The morphological distinction between the two forms is that in the former case (*weqatal*) the final syllable has the accent (e.g., וְנִלְחַם in 1 Sam 17:32), whereas in the latter case (simple conjunction), the penultimate syllable has the accent, but only in 1cs and 2ms (e.g., וְשָׁאַלְתָּ in 1 Kgs 3:11; *IBHS* §32.1.1; Joüon §119). These two distinct forms are purportedly used in distinct ways: whereas *waw* + *qatal* is used to make simple coordinate conjunctions (e.g., 1 Sam 12:2) or to communicate indicative realities (e.g., Judg 3:23), *weqatal* is used to communicate non-indicative (*irrealis*) ideas (like conditions, commands, etc.; e.g., Gen 28:15; Exod 20:9). See Joosten, *The Verbal System*, 288–308.

However, we do not distinguish between *weqatal* and *waw* + *qatal* for several reasons:

type, furthering the discourse mode (foreground or background) and other verbal ideas that are found in the preceding clauses (see pp. 65–68). Therefore, like *wayyiqtol, weqatal* has many possible functions. These functions are grouped below into two groups:

1. Functions that mirror *wayyiqtol*
2. Functions unique to *weqatal*

Note: as with וַיְהִי *in narrative,* וְהָיָה *is a special case and will be discussed below (pp. 81).*

Common Discourse Functions that Mirror wayyiqtol

(Because these functions are so similar to those discussed above for wayyiqtol *[see pp. 68–70], they are listed here more briefly.)*

1. **Next Step** ("and then"): Lev 1:6; Num 5:17; 19:3; Deut 6:15; Josh 15:3; 1 Sam 17:46; 1 Kgs 12:27.
2. **Contrast to Previous Step** ("but"): Deut 4:9, 29; Josh 1:8; 1 Sam 12:20, 23.
3. **Result or Purpose of Previous Steps** ("and thus;" "so that"): Gen 8:17; 9:13; 26:4; 27:10; Lev 1:4; Num 7:5; Deut 5:31. In the case of *weqatal*, it is often *projected* results, and hence "purpose" is sometimes a better label for this discourse relationship.
4. **Simultaneous Step** ("and at the same time"): Gen 26:4; Num 5:15; 1 Sam 8:9; 12:24.
5. **Expansion on Previous Step** ("and what's more;" "that is"): Lev 4:13; Deut 6:18; 1 Kgs 13:6. In practice, the translation of the *weqatal* for an expansion often begins with "by":

first, the only morphological distinction is one of stress and that only occurs in 1cs and 2ms. Even in those cases, the distinction is not absolute: sometimes the expected stress pattern does not appear (see discussion in Cook, *Time and the Biblical Hebrew Verb*, 208–11, esp. 210). Second, when the morphological distinction does not appear, one is required to distinguish between these two forms entirely on the basis of semantic considerations (*IBHS* §32.3a). If this is the case, it makes sense to have one form (*weqatal*) and to add the functions supposedly associated with *waw + qatal* to the list of functions associated with *weqatal*, since one must distinguish those functions on the basis of context anyway.

Deuteronomy 4:15a–16b

15a	וְנִשְׁמַרְתֶּם מְאֹד לְנַפְשֹׁתֵיכֶם	So watch yourselves carefully
16a	פֶּן־תַּשְׁחִתוּן	so that you do not act corruptly
16b	וַעֲשִׂיתֶם לָכֶם פֶּסֶל תְּמוּנַת כָּל־סָמֶל	***by making*** for yourselves an indol in the form of any figure . . .

Common Discourse Functions that Are Unique to weqatal:

1. **Initiate and Continue "If" and "Then" Clauses in an "If-Then" Statement**: this usage is somewhat complex, and the following terms are necessary for discussing it:
   - "Protasis" refers to an "if" or "when" clause.
   - "Apodosis" refers to a "then" clause.

Situation #1: protasis and apodosis with *weqatal*

A *weqatal* verb can initiate both protasis and apodosis:

Genesis 44:22c–d

22c	וְעָזַב אֶת־אָבִיו	***If he*** [***Benjamin***] ***leaves*** his father,
22d	וָמֵת׃	***then he will die.***

The possibility of Jacob's death is conditioned on Benjamin's leaving. (See also: Lev 10:19b; Num 10:3; 14:15; 36:3; Deut 25:8b–9; Ruth 2:9; 1 Sam 19:3.)

Situation #2: apodosis only with *weqatal*

Sometimes a discourse marker is used for the protasis (אִם, כִּי, לוּ, לוּלֵא), and *weqatal* only initiates the apodosis:

Genesis 18:26b–c

26b	אִם־אֶמְצָא בִסְדֹם חֲמִשִּׁים צַדִּיקִם בְּתוֹךְ הָעִיר	If I find in Sodom fifty righteous in the city,
26c	וְנָשָׂאתִי לְכָל־הַמָּקוֹם בַּעֲבוּרָם׃	***then I will spare*** the whole place on their account.

The discourse marker אִם gives the condition for God sparing the city in verse 26c. The apodosis is initiated with *weqatal.* (See also: Gen 43:10; Lev 1:14; 12:8; Judg 4:8; 8:19.)

Situation #3: protasis continued with *weqatal*, apodosis initiated with *weqatal*

Because three functions are possible for *weqatal* in conditional sentences ([1] initiate protasis; [2] initiate apodosis; [3] continue protasis or apodosis), it can be challenging to know which function is in view for a given *weqatal* verb, and you must rely on contextual cues (see the example of Deut 30:1–6 above for another example, pp. 32–35).

1 Kings 12:7b–f

7b	אִם־הַיּוֹם תִּהְיֶה־עֶּבֶד לָעָם הַזֶּה	If you will be a servant to this people today,
7c	וַעֲבַדְתָּם	*and will serve them,*
7d	וַעֲנִיתָם	*and answer them*
7e	וְדִבַּרְתָּ אֲלֵיהֶם דְּבָרִים טוֹבִים	*by speaking* good words to them,
7f	וְהָיוּ לְךָ עֲבָדִים כָּל־הַיָּמִים׃	*then they will be* your servants forever.

Verses 7c–f all begin with *weqatal,* but the first three continue the protasis, while the last one initiates the apodosis. You can only recognize that verse 7f is the beginning of the apodosis (and that the apodosis does not begin earlier) from context. Notice that the *weqatal* in verse 7e not only continues the protasis, it is an expansion on the previous *weqatal* ("answer *by speaking*"; see use [5] above). See also: Lev 4:13–14; Deut 20:12; 30:1–3.

2. **Inference** ("therefore"): the *weqatal* verb concludes something from the foregoing discourse (often the conclusion is a plan of action).

Ruth 3:2b–3c

2b	הִנֵּה־הוּא זֹרֶה אֶת־גֹּרֶן הַשְּׂעֹרִים הַלָּיְלָה׃	Look, he [Boaz] is winnowing barley at the threshing floor tonight.
3a	וְרָחַצְתְּ	***Therefore, wash yourself,***
3b	וָסַכְתְּ	and anoint yourself,
3c	וְשַׂמְתְּ שִׂמְלֹתַיִךְ עָלַיִךְ	and put on your clothes.

Naomi's plan for Ruth (beginning in v. 3a) is a conclusion based on the situation with Boaz explained in the previous verse. (See also: Deut 4:6, 15; 6:3; 7:9; Ruth 3:9; 1 Sam 17:47.)

2. וְהָיָה

וְהָיָה accomplishes in non-narrative many of the tasks that וַיְהִי accomplishes in narrative. (See pp. 76 for וְהָיָה in narrative.)

Common Discourse Functions that Mirror וַיְהִי*:*

1. New Unit ("Now"): Exod 12:14; Deut 26:1; 28:1; 30:1.
2. Shift in Time: Gen 12:12; Exod 13:5; 33:22; Deut 6:10; 1 Sam 25:30.
3. Result or Purpose: Gen 4:14; 6:21; 28:21; Deut 19:10; Jer 40:3.
4. Standard *weqatal*: Gen 28:14; Exod 12:48; 40:9; Num 11:20.

3. *WAW* + *YIQTOL* AFTER AN IMPERATIVAL FORM

This verbal sequence is a common way of communicating a "purpose" relationship, but it can also be a simple conjunction.[2]

Common Discourse Functions:

1. **Purpose**: the following imperatival form gives the purpose or goal for the preceding imperative(s).

---

2. Cohortative and jussive are sometimes marked in ways that morphologically distinguish them from simple *yiqtol*, but often they are not marked (see Joosten, *The Verbal System*, 314–15). And sometimes a paragogic *he* indicates cohortative; other times it does not. For the purpose of this book, we will not note cohortative or jussive as distinct verbal forms but instead will observe the verbal form without determining its function immediately (e.g., *yiqtol* with paragogic *he*). Then, discourse analysis will enable us to determine if a volitional mood is intended by the context.

Genesis 23:4b–c

4b	תְּנ֨וּ לִ֤י אֲחֻזַּת־קֶ֙בֶר֙ עִמָּכֶ֔ם	Give to me property for a grave among you
4c	וְאֶקְבְּרָ֥ה מֵתִ֖י מִלְּפָנָֽי׃	*that I may bury* my dead out of my sight.

Abraham requests property from the sons of Heth (v. 4b) with the purpose of burying Sarah there (v. 4c). (See also: Gen 19:5; Exod 3:18; Num 5:2; Deut 5:31; Ruth 4:11; 1 Sam 11:3; 28:7.)

2. **Simple Conjunction**: sometimes there is no purpose relationship but simply a conjoining of commands or plans (hence the actual relationship is "next step," "expansion," "simultaneous action," or something similar).

Genesis 11:3b–d

3b	הָ֚בָה	Come,
3c	נִלְבְּנָ֣ה לְבֵנִ֔ים	let us make brick,
3d	וְנִשְׂרְפָ֖ה לִשְׂרֵפָ֑ה	*and burn* it thoroughly.

The people of Babel make plans, but the purpose of making brick is not for burning it (v. 3d). Instead, the burning is an expansion on the task of making the brick, detailing one aspect of the larger task. (See also: Gen 1:22; 22:5; Num 23:3; Deut 1:40; 1 Sam 26:11; 2 Sam 3:21.)

4. ASYNDETON WITH A LEADING VERB

Definition: asyndeton is a clause without a conjunction where a verb leads the clause (the verb cannot be *wayyiqtol* or *weqatal*, since these forms have the *waw* conjunction "built in"). There are many instances of asyndeton where the clause begins with a non-verb, and these situations are treated in chapter 6 under Preposing.

Common Discourse Functions:[3]

1. **Reason**: the clause without a conjunction gives the reason for the preceding clause

Ruth 3:10b–c

10b	בְּרוּכָ֨ה אַ֤תְּ לַֽיהוָה֙ בִּתִּ֔י	May you be blessed by YHWH, my daughter,
10c	הֵיטַ֛בְתְּ חַסְדֵּ֥ךְ הָאַחֲר֖וֹן מִן־הָרִאשׁ֑וֹן	***for your last kindness is better than the first.***

The reason why Boaz calls down blessings on Ruth (v. 10b) is because of her most recent kindness (v. 10c).

2. **Inference**: the clause without a conjunction brings the foregoing discussion to a conclusion, which is often an exhortation.

Deuteronomy 4:22a–23b

22a	כִּ֣י אָנֹכִ֥י מֵת֙ בָּאָ֣רֶץ הַזֹּ֔את	For I am about to die in this land;
22b	אֵינֶ֥נִּי עֹבֵ֖ר אֶת־הַיַּרְדֵּ֑ן	I will not cross over the Jordan.
22c	וְאַתֶּם֙ עֹֽבְרִ֔ים	But you will cross over,
22d	וִֽירִשְׁתֶּ֕ם אֶת־הָאָ֥רֶץ הַטּוֹבָ֖ה הַזֹּֽאת׃	and take possession of this good land.
23a	הִשָּׁמְר֣וּ לָכֶ֗ם	***Watch yourselves, therefore,***
23b	פֶּן־תִּשְׁכְּחוּ֙ אֶת־בְּרִ֤ית יְהוָה֙ אֱלֹ֣הֵיכֶ֔ם	so that you do not forget the covenant of YHWH your God.

The command to watch themselves (v. 23a) is the logical conclusion that follows directly from Moses's impending death and the people's impending conquest (v. 22). Notice also how the lack of a conjunction in verse 22b is an instance of "expansion" (see use [1] above). (See also: Deut 5:27, 30; Ruth 1:15.)

---

3. Andersen's seminal treatment of asyndeton (which he calls "apposition sentences") gives a more detailed taxonomy of discourse relationships for this clause type (*The Sentence in Biblical Hebrew*, 36–60).

II. OTHER VERBAL SEQUENCE FUNCTIONS

Before leaving verbal sequences, we note the following important discourse functions that are achieved using verbal sequences. These discourse functions occur in narrative as well as non-narrative.

1. SWITCHING BETWEEN DISCOURSE TYPES AND EMBEDDED DISCOURSE

The discussion about verbal sequences began by distinguishing between two main types of discourse: narrative and non-narrative. Discourses can switch between one type of discourse to another. Often the new discourse is "embedded" in the old discourse, as when a narrative includes a speech from another character and then the narrative resumes after the conclusion of the speech.

Genesis 48:20f–21d, 49:1a

48:20f	וַיָּשֶׂם אֶת־אֶפְרַיִם לִפְנֵי מְנַשֶּׁה׃	Thus he put Ephraim before Manasseh.
48:21a	וַיֹּאמֶר יִשְׂרָאֵל אֶל־יוֹסֵף	*And* Israel *said* to Joseph,
48:21b	הִנֵּה אָנֹכִי מֵת	"Look, I am about to die.
48:21c	וְהָיָה אֱלֹהִים עִמָּכֶם	But God will be with you,
48:21d	וְהֵשִׁיב אֶתְכֶם אֶל־אֶרֶץ אֲבֹתֵיכֶם׃	and he will bring you back to the land of your fathers."
49:1a	וַיִּקְרָא יַעֲקֹב אֶל־בָּנָיו	Then Jacob called to his sons . . .

Situation #1: Speech in Narrative

In the midst of narrative, speech is introduced. The speech is usually preceded by a speech formula (e.g., וַיֹּאמֶר or לֵאמֹר).

The discourse type shifts from the narrative sequence (48:21a and the preceding verses) to an embedded speech (48:21b and following). The narrative is told using *wayyiqtol*, but the direct speech has the signature *weqatal* verb forms. When the speech ends, the narrative resumes with a *wayyiqtol* in 49:1a. The embedded speech should be treated as its own discrete, self-contained discourse.

Situation #2: Procedure or Habitual Action in Narrative

Sometimes narrative is interrupted by a series of *weqatal* forms, recounting a procedure or habitual action where the verbal sequences behave like those found in non-narrative. See the example of Gen 29:2–3 on p. 75. (See also Exod 34:33–35.)

Situation #3: Multiple Levels of Embedding

Embedding can happen in multiple, cascading levels. For example:

<u>Narrative</u>
And YHWH said to Moses,
    <u>Speech level 1</u>
    "When you go back to Egypt,
    see that you do before Pharaoh all the miracles
      that I have put in your power.
    But I will harden his heart,
    so that he will not let the people go.
    Then you shall say to Pharaoh,
        <u>Speech level 2</u>
        'Thus says YHWH,
            <u>Speech level 3</u>
            "Israel is my firstborn son,
            and I say to you,
                <u>Speech level 4</u>
                'Let my son go that he may serve me.'
            If you refuse to let him go,
            behold, I will kill your firstborn son."' "

Exod 4:21–23

2. RESUMPTION OF A PREVIOUS VERBAL SEQUENCE

There are two primary kinds of embedded units:

1. As explained in Situation #1 above, BH can embed speeches into narrative.
2. Another kind of embedding is background comments, which can occur in both narrative and non-narrative.

Regardless of the kind of embedding, when the embedded unit is complete, BH has several ways of returning to a previous verbal sequence:

1. **Resuming the Verbal Forms from the Previous Sequence:** when the embedded unit is of a different discourse type than the outer unit, the writer often simply returns to the different verb forms. For example, the end of a speech is often signaled by a return to the *wayyiqtol* verb forms. The speech (dominated by *weqatal*) is ended and the narrative resumes (dominated by *wayyiqtol*). See the example from Gen 48:20–49:1 above (p. 84).

2. **Repeating the Last Clause of the Previous Unit:** when the last clause from the previous unit is repeated (or closely approximated), this can signal that the previous unit is now resuming:

Genesis 7:12–14a, 17a–c

12	וַיְהִי הַגֶּשֶׁם עַל־הָאָרֶץ אַרְבָּעִים יוֹם וְאַרְבָּעִים לָיְלָה׃	The rain fell on the earth forty days and forty nights.
13	בְּעֶצֶם הַיּוֹם הַזֶּה בָּא נֹחַ וְשֵׁם־וְחָם וָיֶפֶת בְּנֵי־נֹחַ וְאֵשֶׁת נֹחַ וּשְׁלֹשֶׁת נְשֵׁי־בָנָיו אִתָּם אֶל־הַתֵּבָה׃	On that very day Noah entered the ark, along with Shem and Ham and Japeth, the sons of Noah, and the wife Noah, and the three wives of his sons with them.
14a	הֵמָּה וְכָל־הַחַיָּה לְמִינָהּ	They entered, along with every beast after its kind . . .
	. . .	
17a	וַיְהִי הַמַּבּוּל אַרְבָּעִים יוֹם עַל־הָאָרֶץ	***So the flood had been coming for forty days on the earth.***
17b	וַיִּרְבּוּ הַמַּיִם	The waters increased,
17c	וַיִּשְׂאוּ אֶת־הַתֵּבָה	and lifted the ark.

The narrative halts in verse 12 for the narrator to give a lengthy background comment in verses 13–16 about all those who entered the ark. Then the foreground of the narrative resumes in verse 17a. The resumption of the foreground is highlighted by the language of verse 17a, which very closely matches the language of verse 12.

Thus one interpretation of this passage is to see the forty days of the flood in verse 17a as the *same forty days* as are mentioned in verse 12. The repeated language in verse 17a does not indicate a separate event from verse 12 but a resumption of the story from that point. (See also: 1 Kgs 22:35–37.)

3. EPIC RESTATEMENT

Sometimes a clause will restate the previous clause, slowing the discourse down and indicating a climax (or "peak") in the discourse.[4] This phenomenon can occur with a variety of different verbal forms (including asyndeton) and in both discourse types. Andersen notes that the "similar grammatical elements are characteristically placed in chiasmus," as is the case in the example below.[5]

Genesis 1:27a–b

27a	וַיִּבְרָא אֱלֹהִים׀ אֶת־הָאָדָם בְּצַלְמוֹ	Thus God created man in his image;
27b	בְּצֶלֶם אֱלֹהִים בָּרָא אֹתוֹ	*in the image of God he created him.*

The second line says virtually the same thing as the first. This slowing of the pace highlights the climactic significance of the creation of humanity in the Genesis 1 account. (See also: Gen 7:23; 21:1; 25:8; 47:23.)

4. The seminal treatment of this phenomenon appears in Andersen, *The Sentence in Biblical Hebrew*, 39–43.

5. Andersen, *The Sentence in Biblical Hebrew*, 39. For how BH slows down discourse to mark climax, see Randall Buth, "Functional Grammar, Hebrew and Aramaic: An Integrated, Textlinguistic Approach to Syntax," in *Discourse Analysis of Biblical Literature: What It Is and What It Offers*, ed. Walter R. Bodine, Semeia Studies (Atlanta: Scholars Press, 1995), 90–93. Longacre discusses the general principles of climax (which he calls "peak") in "Discourse Peak as Zone of Turbulence," in *Beyond the Sentence: Discourse and Sentential Form*, ed. J. R. Wirth (Ann Arbor, MI: Karoma, 1985), 81–92; idem, *The Grammar of Discourse*, 38–48. Longacre proposes that peak, being the place of highest excitement in the text, is often marked by unusual constructions, unusual uses for common constructions, the absence of typical particles, and in general, linguistic "turbulence." Robar has reservations with Longacre's proposal but ends by suggesting a similar conclusion, namely that unexpected *weqatal* "may suggest a thematic role for the clause in question that would not have been immediately obvious" (*The Verb and the Paragraph*, 159; see also ibid., 65–67, 152–59).

—— *Chapter 6* ——

Element #3 of Biblical Hebrew Prose

Preposing and Verbless Clauses

I. DEFINING PREPOSING AND VERBLESS CLAUSES

1. PREPOSING

In addition to discourse markers and verbal sequences, the word order of a given clause can mark discourse relationships. For the purpose of discourse analysis, the one word order situation that is most important is called *preposing*.[1] Preposing is when "a subject, object, or adverbial is placed before the verb."[2]

This situation is prevalent in both narrative and non-narrative, and the verbal form that follows the preposed element can be of any kind, except for *wayyiqtol* and *weqatal*:

---

1. Dempster argues that the preposing of a non-verb before the verb is the only significant word order variant for the sake of discourse analysis. After the verb, the order is fairly fixed: subject (if present), followed by object (if present), followed by prepositional phrases and other adverbials ("Linguistic Features of Hebrew Narrative," 65).

2. Moshavi, *Word Order*, 1. Note that this definition excludes nominal (verbless) sentences from preposing, because the definition requires a verb.

We are indebted throughout this chapter to Moshavi's excellent work on word order. However, we do not employ her terminology of "focusing" and "topicalization." The reasons are: (1) these terms are used in diverse ways in the literature (compare the sources on p. 38 in footnote 25); (2) Moshavi's own use of these terms, though she clearly defines them and uses them consistently, is idiosyncratic compared to many other scholars (as she admits); and (3) Moshavi's use of the terms do not clearly connect with what their common definitions suggest: "focusing" is not so much about focus as about "a relation between the clause and the context of the addressee's attention state," and "topicalization" is not so much about a new topic as it is about "a relation between the clause and the linguistic context that accompanies it" (*Word Order*, 90). In our taxonomy below, #3 ("Addition") and #4 ("New topic") corresponds to her category of "focusing" and #1 ("Contrast") corresponds to her category of "topicalization."

- (*waw* +) x + *qatal*
- (*waw* +) x + *yiqtol*
- (*waw* +) x + imperative
- (*waw* +) x + participle

Even though the *waw* is almost always present, there are some circumstances where it is missing (e.g., Gen 1:29; 6:4a; Deut 5:13), but the clause should still be considered preposed; hence the parentheses around the *waw* to show that it is optional. In the expressions above, "x" can stand for:

- A noun phrase in all its varieties: a governing noun (which could be a common noun, proper noun, pronoun, substantive participle, or adjective, etc.), along with accompanying modifiers (definite article, direct object marker, adjectives, etc.)
- A prepositional phrase, where a preposition governs another expression (as long as the expression is a noun phrase and not a clause).
- Or some other kind of adverbial expression, such as one involving גַּם:

Genesis 13:5

5a	וְגַם־לְלוֹט הַהֹלֵךְ אֶת־אַבְרָם הָיָה צֹאן־וּבָקָר וְאֹהָלִים׃	And Lot, who went with Abram, also had flocks and herds and tents.

However, putting a noun phrase or prepositional phrase on the front of a clause is only significant when these phrases do not *need* to be on the front of the clause. There are a number of situations where a phrase needs to be on the front, and therefore the preposing is not significant for discourse analysis:[3]

- Adverbs that always occur in a clause-initial position: אוּלַי, עַל־כֵּן ,לָכֵן ,כֹּה ,הֵן ,הִנֵּה ,הֲלוֹא, אוּלָם
- Interrogatives: מָה, מִי, אֵיךְ, etc.
- Fixed expressions such as בִּי נִשְׁבַּעְתִּי. In this expression, the prepositional phrase בִּי always precedes the verb.

3. Summarizing Moshavi, *Word Order*, 109–10.

In short, any time a phrase "needs" to go at the front of a clause (based on the conventions of the language), it should *not* be considered a significant instance of preposing.

In contrast to the scenarios above, when an author does *not* need to front a phrase but does so all the same, we consider this preposed phrase to be "marked." The author fronts the phrase for some reason, often to bring something that was not previously in view into new prominence. For the sake of simplicity, all uses of "preposed" below will be for *marked* preposing.

2. VERBLESS CLAUSES

Verbless clauses are sometimes referred to as "nominal clauses" or "nominal sentences." Nominal sentences include a subject and a predicate, where the predicate is not a verb but a noun. For example:

Deuteronomy 5:6a

6a	אָנֹכִי֙ יְהוָ֣ה	I am YHWH

In this case, the subject is **אָנֹכִי**, and the predicate is the proper noun, יְהוָה. Several variants of this construction exist, including those where the predicate precedes the subject or where a third word, a pleonastic (redundant) pronoun, disambiguates the subject and the predicate (e.g., יְהוָה הוּא הָאֱלֹהִים, "YHWH is God" [Deut 4:35]).[4]

We use the term "verbless clause" instead of a "nominal clause" to incorporate the possibilities that the predicate be an adjective or a prepositional phrase, as in the following examples:[5]

Leviticus 13:36e

36e	טָמֵ֥א הֽוּא	He is unclean (an adjective; predicate-subject order)

4. See the classic study in Francis I. Andersen, *The Hebrew Verbless Clause in the Pentateuch*, JBLMS 14 (Nashville: Abingdon, 1970).

5. Some include participles as a possibility for the predicate in "verbless" clauses, but we believe that participles, though they serve as adjectives and nouns in other contexts (attributive and substantive constructions), should nevertheless be considered "verbal" in a predicate construction and hence are included in our list of preposed clauses above. See the nuanced discussion in Cook, *Time and the Biblical Hebrew Verb*, 223–25.

Genesis 1:2b

2b	וְחֹשֶׁךְ עַל־פְּנֵי תְהוֹם	And darkness was over the surface of the deep (a prepositional phrase; subject-predicate order)

Note: the one kind of clause that lacks a verb but should not be considered under the label "verbless clause" is when the verb has been elided (left out because it can easily be assumed from the previous clause). For example:

1 Samuel 2:16f–h

16f	כִּי עַתָּה תִתֵּן	But you will give [it to me],
16g	וְאִם־לֹא	and if not,
16h	לָקַחְתִּי בְחָזְקָה׃	I will take [it] by force.

In this case, verse 16g assumes the verb נתן: "and if you do not [give]." Technically, this clause is verbless, but it should instead be treated as a verbal clause, with attention given to the discourse marker אִם as the most salient indicator of this clause's discourse function.

Having defined both preposing and verbless clauses, *we observe that they serve a common set of discourse functions*, which are listed below.[6]

II. COMMON DISCOURSE FUNCTIONS FOR PREPOSING AND VERBLESS CLAUSES

1. **Contrast**: the preposed or verbless clause continues the current discourse mode (foreground or background) but predicates something that differs pointedly from a foregoing clause.[7] Even though the two clauses are predicating ideas that in some way oppose each other, they usually have noticeable similarities (note the use of עלה in the example below).

6. Van Wolde gestures in this direction but stops short of it ("The Verbless Clause and Its Textual Function"). In our opinion, she also has too restricted an understanding of the textual function of verbless clauses (restricting them to background comments).

7. Moshavi observes a special kind of contrast achieved through preposing, the *a fortiori* argument: הִנֵּה שְׁנֵי הַמְּלָכִים לֹא עָמְדוּ לְפָנָיו וְאֵיךְ נַעֲמֹד אֲנָחְנוּ "Look, the two kings did not stand against him; how shall we stand?" (2 Kgs 10:4). See additional examples in Moshavi, *Word Order*, 158–59.

Note: in narrative, usually the event in the preposed or verbless clause occurs simultaneously with the previous wayyiqtol *event.*

1 Samuel 1:21a, 22a

21a	וַיַּעַל הָאִישׁ אֶלְקָנָה וְכָל־בֵּיתוֹ	The man Elkanah went up, and all his house,
22a	וְחַנָּה לֹא עָלָתָה	***but Hannah*** did not go up.

(See also: Gen 4:2; Exod 1:7; Deut 4:20; 6:23; Ruth 1:14; 1 Sam 24:23 [ET 22].)

2. **Circumstances/Reason**: this discourse function is much like the previous one ("contrast"), but there is no contrast in view. Instead, the preposed or verbless clause gives the circumstances for the preceding clause. In some cases, the circumstances provide the reason for the preceding clause.

Genesis 24:56b–c

56b	אַל־תְּאַחֲרוּ אֹתִי	Do not delay me
56c	וַיהוָה הִצְלִיחַ דַּרְכִּי	***when*** (***or "for"***) YHWH has prospered my way.

(For circumstances, see also: Gen 19:23. For reasons, see also: Gen 18:13; 24:31; 1 Sam 15:6; Judg 21:7.)

3. **Addition**: the preposed or verbless clause continues the current discourse mode (foreground or background) and says that the predication in the previous clause also applies to another entity. A gloss of "what is more" or "moreover" often captures the transition.

Genesis 35:12

12a	וְאֶת־הָאָרֶץ ... לְךָ אֶתְּנֶנָּה	And I will give you the land,
12b	וּלְזַרְעֲךָ אַחֲרֶיךָ אֶתֵּן אֶת־הָאָרֶץ׃	***and moreover to your offspring after you*** I will give the land.

Not only will Jacob receive the land (v. 12a), but his offspring after him will receive it.

A looser kind of "addition" occurs when the preposed or verbless clause does not predicate exactly the same thing of the new, preposed entity but nevertheless predicates something that builds in the same direction on the previous clause(s). In these cases, the glosses of "what is more" or "moreover" also work. The new, preposed or verbless clause is still "in addition" to the previous clauses, continuing their general direction. The next example is taken from the same context as the previous one.

Genesis 35:11e–12a

11e	גּ֛וֹי וּקְהַ֥ל גּוֹיִ֖ם יִהְיֶ֣ה מִמֶּ֑ךָּ	A nation and a company of nations will come forth from you,
11f	וּמְלָכִ֖ים מֵחֲלָצֶ֥יךָ יֵצֵֽאוּ׃	and ***kings*** will come from your loins,
12a	וְאֶת־הָאָ֗רֶץ . . . לְךָ֣ אֶתְּנֶ֑נָּה	and I will give you ***the land***.

In this promissory context, the initial promise in verse 11e is followed by two other preposed clauses in verses 11f and 12a, which continue the list of promised blessings and state additional blessings Jacob should expect in addition to the one in verse 11e. (See also: Gen 9:5; 11:3; 43:13.)[8]

4. **New Topic (in the Same Episode or a New Episode)**: the preposed or verbless clause continues the current discourse mode (foreground or background) but starts a new direction (a shift within the same episode or an entirely new episode) with a topic that differs from the foregoing. The opening phrase highlights the topic or main actor for the upcoming clauses.

8. These examples are adapted from Moshavi, *Word Order*, 133–35.

Exodus 2:25a–3:1a

2:25a	וַיַּ֥רְא אֱלֹהִ֖ים אֶת־בְּנֵ֣י יִשְׂרָאֵ֑ל	And God saw the sons of Israel,
2:25b	וַיֵּ֖דַע אֱלֹהִֽים׃	and God knew.
3:1a	וּמֹשֶׁ֗ה הָיָ֥ה רֹעֶ֛ה אֶת־צֹ֛אן יִתְר֥וֹ חֹתְנ֖וֹ כֹּהֵ֣ן מִדְיָ֑ן	***Now Moses was*** pasturing the flock of Jethro his father-in-law, the priest of Midian.

After the groaning of the people of Israel at the end of chapter 2, the previous unit concludes with two *wayyiqtol* verbs about how God sees the sons of Israel and "knows." (See also: Gen 6:17; 21:1; 24:1; Deut 6:1; Judg 11:1; Ruth 4:1; 1 Sam 15:1; Jonah 1:4.)

5. **Initiate Background**: an author can use preposing and verbless clauses to pause the main flow of the narrative or discourse (the "foreground") and make a comment that does not propel the story or discourse forward but provides important circumstantial information.[9] The preposed or verbless clause can be a single background comment (after which the foreground resumes), or it can initiate a longer background sequence. On the resumption of foreground after background, see p. 86.

Note: background comments in narrative often require the pluperfect tense, as in Gen 31:34: "Now Rachel had taken the household idols and had put them in the camel's saddle . . ."

Genesis 37:2d–3a

2d	וַיָּבֵ֥א יוֹסֵ֛ף אֶת־דִּבָּתָ֥ם רָעָ֖ה אֶל־אֲבִיהֶֽם׃	And Joseph brought back a bad report about them [his brothers] to their father.
3a	וְיִשְׂרָאֵ֗ל אָהַ֤ב אֶת־יוֹסֵף֙ מִכָּל־בָּנָ֔יו	***Now Israel loved*** Joseph more than all his sons.

In the midst of the narrative about Joseph and his brothers, the narrator pauses to give an aside about how Israel (Jacob) loved Joseph more than all his other sons, an aside that is initiated by

9. See our definition of background above, p. 43.

preposing (*waw* + x + *qatal*). (See also: Gen 12:4; 31:34; Josh 2:6; Ruth 1:22; 1 Sam 9:15.)

6. **Expansion**: when preposed or verbless clauses are asyndetic (without a conjunction), they often communicate an expansion on the previous idea. An expansion provides more detail about the ideas expressed in the preceding clause.

Numbers 5:2a–3b

2a	צַו אֶת־בְּנֵי יִשְׂרָאֵל	Command the sons of Israel
2b	וִישַׁלְּחוּ מִן־הַמַּחֲנֶה כָּל־צָרוּעַ וְכָל־זָב וְכֹל טָמֵא לָנָפֶשׁ׃	that they might send from the camp every leper, and everyone with a discharge, and everyone who is unclean because of the dead.
3a	מִזָּכָר עַד־נְקֵבָה תְּשַׁלֵּחוּ	***Both male and female you shall send out***;
3b	אֶל־מִחוּץ לַמַּחֲנֶה תְּשַׁלְּחוּם	***outside the camp you shall send them.***

Both clauses 3a and 3b begin without a conjunction. They fill out the main command in verse 2b, expanding (1) the people to be sent out (it is to be regardless of gender; v. 3a) and (2) the location to which they are sent (outside of the camp; v. 3b). (See also: Gen 1:29; Deut 5:12–13; Josh 1:2–3.)

7. **Intensification**: finally, preposed or verbless clauses can mark surprise, emphasis, or other forceful effects that in some way intensify the foregoing clause.[10] Intensification is the likely reason for preposing when the preposed element is *already prominent*

10. Bandstra rejects the category of "emphasis" (as do many authors on BH word order) for the following reasons: 1. it is too vague; 2. it is an ad-hoc solution that is impossible to verify ("Word Order and Emphasis," 112–13). Bandstra argues that a more precise category is needed, and he presents an idea of "topicalization" based on what is new and old in the discourse. This is a useful beginning, but does not account for situations like Deut 6:12–13 discussed shortly. We believe "intensification" is a helpful category that is readily identified (by the preposed entity being already prominent in the discourse) and that is well defined (when a clause forcefully reiterates a previous clause, intensifying it).

in the discourse (and hence the preposed element is not needed to signal a new topic). In this situation, preposing makes the prominent element even more prominent.

Deuteronomy 6:12–13

12a	הִשָּׁמֶר לְךָ	Watch yourself
12b	פֶּן־תִּשְׁכַּח אֶת־יְהוָה אֲשֶׁר הוֹצִיאֲךָ מֵאֶרֶץ מִצְרַיִם מִבֵּית עֲבָדִים׃	so that you do not forget YHWH who brought you out from the land of Egypt, from the house of slaves.
13a	אֶת־יְהוָה אֱלֹהֶיךָ תִּירָא	*It is YHWH your God* you must fear,
13b	וְאֹתוֹ תַעֲבֹד	*and him* you must serve,
13c	וּבִשְׁמוֹ תִּשָּׁבֵעַ׃	*and in his name* you must swear.

Although YHWH is already prominent in verse 12b, this forceful exhortation concludes with three clauses where YHWH is preposed. Hence the speaker emphatically identifies YHWH as the one whom Israel should fear and serve, and by whom they should swear.[11] (See also: Gen 9:5.)

11. Moshavi (*Word Order*, 118–19) notes similar instances where a preposed noun serves an emphatic function, but in these cases there is no preceding clause which is intensified: Gen 14:23; 21:24; 47:30; 2 Sam 1:16.

Chapter 7

A Process for Discourse Analysis with Hebrew Prose

Chapters 3–6 provide a general understanding of how BH prose communicates relationships between clauses. How can we use this knowledge to understand specific BH texts? This section outlines a simple process that constitutes the foundation for Hebrew exegesis. Although this process helps to provide rigor to our reading, good reading is not mechanical but relies on balanced, sympathetic attention to all kinds of contextual cues.

I. STEP 1: SEPARATE THE TEXT BY CLAUSES

Separating a text by clauses enables us to see clearly the constituent parts of a text and to consider how these parts interrelate. Recall that a "clause" has a subject (usually a noun) and a predicate (usually a verb). Clauses can be independent clauses or dependent clauses:

- *Independent* (can stand by themselves): "He wrote a book."
- *Dependent* (require an independent clause for them to make sense):
  - Temporal clauses: "When he did that, . . ."
  - Relative clauses: ". . . which he wrote"
  - Purpose clauses: ". . . so that he could see it"
  - Participial clauses: "Saying these things, . . ."
  - Conditional clauses: "If I get there in time, . . ."
  - (Other kinds of dependent clauses exist.)

Clauses are distinct from phrases, which are groups of words that do not have both a subject and a predicate (e.g., a prepositional phrase like "in the house").[1] Expressions governed by prepositions should not be considered clauses.[2]

The following is a simple approach to diagramming Hebrew texts in a word processor. It cannot handle every scenario, and it does not give the wealth of insight that traditional sentence diagramming provides, but it has the advantage of being fast (once you get the hang of it!) and also of highlighting the information most important to discourse analysis.

1. Each clause (independent or dependent) should receive its own box in a table.
   - Clarification #1: Even short temporal clauses like כְּשָׁמְעוֹ ("when he heard") or short purpose clauses like לִשְׁמֹר ("in order to keep") should have their own box.
   - Clarification #2:
     - When participles function as substantives (as in Deut 16:18: שֹׁפְטִים וְשֹׁטְרִים תִּתֶּן־לְךָ; "*judges* and *officials* you shall appoint") or as attributive adjectives (as in Deut 4:34: וּבִזְרוֹעַ נְטוּיָה; "with an *outstretched* arm"), they *do not* get their own box.
     - When participles predicate something (as in Deut 16:4: אֲשֶׁר־יְהוָה אֱלֹהֶיךָ נֹתֵן לָךְ; "which YHWH your God is giving to you"), or when they are used to create a relative clause (as in Gen 47:14: אֶת־כָּל־הַכֶּסֶף הַנִּמְצָא בְאֶרֶץ־מִצְרַיִם; "all the money *which was found* in the land of Egypt"), they *do* get their own box.
   - Exception #1: when a sentence begins with וַיְהִי or וְהָיָה (or a similar construction), put the היה verb in the same box with the phrase or clause that follows, since the היה verb is preparatory for a larger construction (note: this only applies to "discourse"

1. Waltke and O'Connor offer two complementary definitions of phrases: 1. "A *phrase* is, in one sense, a group of words used as an equivalent of a single word class" (*IBHS* §4.3a). 2. "a phrase includes a governing word and all it governs [for example, a preposition and the words it governs]" (*IBHS* §4.3b).

2. Moshavi (*Word Order*, 51–52) summarizes a debate regarding how one should handle expressions headed by a preposition, where the preposition governs a clause ("until your beards grow") not a noun phrase ("until this day"). Should the former category be considered a kind of subordinate clause? For our purposes, we will consider all expressions headed by prepositions to be prepositional phrases, not clauses.

uses of היה, not when it is functioning as a "to be" verb. See pp. 72–73, 81).

Numbers 10:35a–b

35a	וַיְהִי בִּנְסֹעַ הָאָרֹן	When the ark set out,
35b	וַיֹּאמֶר מֹשֶׁה	Moses said . . .

- Exception #2: if the clause in question is לֵאמֹר, it can be included in the box with the main clause on which it depends (but indented to show its dependency).
- Exception #3: sometimes relative clauses (usually beginning with אֲשֶׁר) are so inconsequential that it does not make sense to give them their own box. In these cases, one can leave them indented as though they were dependent phrases, not clauses (see two examples of this in Example C below; Exod 12:22b, c).

2. Always preserve the Hebrew word order.
   - Exception: sometimes, for clarity's sake, you may want to take out a prepositional phrase or a subordinate clause from the midst of a main clause and move it below. In this case, use ellipses ". . ." to indicate the place from which the words have been removed, and put brackets ("["and"]") around the phrase that has been moved.

     For example, Deut 8:1 begins with כָּל־הַמִּצְוָה אֲשֶׁר אָנֹכִי מְצַוְּךָ הַיּוֹם תִּשְׁמְרוּן. This could be diagrammed as follows:

כָּל־הַמִּצְוָה . . . תִּשְׁמְרוּן
[אֲשֶׁר אָנֹכִי מְצַוְּךָ הַיּוֹם]

3. Indent subordinate phrases and clauses to show how they relate to the main clause.
   - Clarification #1: This even applies to subordinate clauses, which will have their own box. See the example of Deut 8:1 directly above.

- Clarification #2: This means that on the unindented main line there will be: (1) the subject (if present); (2) the predicate; (3) the direct object (if present).
- Clarification #3: Sometimes the direct object is so long it needs to be included on an indented line below the governing clause.
- Clarification #4: One shortcoming of this indenting scheme is that it does not identify the precise words in the governing phrase or clause that the indented words depend on (e.g., does a prepositional phrase modify the verb or the subject or the direct object?).

4. Sometimes the dependence is downward (e.g., a dependent phrase precedes the main clause on which it depends). In this instance, indent the dependent phrase and indicate the direction of dependence with an arrow: ↓.

5. Grey shading is used for embedded discourse (e.g., quotations) to set it apart. If there is embedding within an embedded discourse (e.g., a quote within a quote), then the doubly embedded discourse is darker in color.

This diagramming scheme will not cover every situation. Strive to be consistent with how you handle unusual circumstances.

EXAMPLE:

Genesis 2:15–18

	Text	Translation	Notes
15a	וַיִּקַּח יְהוָה אֱלֹהִים אֶת־הָאָדָם	And YHWH God took the man	• Simple scenario: verb—subject—object.
15b	וַיַּנִּחֵהוּ בְגַן־עֵדֶן	and set him in the garden of Eden	• Main verb • Indent for prepositional phrase beginning with בְּ.
15c	לְעָבְדָהּ	to serve it	• Indent for the inf c because it is dependent on the main verb, but give it its own box because (even though it is technically an infinitive phrase) we are treating it as a dependent purpose clause (see p. TODO, footnote TODO).
15d	וּלְשָׁמְרָהּ	and to keep it.	• Same as v. 15c
16a	וַיְצַו יְהוָה אֱלֹהִים עַל־הָאָדָם לֵאמֹר	And YHWH God commanded the man, saying,	• Main verb—subject. • Prepositional phrase (indent) • לֵאמֹר: minor dependent clause (indent)
16b	↓מִכֹּל עֵץ־הַגָּן אָכֹל תֹּאכֵל	"From every tree of the garden you may certainly eat,	• Shading the box to set off the speech as its own discourse unit. • Dependent prepositional phrase precedes the main verb, so using downward arrow to show that it is dependent on what follows. • We are treating the infinitive absolute as basically part of the main verb, and thus are leaving it on the unindented main line.

(cont.)

	Text	Translation	Notes
17a	↓וּמֵעֵץ הַדַּעַת טוֹב וָרָע לֹא תֹאכַל מִמֶּנּוּ	but from the tree of the knowledge of good and evil you may not eat,	• The dependent prepositional phrase at the beginning depends on the main verb that follows it. • The main verb has another dependent prepositional phrase following it (מִמֶּנּוּ).
17b	כִּי ↓בְּיוֹם אֲכָלְךָ מִמֶּנּוּ מוֹת תָּמוּת	for in the day you eat from it, you will surely die."	• The כִּי starts a new dependent clause, so it gets its own box. Everything after it is indented to show it depends on the כִּי. • The temporal phrase starting with בְּ depends on the verb תָּמוּת, so we have a downward arrow. • But the prepositional phrase מִמֶּנּוּ depends on אֲכָלְךָ, so there is no downward arrow.
18a	וַיֹּאמֶר יְהוָה אֱלֹהִים	And YHWH God said,	
18b	לֹא־טוֹב הֱיוֹת הָאָדָם לְבַדּוֹ	"It is not good for the man to be alone.	• The infinitive construct is part of the predicate, so it stays on the main line.
18c	אֶעֱשֶׂה־לּוֹ עֵזֶר כְּנֶגְדּוֹ	I will make for him a helper suitable for him."	• The לּוֹ is a prepositional phrase, but it is kept on the main line for simplicity, since it occurs between the main verb and the direct object.

II. STEP 2: ANALYZE EACH CLAUSE

The diagramming step has prepared us to do discourse analysis by separating the clauses and highlighting the main verbs in each clause. Now we can proceed through each clause, working to understand how the text flows from one clause to the next.

STEP 2.A: OBSERVE KEY FACTORS IN A GIVEN CLAUSE

1. Observe the Clause

In this substep, we look for the elements of discourse discussed in chapters 3–6.

1. Discourse Markers: are any discourse markers (like וְעַתָּה) used in this clause?
2. Verbal Sequences: what verbal construction is used (*wayyiqtol, weqatal*, verbless, etc.)? What verbal construction immediately precedes it?
3. Word Order: is there a noun phrase or prepositional phrase in the first position?
4. Verbless Clauses: does the clause lack a verb?

All four of these questions must be answered before proceeding. To assist in answering (2) Verbal Sequences, we develop a second column next to our diagram of the Hebrew text. Verbal sequences require us to observe a pattern of verbs (or departures from a pattern), so we track the construction of each clause in the Construction column of our discourse analysis tables.

A list of common constructions is as follows:

1. Simple verb-first clauses
    A. *wayyiqtol*
    B. *qatal*
    C. *yiqtol*
    D. *weqatal*
    E. *waw* + *yiqtol*
    F. (*waw* +) imv

2. Noun-first clauses (in all of these, x can be single noun, a noun phrase, a prepositional phrase, etc.)
   - A. (*waw* +) x + ptc
   - B. (*waw* +) x + *qatal*
   - C. (*waw* +) x + *yiqtol*
3. Particle-first clauses
   - A. *hinneh* + . . .
   - B. *'asher* + . . .
   - C. *l* + inf c
   - D. *'im* + . . .
   - E. *lo'* + . . .
   - F. *ki* + . . .

In general, we observe the following rules for the Construction column:

- Everything before the verb is included, but all noun phrases, prepositional phrases, and adverbial phrases are replaced with "x."
- Everything after the verb is not included.
- Conjunctions and important discourse-related particles are included in transliterated form (see #3 above).
- Verbless clauses are noted simply as "verbless."
- If a verb is assumed from a previous clause, we use "elliptical."

The following table shows the Construction column for our example diagram:

Genesis 2:15–18

	Text	Construction
15a	וַיִּקַּח יְהוָה אֱלֹהִים אֶת־הָאָדָם	*wayyiqtol*
15b	וַיַּנִּחֵהוּ בְגַן־עֵדֶן	*wayyiqtol*
15c	לְעָבְדָהּ	*l* + inf c
15d	וּלְשָׁמְרָהּ	*waw* + *l* + inf c
16a	וַיְצַו יְהוָה אֱלֹהִים עַל־הָאָדָם לֵאמֹר	*wayyiqtol*
16b	↓מִכֹּל עֵץ־הַגָּן אָכֹל תֹּאכֵל	x + inf a + *yiqtol*
17a	↓וּמֵעֵץ הַדַּעַת טוֹב וָרָע לֹא תֹאכַל מִמֶּנּוּ	*waw* + x + *lo*ʾ + *yiqtol*
17b	כִּי ↓ בְּיוֹם אֲכָלְךָ מִמֶּנּוּ מוֹת תָּמוּת	*ki* + x + inf a + *yiqtol*
18a	וַיֹּאמֶר יְהוָה אֱלֹהִים	*wayyiqtol*
18b	לֹא־טוֹב הֱיוֹת הָאָדָם לְבַדּוֹ	*lo*ʾ + verbless
18c	אֶעֱשֶׂה־לּוֹ עֵזֶר כְּנֶגְדּוֹ	*yiqtol*

2. Observe the Context

- In what discourse type does this clause appear, narrative or non-narrative?
- What verbal sequence precedes this clause? Does this preceding sequence suggest a significant verbal pattern (e.g., imperatives followed by *yiqtol*)?
- Special situations:
  - Is this clause in the context of background material? If so, are there suggestions that the background is continued or halted (see pp. 85–86)?
  - Does this clause reiterate a previous clause, suggesting the resumption of a previous sequence (see pp. 86–87)?

- Was this clause preceded by לֵאמֹר or some other phrase that introduces embedded discourse?
- Does this clause switch expected verb forms (e.g., a *weqatal* in a *wayyiqtol* chain), suggesting a change in discourse type (see pp. 84–85)?

STEP 2.B: CONCLUDE WITH HOW THE CLAUSE RELATES TO THE PREVIOUS CLAUSES

The preceding observations culminate in the following question: how does the clause under examination relate to the previous ones? This step is the heart of discourse analysis and the most challenging. You must draw together:

1. All that you have observed in step 2.A;
2. Your knowledge of how the elements of BH prose (discourse markers, verbal sequences, word order) convey meaning (see chapters 3–6 above; a summary is provided in chapter 9);
3. Your sense of the text's inner logic; and
4. All kinds of relevant broader contexts (literary, historical, theological) that help establish logical unity.

Understanding the flow of a text is the product of all these considerations! Discourse analysis is the rigorous art of weighing these factors well in the pursuit of an intelligent understanding of the text.

You will then record your conclusion about how a clause relates to the others by giving a name to the relationship. If, for example, the clause in Deut 5:25a brings the foregoing three clauses to a conclusion, you might write "inference on the basis of 24b–d." However, naming discourse relationships is only the beginning of exegesis. Much more could be said about the relationship between individual clauses than the simple word "inference." How precisely do the first three lines provide the basis for the conclusion in the final line? More can be done from this point, but the names we give to discourse relationships summarize important observations we have made about the discourse, and lay the foundation for deeper exegesis.

One simple example will illustrate how the four factors above can be weighed together:[3]

Joshua 18:8a–c

8a	וַיָּקֻמוּ הָאֲנָשִׁים	Then the men arose
8b	וַיֵּלֵכוּ	and went.
8c	וַיְצַו יְהוֹשֻׁעַ אֶת־הַהֹלְכִים לִכְתֹּב אֶת־הָאָרֶץ לֵאמֹר	Then Joshua commanded those who went to write [a description of] the land, saying . . .

The key question is how to understand the relationship of verse 8c to the foregoing. Taking into account the context of verses 8a–b, which are two *wayyiqtol* forms operating in the foreground, our expectation when we encounter the next *wayyiqtol* in verse 8c is that it will continue the foreground (based on our discussion above about *wayyiqtol* as a continuative form and the list of common discourse functions for *wayyiqtol*). Our first guess might be that verse 8c is the "next event" after verse 8b (this is reflected in the translation in the table above).

But when we take into account what is being said, we must revise our interpretation. For verses 8a–b indicate that the men have already departed (and as vv. 3–7 tell us, their mission is to investigate the land). Based on our understanding of what is taking place (#3–4 in our list above), it does not make sense that Joshua would command people *after* they have left. Therefore, we must understand verse 8c as a pluperfect ("Now, Joshua *had commanded* . . .") and that verse 8c is introducing a background comment, where we flashback to the commands Joshua had given *before* the spies left. Even though this is an unusual use of *wayyiqtol* and no cue signals this relationship besides these contextual considerations (we might have expected a *waw* + x + *qatal* or the use of וַיְהִי with a temporal phrase), we can still be reasonably certain that our interpretation is correct. The pursuit of intelligibility caused us to regard factors #3–4 (text flow and context) as more important than factor #2 (normal uses of the *wayyiqtol*).

3. This example is adapted from C. John Collins, "The Wayyiqtol as 'Pluperfect': When and Why," *TynBul* 46 (1995): 123–24.

PRACTICAL HELPS FOR STEP 2.B

The question of how two clauses relate (Step 2.B) is the heart of discourse analysis, and this step will be the place where you will most often encounter difficulty. Here we provide some practical helps for doing this vital step.

1. **Ask what the speaker is *doing* with this clause.** Sometimes the answer will be, "he's giving advice" or "she's asking a rhetorical question." These are useful labels for clauses when doing discourse analysis, and we employ them below, but it should be noticed that these answers are not the heart of discourse analysis, which is to focus on the *relationship* between clauses. One must not stop until the relationship of this clause to the larger whole has been discovered. For example: "Advice *based on vv. 23a–b.*"

   The one exception to the previous point occurs when a clause begins a new unit in a discourse or a new discourse altogether (something that happens quite frequently in narrative, since each direct speech is a new discourse unit). In this situation, it is often sufficient to mark what the author is doing with this individual initial clause without necessarily relating it to the foregoing clauses (e.g., "Rhetorical question regarding idolatry"). Or, if you prefer, you can also identify the clause as the beginning of a new unit: "*New topic*: Rhetorical question regarding idolatry."
2. **Scan lists of possible relationships.** Sometimes looking over lists of possible relationships can help stimulate ideas about how clauses relate. The process of elimination can bring you to two or three strong exegetical options.

   First, you can scan the list of possible relationships in chapter 2 above. At the same time, these are not exhaustive lists and sometimes it is appropriate to express the relationship you see between the clauses in your own words. However, for consistency's sake, first try to use the list of relationships provided.

   Second, you can scan the lists of possible relationships for the particular discourse marker, verbal sequence, or word-order situation in chapters 3–6. If you are considering a *wayyiqtol*, then look through the possible uses of *wayyiqtol*.

3. **Be prepared for unusual situations.** The lists in chapters 3–6 are not complete. As was just demonstrated above with the *wayyiqtol* in Joshua 18:8c, in some rare situations *wayyiqtol* can initiate background, a scenario that was not in the list in chapter 3. Allow for the possibility that context will overrule your expectations for how a specific element will be used.

Also, the lists in chapters 3–6 are not complete in that not every discourse marker or verbal sequence is listed. How should you handle a situation that is not discussed above? Here are three rules of thumb:

1. *Rule of Thumb #1*: Look for analogies with the verbal sequences you know already. For example, וְהָיָה has many discourse functions in common with וַיְהִי. And *waw* + x + *yiqtol* behaves similarly to *waw* + x + *qatal*. Asyndeton in narrative (which we did not treat above) functions similarly to how it functions in non-narrative (which we did treat; pp. 82–83).
2. *Rule of Thumb #2*: Be aware of special constructions. For example, BH has special discourse markers and verbal sequences for expressing oaths and curses.[4] (Other examples include: questions, exclamations, etc.). Understanding how these constructions operate is vital to a correct discourse analysis, and many advanced grammars provide thorough descriptions of these special situations.[5]
3. *Rule of Thumb #3*: Sometimes a line has none of the main elements of discourse: there is no discourse marker nor any well-attested verbal sequence or word-order pattern. In this situation, we must remember how each verbal form (*qatal*, *yiqtol*, etc.) has its own default meaning in terms of the verbal semantics: tense, aspect, and mood.[6] Knowing the default meaning of a verb's tense, aspect, and mood helps to identify the discourse function of a line.

---

4. See a full account in Blane Conklin, *Oath Formulas in Biblical Hebrew*, LSAWS 5 (Winona Lake, IN: Eisenbrauns, 2011).
5. See *GBHS*, 162–92; Joüon §§157–75; GKC §§148–67.
6. For a brief introduction to verbal semantics, see pp. 62–65.

The following example has a situation where we apply the first and third rules of thumb.

Exodus 33:6–7b

6	וַיִּֽתְנַצְּל֧וּ בְנֵֽי־יִשְׂרָאֵ֛ל אֶת־עֶדְיָ֖ם מֵהַ֥ר חוֹרֵֽב׃	So the sons of Israel stripped themselves of their ornaments, from Mount Horeb onward.
7a	וּמֹשֶׁ֡ה יִקַּ֣ח אֶת־הָאֹ֠הֶל	Now Moses used to take his tent
7b	וְנָֽטָה־ל֣וֹ מִח֣וּץ לַֽמַּחֲנֶ֗ה הַרְחֵק֙ מִן־הַֽמַּחֲנֶ֔ה	and would pitch it outside the camp, far from the camp.

Exodus 33:1–6 has a *wayyiqtol* chain, the last verse of which is given above. In this *wayyiqtol* chain, how are we to understand *waw* + x + *yiqtol* in verse 7a?

- Using Rule of Thumb #1: on the one hand, the *waw* + x + *yiqtol* interrupts the *wayyiqtol* chain with a preposed clause and a new verb form (*yiqtol*). Based on our word order discussion, this suggests that it may be a background comment, which is true in this case.
- Using Rule of Thumb #3: part of the default meaning of *yiqtol* is imperfective aspect (see the default verbal semantics table above). In this case the clause makes sense when understood as a habitual action (a particular kind of imperfective idea) on Moses's part: his taking and pitching his tent was a regular practice. This hunch is confirmed as we read on and discover in verses 7d–11 a description of a habitual state of affairs near the camp of Israel, a description that is carried on with *weqatal.*
- Verse 7a therefore initiates a background comment about Moses's habit in pitching his tent, a background comment that ends in verse 11, when the foreground resumes in verse 12 with a return to *wayyiqtol.*

III. STEP 3: REASSESS YOUR ANALYSIS

1. REVISE RELATIONSHIPS IN LIGHT OF THE WHOLE DISCOURSE

Quite often, the function of a clause within a discourse only emerges later, when the discourse as a whole is in view (as we saw above in Josh 18:8). As interpreters, we make our best first attempt as we move through the text (in Steps 2–3 above), relying on background knowledge, schemas, and scripts to fill the gaps and achieve intelligibility.[7] But when we have reached the end of the discourse, we sometimes realize we have filled these gaps erroneously. Therefore, our analysis is not complete until we have reassessed each discourse relationship in light of the whole. Indeed, we are always reevaluating our interpretations in light of new context from elsewhere in Scripture or other theological and historical contexts.

2. DETERMINE BOUNDARIES OF LARGER SECTIONS

When the discourse is viewed as a whole, we can observe larger subdivisions of the text (e.g., paragraphs and larger sections). Although our focus in this book has been on clausal relationships, much of this book is useful for determining higher-level relationships. For example, several constructions (*wayyiqtol*, וַיְהִי, and preposing) are used to begin new episodes or discourse units. New topics or themes suggest the beginning of a new paragraph. Examples B and D below, being longer, demonstrate how we can discern larger sections in a discourse.

IV. CRITERIA FOR A COMPELLING DISCOURSE RELATIONSHIP

While there is a large subjective component to every interpretation, discourse analysis helps to limit and inform the interpretive options by taking into account more than just sentence syntax. Especially important is the recognition that BH often conveys discourse relationships through

7. See an excellent example of this process in George Yule, *The Study of Language*, 6th ed. (Cambridge: Cambridge University Press, 2017), 166–67.

verbal sequences (like a *wayyiqtol* chain interrupted by *waw* + x + *qatal*) and alterations in word order, features not as salient in English.[8]

How certain can you be that your proposed discourse relationships are correct? A good proposal for a discourse relationship usually will:

1. Not contravene the typical uses of discourse markers, verbal sequences, or word order.
2. Account for *all* elements of a clause, including the usual meanings of each individual word.
3. Fit comprehensibly with the surrounding context.

The final criterion is especially important. As we saw in the example of Joshua 18:8a–c above, we opted for an unusual interpretation of the *wayyiqtol* in verse 18c because it was more *intelligible* than the other interpretations. The question of textual meaning and the principles of intelligibility leads us into the discipline of hermeneutics and is beyond the scope of this book.[9] But notice: discourse analysis teaches us to attend well to texts so we can approach the interpretive question of logical unity with as much information as possible.

There may be more than one discourse relationship that meets these criteria equally well. BH clauses are often simply laid next to each other with no discourse marker (like פֶּן or לָכֵן) to clarify the discourse relationship. Moreover, discourse markers and verbal sequences can evoke several meanings (e.g., וְהִנֵּה or *wayyiqtol* in a *wayyiqtol* sequence). In these situations, our discourse analysis must be held lightly. Sometimes we can only suggest the relationship between two clauses because its precise relationship is not clearly encoded in the text.

8. Regarding word order, Goldfajn points out that in BH it conveys "the sort of temporal meanings which in many languages are more often indicated lexically, for instance by special forms of the verb or by a range of adverbials" (*Word Order*, 141).

9. On the distinct question of "coherence" in linguistics, see Brown and Yule, *Discourse Analysis*, 223–71.

Chapter 8

Examples of Discourse Analysis with Hebrew Prose

EXAMPLE A: JONAH 1:4A–6B

This example shows a variety of discourse relationships in narrative.

	Text	Construction	Discourse Analysis	Translation
4a	וַיהוָה הֵטִיל רֽוּחַ־גְּדוֹלָה אֶל־הַיָּם	*waw* + x + *qatal*	New episode: YHWH hurled a great wind	Now YHWH hurled a great wind on the sea,
4b	וַיְהִי סַֽעַר־גָּדוֹל בַּיָּם	*wayyiqtol*	Result of v. 4a: a tempest arose	and a great tempest arose on the sea.
4c	וְהָאֳנִיָּה חִשְּׁבָה לְהִשָּׁבֵר׃	*waw* + x + *qatal*	Result of v. 4b: the ship is about to break	And the ship was about to break (literally, "thinking to be broken").
5a	וַיִּֽירְאוּ הַמַּלָּחִים	*wayyiqtol*	Result of v. 4a–c: the sailors became afraid	Then the sailors became afraid,
5b	וַֽיִּזְעֲקוּ אִישׁ אֶל־אֱלֹהָיו	*wayyiqtol*	Simultaneous with v. 5a: they cried out	and they cried out, each to his gods,

(cont.)

- **v. 4a**: The *waw* + x + *qatal* construction initiates a new topic. In the previous verse, Jonah was the main actor and had just boarded a ship in disobedience to YHWH. Now the narrator brings a new actor to the fore, YHWH, whose hurling of the storm initiates a new sequence of events.
- **v. 4c**: The *waw* + x + *qatal* construction is another instance of a new topic being highlighted. Attention now focuses on the ship that is about to be broken.
- **vv. 5a–c**: The next three clauses are narrated with simple *wayyiqtol* verbs. They could be a temporal sequence (they feared, *then* they cried out, *then* they hurled). But they could also be simultaneous actions, where the fearing, the crying out, and the hurling of the cargo are all happening at the same time (we opted for this understanding).

	Text	Construction	Discourse Analysis	Translation
5c	וַיָּטִ֨לוּ אֶת־הַכֵּלִ֜ים	*wayyiqtol*	Simultaneous with v. 5a–b: they hurled the cargo	and they hurled the cargo
5d	אֲשֶׁ֤ר בָּֽאֳנִיָּה֙ אֶל־הַיָּ֔ם	*ʾasher* + verbless	Expansion on the cargo: it was in the ship [Prepositional phrase modifies וַיָּטִ֨לוּ in v. 5c]	in the ship into the sea
5e	לְהָקֵ֖ל מֵעֲלֵיהֶ֑ם	*l* + inf c	Purpose of the hurling in v. 5c: to lighten the ship	in order to lighten it.
5f	וְיוֹנָ֗ה יָרַד֙ אֶל־יַרְכְּתֵ֣י הַסְּפִינָ֔ה	*waw* + x + *qatal*	Background: Episode prior to the events in vv. 4a–5c: Jonah had gone down	Now Jonah had gone down to the inner parts of the ship,
5g	וַיִּשְׁכַּ֖ב	*wayyiqtol*	Next after v. 5f: he had lain down	and had lain down

(cont.)

- **vv. 5c–e**: These three lines are a little challenging to diagram according to our scheme. Each is its own clause: an independent clause (v. 5c), a relative clause (v. 5d), and a purpose clause (v. 5e). The latter two (vv. 5d–e) depend on the first one (v. 5c), which is why they are indented. The prepositional phrase in verse 5d (אֶל־הַיָּ֔ם) really belongs with the main verb in verse 5c (וַיָּטִ֨לוּ), but in the interest of preserving Hebrew word order we keep it in verse 5d.
- **v. 5g**: Another *waw* + x + *qatal* construction suggests two options:
  1. The foreground continues but with a new topic, Jonah. In this case, Jonah's going down into the hold of the ship is subsequent to the sailors' actions in verses 5a–c.
  2. A background sequence has begun. Looking ahead, this sequence continues until verse 6a, when the captain approaches the sleeping Jonah.

  We adopt option (2) because option (1) has Jonah descending and going to sleep in the midst of the storm, an unlikely situation. Under option (2), the sequence in verses 5f–h took place at some unspecified time prior to the events of verses 4a–5c.

	Text	Construction	Discourse Analysis	Translation
5h	וַיֵּרָדַם׃	*wayyiqtol*	Next after v. 5g: he had fallen asleep	and fallen asleep.
6a	וַיִּקְרַב אֵלָיו רַב הַחֹבֵל	*wayyiqtol*	Resumption of foreground, next after v. 5c: the captain approaches him	So the captain approached him
6b	וַיֹּאמֶר	*wayyiqtol*	Simultaneous with v. 6a: he says	and said . . .

- **vv. 5g–h**: Once we have determined that verse 5f initiates a background statement, the function of these two clauses becomes clear. These *wayyiqtol* statements continue the background statement, explaining what Jonah did when he descended into the ship.
- Regarding tense, once we conclude that verses 5f–h are background statements about what Jonah did prior to the storm, this determines the tense of our English translation as pluperfect ("Jonah *had gone down*").
- **vv. 6a–b**: Now that verses 5f–h have set the scene with Jonah sleeping in the hold, the foreground resumes with the captain approaching him. Since the foreground was suspended in verses 5f–h, the event in verse 6a follows immediately after the chaotic actions of the sailors in verses 5a–c.

Summary: Discourse analysis enabled us to think clearly about three instances where *waw* + x + *qatal* occurs in a *wayyiqtol* sequence (vv. 4a, 4c, 5f). The first two instances shift the focus of attention from one topic to another. The third instance initiates a background sequence. Discourse analysis also allowed us to piece the temporal sequence together properly, understanding verses 5f–h as a flashback about Jonah falling asleep, which sets the stage for the next event in verse 6a.

EXAMPLE B: 1 KINGS 20:23–25

This example shows the discourse relationships between each clause of a direct speech embedded in a narrative. This example also shows how we can delineate subsections of a discourse.

	Text	Construction	Discourse Analysis	Translation
23a	וְעַבְדֵ֨י מֶֽלֶךְ־אֲרָ֜ם אָמְר֣וּ אֵלָ֗יו	*waw* + x + *qatal*	New topic: the servants of the king of Aram speak	Now the servants of the king of Aram said to him,
		Embedded Discourse (vv. 23b–25c): Advice of the King's Servants		
23b	אֱלֹהֵ֤י הָרִים֙ אֱלֹ֣הֵיהֶ֔ם	verbless	vv. 23b–c: Reasoning about the recent loss: Initial assertion: Israel's gods are gods of the mountains.	"Their gods are gods of the mountains,

(cont.)

- **v. 23a**: The *waw* + x + *qatal* construction initiates a new topic, the servants of the king and their speech.
- **vv. 23b–25c**: The direct speech here is marked off by the grey shading. It is embedded discourse, and hence is its own discourse unit, distinct from the narrative flow in which it is embedded.
- Discourse relationships can operate on a clause-by-clause level, but they can also operate from a broader perspective.
  - The relationship between verse 23b ("their gods are gods of the mountains") and verse 23c ("therefore they were stronger than we") is a simple clause-by-clause relationship.
  - The detailed instructions in verses 24a–25c are a specification of the basic instruction in verse 23d. This is a broader, more macroscopic relationship.
  - When these broader, macroscopic relationships exist, it can be helpful to indent the discourse analysis of the sub-sections (e.g., vv. 23b–c) to make the larger sections clearer (in examples below, we will show larger macroscopic relationships with headings).

	Text	Construction	Discourse Analysis	Translation
23c	עַל־כֵּן חָזְקוּ מִמֶּנּוּ	*ʿal-ken* + *qatal*	Inference based on v. 23b: they were stronger than us.	therefore they were stronger than we;
23d	וְאוּלָם נִלָּחֵם אִתָּם בַּמִּישׁוֹר	*waw* + *ʾulam* + *yiqtol*	vv. 23d–25c: Advice based on vv. 23b–c Contrast with previous actions in 20:1ff: instead, let us fight in the plain.	but rather let us fight against them in the plain,
23e	אִם־לֹא נֶחֱזַק מֵהֶם׃	*ʾim* + *loʾ* + *yiqtol*	Hoped-for result from v. 23d: we will be stronger	and surely we will be stronger than they.

(cont.)

- It is perfectly acceptable to name new discourse relationships on an as-needed basis. For example, we describe verse 23e as the "hoped-for result" of verse 23d, even though that relationship is not in our lists of suggested relationships above.
- Remember, naming discourse relationships is only the beginning of exegesis. Much more could be said about the relationship between individual clauses than the simple words in the table above. For example, how precisely is the advice of verses 23d–25c "based on" the reasoning in verses 23b–c? Are there clues in the narrative for why the Arameans would think they would have more success in the plain rather than the mountains?
- **v. 23c** begins with עַל־כֵּן. This is an example of a discourse marker, where verse 23c is explicitly marked as a conclusion on the basis of the preceding clause. Another discourse marker is אִם־לֹא in verses 23e and 25c.

	Text	Construction	Discourse Analysis	Translation
24a	וְאֶת־הַדָּבָר הַזֶּה עֲשֵׂה	*waw* + x + imv	vv. 24a–25a: Expansion on the advice in v. 23d: Introduction to vv24b–25a: do this thing	Do this thing:
24b	הָסֵר הַמְּלָכִים אִישׁ מִמְּקֹמוֹ	imv	Initial step: remove the kings	remove the kings, each from his place,
24c	וְשִׂים פַּחוֹת תַּחְתֵּיהֶם׃	*waw* + imv	Simultaneous to v. 24b: put captains in their place	and put captains in their place,
25a	וְאַתָּה תִמְנֶה־לְךָ חַיִל כַּחַיִל הַנֹּפֵל מֵאוֹתָךְ וְסוּס כַּסּוּס וְרֶכֶב כָּרֶכֶב	*waw* + x + *yiqtol*	Simultaneous with vv. 24b–c: muster an army like the one you lost	and as for you, muster an army like the army that you have lost, horse for horse, and chariot for chariot.
25b	וְנִלָּחֲמָה אוֹתָם בַּמִּישׁוֹר	*waw* + *yiqtol*	Inference on the basis of vv. 24b–25a: in this manner we will fight	Thus we will fight against them in the plain,

(cont.)

- **v. 24a**: The noun phrase וְאֶת־הַדָּבָר הַזֶּה is preposed before עֲשֵׂה. The most likely explanation here is "emphasis": do *this* thing (as opposed to the previous failed approaches).
- **v. 25a**: The placement of וְאַתָּה before תִמְנֶה is another instance of preposing, in this case perhaps to focus on a new actor, where the king is the one carrying out the actions.
- **v. 25b**: *waw* + *yiqtol* after a series of imperative forms could indicate purpose, but the repetition of words from verse 23d suggests that this clause draws a conclusion on the basis of the foregoing plan.

	Text	Construction	Discourse Analysis	Translation
25c	אִם־לֹ֖א נֶחֱזַ֥ק מֵהֶֽם	*'im* + *lo'* + *yiqtol*	Hoped-for result from v. 25b: we will be stronger	and surely we will be stronger than they."
25d	וַיִּשְׁמַ֥ע לְקֹלָ֖ם	*wayyiqtol*	Next after vv. 23a–25c: the king listened	And he listened to their voice
25e	וַיַּ֥עַשׂ כֵּֽן׃	*wayyiqtol*	Simultaneous with v. 25d: and he did so	and did so.

Summary: Discourse analysis uncovered the inner logic of the king's counselors. The instructions in verse 23d about fighting in the plain is an overview of the more detailed instructions in verses 24a–25a. All of these instructions are based on the assumption about Israel's gods being gods of the mountains (v. 23b).

EXAMPLE C: EXODUS 12:21C–23F

This non-narrative example shows some of the flexibility of *weqatal*.

	Text	Construction	Discourse Analysis	Translation
		The Passover Rite (vv. 21c–22d)		
21c	מִשְׁכוּ	imv	New command sequence: draw out	Draw out
21d	וּקְחוּ לָכֶם צֹאן לְמִשְׁפְּחֹתֵיכֶם	*waw* + imv	Simultaneous to v. 21c: take a sheep	and take for yourselves a sheep for each of your families,
21e	וְשַׁחֲטוּ הַפָּסַח׃	*waw* + imv	Next after vv. 21c–d: slaughter	and then slaughter the passover lamb.
22a	וּלְקַחְתֶּם אֲגֻדַּת אֵזוֹב	*weqatal*	Next after v. 21e / shift of topic to hyssop: take a bunch of hyssop	Take a bunch of hyssop,

(cont.)

- **vv. 21c–e** has a series of three imperative verbs chained together. The second and third imperative forms could have a result ("so that") relationship with the previous imperative(s). But the chain makes better sense as two simultaneous actions ("draw out" and "take"), followed by a subsequent action ("slaughter").
- **v. 22a** switches from imperative forms to *weqatal*. There is no apparent reason for the shift, although Moses now speaks of hyssop instead of lambs. The *weqatal* continues the imperative mood from the previous clauses.

	Text	Construction	Discourse Analysis	Translation
22b	וּטְבַלְתֶּם֙ בַּדָּ֣ם אֲשֶׁר־בַּסַּ֔ף	*weqatal*	Next after v. 22a: dip it in the blood	dip it in the blood in the basin,
22c	וְהִגַּעְתֶּ֨ם אֶל־הַמַּשְׁקוֹף֙ וְאֶל־שְׁתֵּ֣י הַמְּזוּזֹ֔ת מִן־הַדָּ֖ם אֲשֶׁ֣ר בַּסָּ֑ף	*weqatal*	Next after v. 22b: apply it to the lintel and the two door posts	and apply some of the blood in the basin to the lintel and the two door posts.
22d	וְאַתֶּ֗ם לֹ֥א תֵצְא֛וּ אִ֥ישׁ מִפֶּֽתַח־בֵּית֖וֹ עַד־בֹּֽקֶר׃	*waw* + x + *yiqtol*	Prohibition for the time after v. 22c / shift in topic to the people: do not go outside	None of you must go out of the door of the house until morning.

(cont.)

- **vv. 22b–c**: The *weqatal* chain, along with the nature of each of these activities, indicates a sequence of actions, one following another.
- **vv. 22b–c**: The two instances of the phrase אֲשֶׁר־בַּסַּף require special mention. Although technically they are relative clauses with an assumed "to be" verb (i.e., "which [are] in the basin"), they are so minor as not to warrant giving them their own box in the diagram.
- **v. 22d**: The *waw* + x + *yiqtol* departs from *weqatal* and suggests a new direction, which is confirmed by the shift from a series of prescribed actions to a prohibition. The preposed וְאַתֶּם makes the prohibition emphatic and serious. It also signals a new topic (the people) and what they are to do with themselves (as opposed to what they must do with the lamb and the hyssop).

	Text	Construction	Discourse Analysis	Translation
		Result of the Rite in Verses 21c–22d: YHWH Sparing Them (v. 23)		
23a	וְעָבַ֣ר יְהוָ֮ה	*weqatal*	Next after v. 21c / circumstances for vv. 23b–c: YHWH passes through	Then, when YHWH passes through
23b	לִנְגֹּ֣ף אֶת־מִצְרַ֒יִם֒	*l* + inf c	Purpose for v. 23a: to plague Egypt	to plague Egypt,
23c	וְרָאָ֤ה אֶת־הַדָּם֙ עַל־הַמַּשְׁק֔וֹף וְעַ֖ל שְׁתֵּ֣י הַמְּזוּזֹ֑ת	*weqatal*	During v. 23a–b: Initial action: YHWH sees the blood	he will see the blood on the lintel and the two door posts,
23d	וּפָסַ֤ח יְהוָה֙ עַל־הַפֶּ֔תַח	*weqatal*	Result of v. 23c: YHWH passes over the door	and YHWH will pass over the door,

(cont.)

- **v. 23**: This verse as a whole stands in a relationship to verses 21c–22d that surpasses the level of individual clauses. These macro-relationships can be expressed through headings, as above for verses 21c–22d and verse 23.
- **v. 23a**: The *weqatal* form suggests the continuation of the chain in verse 22c. However, the new subject (יְהוָה) indicates another new direction, focusing on how YHWH will respond to the rite in verses 21c–22d.
- **v. 23b**: The "seeing" is something that takes place when YHWH is "passing through" Egypt (v. 23a). A "when . . . then" construction captures this relationship.
- **vv. 23c–f** give the results of YHWH seeing the blood. Another way of construing this verse is that verses 23a–b give the circumstances for the main actions in verses 23c–d, yielding something like: "When YHWH passes through . . . and sees the blood . . . , then he will pass over . . . and not allow . . . ."

	Text	Construction	Discourse Analysis	Translation
23e	וְלֹא יִתֵּן הַמַּשְׁחִית לָבֹא אֶל־בָּתֵּיכֶם	*waw* + *lo'* + *yiqtol*	Expansion on v. 23d: YHWH will not allow the destroyer to enter	and he will not allow the destroyer to enter into your houses
23f	לִנְגֹּף׃	*l* + inf c	Purpose of entering in v. 23e: to plague	to plague them.

- **v. 23e**: The phrase beginning with לָבֹא is the complement of the main verb יִתֵּן and should not have its own box, since it forms one verbal idea: "he did not allow to enter." In verse 23f, however, we have a very short purpose clause that modifies לָבֹא: לִנְגֹּף "in order to plague."

Summary: This example showed how discourse analysis gives criteria for understanding highly flexible verbal forms like *weqatal*. Sometimes *weqatal* continues a sequence of instructions (vv. 22b–c); other times its use with a new subject denotes a new beginning (v. 23a). One complex instance can legitimately be taken several ways (see comments above on vv. 23c–f). Discourse analysis helps expose the interpretive options for a text.

EXAMPLE D: 1 SAMUEL 9:26–10:13

This extended example shows how discourse analysis operates on a larger pericope.

Note: there are many text-critical issues in this text, where the LXX may preserve a better reading than MT. We conduct our discourse analysis on the MT, which is intelligible as it stands.

	Text	Construction	Discourse Analysis	Translation
9:26a	וַיַּשְׁכִּמוּ	*wayyiqtol*	New episode (the next day after 9:5–25): they arose early	They [Samuel and Saul] arose early,
26b	וַיְהִי כַּעֲלוֹת הַשַּׁחַר	*wayhi* + *k* + inf c	↓Circumstances of v. 26c: when the dawn was rising	and at the break of day
26c	וַיִּקְרָא שְׁמוּאֵל אֶל־שָׁאוּל הַגָּגָה לֵאמֹר	*wayyiqtol*	Next after v26a: Samuel called	Samuel called to Saul on the roof, saying,

(cont.)

- **vv. 26b–c**: A *wayhi* introduces a temporal clause that describes the circumstances for the *wayyiqtol* that follows in verse 26c. The *wayhi* and temporal clause have one row in the table (see p. 99). The discourse purpose of verse 26b is dependent on the main action that follows in verse 26c, so we indent verse 26b and use a down arrow to show this dependency.

	Text	Construction	Discourse Analysis	Translation
		Embedded Discourse (vv. 26d–e): Samuel's Early Morning Commands		
26d	קוּמָה	imv	Samuel's command to Saul: arise	"Arise,
26e	וַאֲשַׁלְּחֶךָּ	*waw* + *yiqtol*	Purpose of v. 26d: that I might send you	so I might send you [on your way]."
26f	וַיָּקָם שָׁאוּל	*wayyiqtol*	Result of vv. 26d–e: Saul arose	So Saul arose,
26g	וַיֵּצְאוּ שְׁנֵיהֶם הוּא וּשְׁמוּאֵל הַחוּצָה׃	*wayyiqtol*	Next after v. 26f: they went out	and the two of them, both he and Samuel, went out into the street.
27a	הֵמָּה יוֹרְדִים בִּקְצֵה הָעִיר	x + Ptc	↓Circumstance for v. 27b: as they were going down	As they were going down to the edge of the city,

(cont.)

- **vv. 26d–e**: The *yiqtol* follows the imperative, suggesting that the *yiqtol* gives the purpose for the command to Saul to arise.
- **v. 26f**: The *wayyiqtol* signals the end of the short speech in verses 26d–e and the resumption of the foreground narrative. This situation will recur several times in this text.
- **v. 26g**: The phrase **הוּא וּשְׁמוּאֵל** is in apposition to **שְׁנֵיהֶם**, so it is indented.
- **v. 27a**: This construction is not discussed in chapters 3–6, but it can be readily understood. Participial clauses commonly convey an imperfective (ongoing) aspect (see the table of default verbal semantics, p. 64). However, the default tense for participles (present) is overridden here, since the context is in the past; hence: "they were going down." Then, when we coordinate this clause with verse 27b, it becomes clear that this gives the circumstance for the main action: Samuel speaking to Saul.

	Text	Construction	Discourse Analysis	Translation
27b	וּשְׁמוּאֵל אָמַר אֶל־שָׁאוּל	*waw* + x + *qatal*	Next after v. 26g: Samuel said	Samuel said to Saul,
		Embedded Discourse (vv. 27c–d, f–g): Preparatory Commands		
27c	אֱמֹר לַנַּעַר	imv	Command: speak to the servant	"Speak to the servant
27d	וְיַעֲבֹר לְפָנֵינוּ	*waw* + *yiqtol*	Purpose: that he might pass on	so that he might pass on ahead of us"
27e	וַיַּעֲבֹר	*wayyiqtol*	Interruption of the speech in vv. 27c–d / next after vv. 27b–d: the servant complies	—and he passed on—

(cont.)

- **vv. 27c–d**: Similar to verses 26d–e, a *waw* + *yiqtol* following an imperative implies purpose.
- **v. 27e**: The sudden introduction of a *wayyiqtol* form in the midst of Samuel's speech indicates a quick shift back to the narrative foreground, showing concisely (without reporting Saul speaking to the servant) that Samuel's first command in verse 27c has now been carried out. Thus, Samuel is alone with Saul as he speaks verses 27f–g. Some translations have this clause as part of Samuel's speech (e.g., ESV: "Tell the servant to pass on before us, *and when he has passed on*, stop here yourself . . ." [emphasis added]). But this is unlikely, first, because *wayyiqtol* is less common in non-narrative than in narrative, and second, if the author wanted to convey the idea of the ESV, he could have done so using non-narrative verbal patterns (e.g., a *wehayah* or *weqatal* clause). Notice also that this line has two discourse relationships: "Interruption of the speech in verses 27c–d" *and* "next after verses 27b–d." Sometimes a clause stands in a multifaceted, complex relationship with the surrounding verses.

	Text	Construction	Discourse Analysis	Translation
27f	וְאַתָּה עֲמֹד כַּיּוֹם	*waw* + x + imv	Resumption of the speech from v. 27d / shift of topic from the servant to Saul: Command: stand	"but you, stand a while,
27g	וְאַשְׁמִיעֲךָ אֶת־דְּבַר אֱלֹהִים׃	*waw* + *yiqtol*	Purpose: that I might make you hear	that I might make you hear the word of God."
10:1a	וַיִּקַּח שְׁמוּאֵל אֶת־פַּךְ הַשֶּׁמֶן	*wayyiqtol*	Next after vv. 27f–g: Samuel took	Then Samuel took the flask of oil,
1b	וַיִּצֹק עַל־רֹאשׁוֹ	*wayyiqtol*	Next: he poured	poured it on his head,
1c	וַיִּשָּׁקֵהוּ	*wayyiqtol*	Next: he kissed	kissed him,
1d	וַיֹּאמֶר	*wayyiqtol*	Next: he said	and said,
		Embedded Discourse (vv. 1e–8g): Samuel's Anointing Speech		
1e	הֲלוֹא כִּי־מְשָׁחֲךָ יְהוָה עַל־נַחֲלָתוֹ לְנָגִיד׃	*h* + *lo'* + *ki* + *qatal*	Rhetorical question, explaining vv. 1a–c: has not YHWH anointed?	"Has not YHWH anointed you as ruler over his inheritance?

(cont.)

- **v. 27f**: The preposing of "you" (וְאַתָּה) indicates a new topic. In contrast to the words about the servant in verses 27c–d, Samuel is now addressing Saul.
- **10:1a–d**: These actions are in swift succession, lending themselves to a list (the conjunction "and" is not necessary between each action).

	Text	Construction	Discourse Analysis	Translation
2a	בְּלֶכְתְּךָ הַיּוֹם מֵעִמָּדִי	*b* + inf c	↓Circumstance for v. 2b: when you go,	When you go away today from me,
2b	וּמָצָאתָ שְׁנֵי אֲנָשִׁים עִם־קְבֻרַת רָחֵל בִּגְבוּל בִּנְיָמִן בְּצֶלְצַח	*weqatal*	Prediction / shift in time to the future: you will find	you will find two men by the tomb of Rachel, which is in the territory of Benjamin at Zelzah.
2c	וְאָמְרוּ אֵלֶיךָ	*weqatal*	Next after v. 2b: they will say	And they will say to you,
		Doubly Embedded Discourse (vv. 2d–i): The Men Speak to Saul		
2d	נִמְצְאוּ הָאֲתֹנוֹת	*qatal*	Initial report: The donkeys were found	'The donkeys have been found
2e	אֲשֶׁר הָלַכְתָּ	*'asher* + *qatal*	Expansion on the donkeys: the ones you went	which you went
2f	לְבַקֵּשׁ	*l* + inf c	Purpose of going in v. 2e: to seek	to seek.

(cont.)

- **v. 2a**: The asyndetic, preposed temporal clause ("when you go away"; בְּלֶכְתְּךָ) introduces a new unit and moves the temporal frame to the future.
- **v. 2c**: Now that the temporal frame is set in the future, *weqatal* carries the predictive speech forward in the future tense.
- **v. 2d**: The speech within a speech is marked off by an even darker shading than that used for Samuel's speech.

	Text	Construction	Discourse Analysis	Translation
2g	וְהִנֵּה נָטַשׁ אָבִיךָ אֶת־דִּבְרֵי הָאֲתֹנוֹת	*wehinneh* + *qatal*	New topic: your father has ceased	Now look, your father has ceased to care about the donkeys,
2h	וְדָאַג לָכֶם לֵאמֹר	*weqatal*	Contrast to v. 2g: and he is worried	and is worried about you, saying,
		Triply Embedded Discourse (v. 2i): Saul's Father's Worry		
2i	מָה אֶעֱשֶׂה לִבְנִי׃	x + *yiqtol*	Worried question: what shall I do?	"What shall I do about my son?"'
3a	וְחָלַפְתָּ מִשָּׁם וָהָלְאָה	*weqatal*	Next after vv. 2c–g / command to Saul: you shall pass on	Then you shall pass on further from there,
3b	וּבָאתָ עַד־אֵלוֹן תָּבוֹר	*weqatal*	Next after v. 3b: you shall come	and when you come to the oak of Tabor,

(cont.)

- **v. 2g**: וְהִנֵּה signals a new topic: the concern of Saul's father for Saul.
- **v. 3a**: The *weqatal* signals the end of the men's speech (including the quotation of Saul's father) and the resumption of Samuel's predictive speech.

	Text	Construction	Discourse Analysis	Translation
3c	וּמְצָאוּךָ שָׁם שְׁלֹשָׁה אֲנָשִׁים עֹלִים אֶל־הָאֱלֹהִים בֵּית־אֵל אֶחָד נֹשֵׂא שְׁלֹשָׁה גְדָיִים וְאֶחָד נֹשֵׂא שְׁלֹשֶׁת כִּכְּרוֹת לֶחֶם וְאֶחָד נֹשֵׂא נֵבֶל־יָיִן׃	*weqatal*	Simultaneous to v. 3b: three men will find you • Expansion on the men: they are going up • Expansion on first man: carrying three goats • Expansion on second man: carrying three loaves • Expansion on third man: carrying a jug	three men will find you there. They will be going up to the God of Bethel, one carrying three three young goats, one carrying three loaves of bread, and one carrying a jug of wine.
4a	וְשָׁאֲלוּ לְךָ לְשָׁלוֹם	*weqatal*	Next after vv. 3b–c: they will greet	Then they will greet you,
4b	וְנָתְנוּ לְךָ שְׁתֵּי־לֶחֶם	*weqatal*	Next after v. 4b: and give you	and give you two [loaves] of bread.
4c	וְלָקַחְתָּ מִיָּדָם׃	*weqatal*	Next after v. 4c / command to Saul: you shall take	You shall then take [them] from their hand.

(cont.)

- **v. 3c**: Because the men finding Saul is simultaneous to him arriving at the oak in verse 3b, we can render verses 3b–c using a "when . . . [then] . . ." construction.
- **v. 3c**: The participle **עֹלִים** belongs in the same box as **וּמְצָאוּךָ** because it is not its own clause. Instead, it modifies **אֲנָשִׁים**, expanding on the men. However, it and the following three participial phrases are sufficiently detailed to deserve their own lines in the discourse analysis box.
- **v. 4c**: Although the verb is the same form as the preceding verbs (*weqatal*), it has an imperatival force because of the shift to second person. In a mixture of prediction and command, Samuel directly addresses Saul with what he must do at this juncture. The same situation occurred previously in verse 3a.

	Text	Construction	Discourse Analysis	Translation
5a	↓אַ֣חַר כֵּ֗ן תָּבוֹא֙ גִּבְעַ֣ת הָאֱלֹהִ֔ים	x + *yiqtol*	New unit / command to Saul: after this, you shall come	After this you shall come to the hill of God,
5b	אֲשֶׁר־שָׁ֖ם נְצִבֵ֣י פְלִשְׁתִּ֑ים	*ʾasher* + verbless	Expansion on the hill of God: there is a Philistine garrison there	where there is a Philistine garrison.
5c	וִיהִ֣י כְבֹאֲךָ֩ שָׁ֨ם הָעִ֜יר	*wihi*	↓Circumstances for v. 5d: as you enter	As you enter the city there,
5d	וּפָגַעְתָּ֜ חֶ֣בֶל נְבִאִ֗ים יֹרְדִ֤ים מֵהַבָּמָה֙	*weqatal*	Next after v. 5a–b: you will encounter a group of prophets Expansion on the group of prophets: they are going down	you will encounter a group of prophets going down from the high place.
5e	וְלִפְנֵיהֶ֞ם נֵ֤בֶל וְתֹף֙ וְחָלִ֣יל וְכִנּ֔וֹר	*waw* + verbless	Background: Expansion on the group of prophets: Instruments [go] before them	Now they will have harp, tambourine, flute, and lyre going before them,

(cont.)

- **v. 5a**: The shift from a *weqatal* chain to x + *yiqtol* signals a new unit in Samuel's speech. In this case, the phrase אַחַר כֵּן moves the time referent forward an unspecified amount of time.
- **v. 5c–d**: This instance of וִיהִי + temporal clause + *weqatal* is handled much like 9:26b–c above. Note: וִיהִי is a particular kind of *waw* + *yiqtol*, distinct from וַיְהִי.
- **v. 5e**: The shift from *weqatal* to *waw* + verbless introduces a background statement, where the predictive narrative in the foreground pauses so Samuel can describe the group of prophets.

	Text	Construction	Discourse Analysis	Translation
5f	וְהֵ֫מָּה מִֽתְנַבְּאִֽים׃	*waw* + x + Ptc	Continuation of background / shift of topic from those bearing instruments to the prophets: they are prophesying	and they will be prophesying.
6a	וְצָלְחָ֤ה עָלֶ֙יךָ֙ ר֣וּחַ יְהוָ֔ה	*weqatal*	Next after v. 5d: the Spirit of YHWH will rush	Then the Spirit of YHWH will rush upon you,
6b	וְהִתְנַבִּ֖יתָ עִמָּ֑ם	*weqatal*	Result of v. 6a: you will prophesy	and you will prophesy with them,
6c	וְנֶהְפַּכְתָּ֖ לְאִ֥ישׁ אַחֵֽר׃	*weqatal*	Simultaneous to v. 6b: you will be changed	and you will be changed into a different man.
7a	וְהָיָ֗ה כִּ֥י תָבֹ֛אנָה הָאֹת֥וֹת הָאֵ֖לֶּה לָ֑ךְ	*wehayah* + *ki* + *yiqtol*	↓Condition for command in v. 7b: when these signs come	When these signs come upon you,
7b	עֲשֵׂ֤ה לְךָ֙	imv	Command: do	do
7c	אֲשֶׁ֣ר תִּמְצָ֣א יָדֶ֔ךָ	*ʾasher* + *yiqtol*	Expansion on what you are to do in v. 7b: whatever your hand finds	whatever your hand finds [to do],

(cont.)

- **v. 5f**: Another similar construction continues the background. The preposed הֵ֫מָּה indicates a shift in topic from the instruments that go at the front of the group to the prophets in the heart of the group.
- **v. 6a**: The return to *weqatal* resumes the narrative where it left off in verse 5d, before the background sequence in verses 5e–f.

	Text	Construction	Discourse Analysis	Translation
7d	כִּ֥י הָאֱלֹהִ֖ים עִמָּֽךְ׃	*ki* + verbless	Reason for v. 7b–c: God is with you	for God is with you.
8a	וְיָרַדְתָּ֣ לְפָנַי֮ הַגִּלְגָּל֒	*weqatal*	Next after vv. 7b–c: go down	Then go down before me to Gilgal,
8b	וְהִנֵּ֤ה אָנֹכִי֙ יֹרֵ֣ד אֵלֶ֔יךָ	*wehinneh* + x + Ptc	Reason for v. 8a / shift point of view to Samuel: I will be going down	for I will be going down to you
8c	לְהַעֲל֣וֹת עֹל֔וֹת	*l* + inf c	Purpose for v. 8b: to offer burnt offerings	to offer burnt offerings
8d	לִזְבֹּ֖חַ זִבְחֵ֣י שְׁלָמִ֑ים	*l* + inf c	Second purpose for v. 8b: to sacrifice peace offerings	and to sacrifice peace offerings.
8e	שִׁבְעַ֨ת יָמִ֤ים תּוֹחֵל֙	x + *yiqtol*	Shift back to Saul / command while he waits for the event predicted in v. 8b: wait	Seven days you shall wait
8f	עַד־בּוֹאִ֣י אֵלֶ֔יךָ	ʻ*ad* + inf c	Temporal clause restricting v. 8e: until I come	until I come to you

(cont.)

- **v. 8b**: Although "reason" is not a common discourse function for וְהִנֵּה, Samuel's command in verse 8a seems to be grounded in his intentions in verse 8b and following.
- **v. 8e**: This asyndetic preposed clause does not fit neatly in our list of common uses above, but the discourse relationship here is clear from context. Samuel has promised he will come to Gilgal in verse 8b. Verse 8e shifts back to Saul, to what he is to be doing until Samuel comes (see v. 8f).

	Text	Construction	Discourse Analysis	Translation
8g	וְהוֹדַעְתִּי לְךָ אֵת אֲשֶׁר תַּעֲשֶׂה׃	*weqatal*	Continuation of temporal clause in v. 8f / simultaneous to v. 8f: and make known	and make known what you are to do."
9a	וְהָיָה כְּהַפְנֹתוֹ שִׁכְמוֹ	*wehayah* + *k* + inf c	↓Circumstances for v. 9c: as he [Saul] turned his shoulder	Then, as [Saul] turned his shoulder
9b	לָלֶכֶת מֵעִם שְׁמוּאֵל	*l* + inf c	Purpose for v. 9a: to go from Samuel	to go from Samuel,
9c	וַיַּהֲפָךְ־לוֹ אֱלֹהִים לֵב אַחֵר	*wayyiqtol*	Next after speech in vv. 1e–8g: God changed his heart	God changed his heart,
9d	וַיָּבֹאוּ כָּל־הָאֹתוֹת הָאֵלֶּה בַּיּוֹם הַהוּא׃	*wayyiqtol*	Next after v. 9c / summary of vv. 10–12: all these signs happened	and all these signs happened on that day.
		Expansion on Verse 9d (vv. 10–12): Narration of How These Signs Happened		
10a	וַיָּבֹאוּ שָׁם הַגִּבְעָתָה	*wayyiqtol*	Initial event (after the predictions in vv. 2–4 took place): they came	When they came to the hill,
10b	וְהִנֵּה חֶבֶל־נְבִאִים	*wehinneh* + verbless	Next after v. 10a / shift in topic: the band of prophets [came]	look, the band of prophets [came]

(cont.)

- **vv. 10–12**: These three verses stand together in one big relationship to verse 9d, which says that all these signs happened on that day. All three verses expand on verse 9d, narrating how the signs took place. We can represent a big discourse relationship like this using a heading (see between v. 9d and v. 10a).

	Text	Construction	Discourse Analysis	Translation
10c	לִקְרָאתוֹ	*l* + inf c	Purpose: to meet him	to meet him.
10c	וַתִּצְלַח עָלָיו רוּחַ אֱלֹהִים	*wayyiqtol*	Next: the Spirit rushed	And the Spirit rushed on him
10d	וַיִּתְנַבֵּא בְּתוֹכָם׃	*wayyiqtol*	Result: he prophesied	such that he prophesied in their midst.
11a	וַיְהִי כָּל־יוֹדְעוֹ מֵאִתְּמוֹל שִׁלְשׁוֹם	*wayhi*	Shift in topic: ↓subject of v. 11b: all who knew him	Now all who knew him formerly
11b	וַיִּרְאוּ	*wayyiqtol*	Next after v. 10d:	looked,
11c	וְהִנֵּה עִם־נְבִאִים נִבָּא	*wehinneh*	Result of looking in v. 11b: they saw Saul prophesying	and there he was, prophesying with the prophets!
11d	וַיֹּאמֶר הָעָם אִישׁ אֶל־רֵעֵהוּ	*wayyiqtol*	Result of vv. 11a–c: the people said	And the people said, each to his neighbor,

(cont.)

- **v. 10a**: Discourse analysis helps understand the purpose of the narrator here. He skips the events predicted in verses 2–4. On the basis of verse 9d, one can assume they took place as Samuel predicted. He picks up in the middle, at the "hill of God." Hence "when" is a good way to begin our translation of verse 10a (the idea being: "When they came to the part about the hill . . .").
- **v. 10b**: This clause is verbless, but a verb is assumed (perhaps a participle, "coming").
- **v. 11a**: This *wayhi* introduces a noun phrase which will become the subject of verse 11b. The noun phrase is not technically a clause, but we give it its place in the *wayhi* box like we would for a temporal clause.

	Text	Construction	Discourse Analysis	Translation
		Embedded Discourse (vv. 11e–f): The People's Wonder		
11e	מַה־זֶּה הָיָה לְבֶן־קִישׁ	*mah* + x + *qatal*	Wondering question: what has happened?	"What has happened to the son of Kish?
11f	הֲגַם שָׁאוּל בַּנְּבִיאִים׃	*h* + verbless	Wondering question: is Saul also among the prophets?	Is Saul also among the prophets?"
12a	וַיַּעַן אִישׁ מִשָּׁם	*wayyiqtol*	Next: a man answered the people	And a man from there answered
12b	וַיֹּאמֶר	*wayyiqtol*	Expansion on v. 12a: he said	and said,
12c	וּמִי אֲבִיהֶם	*waw* + verbless	Embedded discourse / Rhetorical question: who is their father?	"And who is their father?"
12d	עַל־כֵּן הָיְתָה לְמָשָׁל	*ʿal-ken* + *qatal*	Background comment / result of this event: thus it became a proverb	Thus it became a proverb,
12e	הֲגַם שָׁאוּל בַּנְּבִאִים	*h* + verbless	Embedded discourse / content of the proverb: is Saul also among the prophets?	"Is Saul also among the prophets?"
13a	וַיְכַל מֵהִתְנַבּוֹת	*wayyiqtol*	Next: he finished prophesying	Then he finished prophesying
13b	וַיָּבֹא הַבָּמָה׃	*wayyiqtol*	Next: he came to the high place	and came to the high place.

A discourse analysis of a longer text shows how useful discourse analysis is for understanding the macrostructure of a text. Using the discourse analysis column, we can readily organize the main sections of the text into an outline. This outline allows us to do discourse analysis at a higher level than clauses, examining how larger sections of text relate to each other.

- I. Preparation for the Anointing and Speech (9:26–27)
  - A. Saul Arises and Goes out with Samuel (9:26)
  - B. Samuel's Request to Be Alone with Saul (9:27)
- II. Samuel's Anointing of Saul and Consequent Speech (10:1–8)
  - A. The Anointing (10:1a–c)
  - B. The Speech (10:1d–8g)
    - 1. Summary of What Has Just Happened (10:1e)
    - 2. Predictive Narrative (10:2–7)
      - a. The Two Men at Rachel's Tomb (10:2)
      - b. The Three Men at the Oak (10:3–4)
      - c. The Prophets at the Hill (10:5–7)
    - 3. Final Instructions (10:8)
- III. The Fulfillment of Samuel's Predictions, and the People's Response (10:9–13)
  - A. Saul's Changed Heart (10:9a–c)
  - B. Summary of Samuel's Words Fulfilled (10:9d)
  - C. Details of How 10:5–7 Were Fulfilled (10:10–13)
    - 1. Saul Prophesies (10:10)
    - 2. The People's Response (10:11–12)
    - 3. Closing Denouement (10:13)

Summary: This extended example shows the power and the challenges of discourse analysis. Discourse analysis cultivates the simple discipline of asking, clause after clause: how does *this* clause fit in the larger whole? When this process is followed, the bigger relationships stand out with clarity (e.g., that 10:10–12 give the details for the summary statement in 10:9d). This clarity allows us to map the larger flow of a text (see the outline above). But there are many challenges: sometimes a single clause has more than one purpose in a discourse (as in v. 3a, which was both a command to Saul and the next part of the predictive sequence). Other times a clause will not fit neatly in the lists of discourse relationships provided in this chapter (as in v. 8e). Even if it cannot resolve all these difficulties, discourse analysis fruitfully disciplines us to move beyond the sentence to the text as a whole in our search for meaning.

Chapter 9

Prose Discourse Analysis Summary Chart

The following seeks to distill all the information in the foregoing chapters into one handy summary.

Step 1. Separate the text by clauses		
Rules:	1. Each clause gets its own box. 2. Preserve word order. 3. Indent dependent phrases to show dependence. 4. If the dependence is downward, add an arrow: ↓ 5. Use grey shading for embedded discourse.	
Step 2. Analyze each clause		
Step 2.A. For each clause, observe the following factors:		
	Form / situation	**Possible discourse functions**
1. Discourse Markers	Conjunctions (e.g., כִּי; לְמַעַן; אִם; פֶּן)	The lexical meaning(s) of the conjunction. For example, possible meanings in the case of כִּי: 1. Cause ("for", "because") 2. Circumstance ("when") 3. Condition ("if") 4. Expansion ("that") (as a complement to a verb of seeing or knowing) 5. Contrast ("but instead")
	Relatives (e.g., אֲשֶׁר; שֶׁ; זוּ)	Often introducing relative clauses. Possible meanings in the case of אֲשֶׁר: 1. Expansion ("which"; etc.) 2. Cause ("because") 3. Result ("such that") 4. Condition ("if")
	Interrogatives (e.g., הֲ-; אֵי; אֵיפֹה)	Introducing a question.

	Adverbs (e.g., אַךְ; רַק)	The lexical meaning(s) of the adverb
	Interjections (e.g., אוֹי; הִנֵּה)	The lexical meaning(s) of the interjection
	וְעַתָּה	1. Inference ("now therefore") 2. Shifts time reference to the present ("and now")
	וְהִנֵּה	1. New point of view 2. Imperative to consider a new topic ("now look") 3. Results of looking 4. Inference ("therefore")
2. Verbal Sequences	**Narrative Sequences**	
	wayyiqtol	1. Next event ("and then") 2. Contrast ("but") 3. Result ("and so") 4. Simultaneous ("and at the same time") 5. Expansion ("and what's more" or "who" or "which") 6. New episode / initiate foreground ("now") Remember *wayyiqtol*'s tendency to continue whatever semantic ideas (like tense, aspect, mood, background) preceded it.
	וַיְהִי	1. New unit 2. Shift in time (but same unit) 3. Result 4. Standard *wayyiqtol* (when it has the non-discourse meaning of "to be" or "to happen" or "to become")
	waw + x + *qatal* in a *wayyiqtol* sequence	See below under preposing

(cont.)

	weqatal in a *wayyiqtol* sequence	1. Marks a foreground event as climactic or final 2. Initiate a background *weqatal* sequence conveying habitual information 3. Indistinguishable from *wayyiqtol*
	וְהָיָה in a *wayyiqtol* sequence	Initiate a background comment about a habitual action ("whenever")
	Non-narrative Sequences	
	weqatal	1. Next step ("and then") 2. Contrast ("but") 3. Result or purpose ("and thus"; "so that") 4. Simultaneous step ("and at the same time") 5. Expansion ("and what's more" or "who" or "which") 6. Initiate and continue "if" and "then" clauses in an "if-then" statement 7. Inference ("therefore") Remember *weqatal*'s tendency to continue whatever semantic ideas (like tense, aspect, mood, background) preceded it.
	וְהָיָה	1. New unit ("now") 2. Shift in time 3. Result or purpose 4. Standard *weqatal* (when it has the non-discourse meaning of "to be" or "to happen" or "to become")
	waw + *yiqtol* after an imperatival form	1. Purpose ("so that") 2. Next step
	Asyndeton (no conjunction on the front) with a leading verb (For asyndetic clauses led by non-verbs, see "preposed clauses" under #3)	1. Reason ("for") 2. Inference ("therefore")

3. Word Order and Verbless Clauses	Preposed clauses and verbless clauses	1. Contrast 2. Circumstances or Reason 3. Addition ("what is more", "moreover") 4. New topic or new episode 5. Initiate background 6. Expansion (when the preposed clause is asyndetic) 7. Intensification
4. Special Situations	In background or other embedded discourse, when verbal forms from the foreground reappear. (E.g., background is being conveyed by *weqatal*, but then *wayyiqtol* is used, which was the verbal form from the foreground)	Termination of the embedded discourse, resumption of the foreground
	In background or other embedded discourse, when the last sentence from the foreground is repeated	Termination of the embedded discourse, resumption of the foreground
	Restatement of immediately prior clause	Climax of discourse
Step 2.B. Based on your analysis of this clause, conclude with how it relates to the previous clauses		
The key question	Ask: how does this clause relate to the previous ones? Answer using: 1. All that you have observed in step 2.A, 2. Your knowledge of how the elements of BH prose (discourse markers, verbal sequences, word order) convey meaning, 3. Your sense of the text's inner logic, and 4. All kinds of relevant broader contexts (literary, historical, theological) that help establish logical unity.	

(cont.)

<table>
<tr><td rowspan="1">Practical helps</td><td colspan="4">Ask: what is the speaker doing with this clause?

1. Scan lists of possible relationships.
2. Be prepared for unusual situations.

Rule of thumb #1: Look for analogies with the verbal sequences you know already.
Rule of thumb #2: Be aware of special constructions, like oaths or curses.
Rule of thumb #3: When no element of discourse seems prominent, remember the default meaning of each verbal form provided below.</td></tr>
<tr><td rowspan="10">Default verbal semantics</td><td>Form</td><td colspan="3">Default Semantics</td></tr>
<tr><td></td><td>Tense</td><td>Aspect</td><td>Mood</td></tr>
<tr><td>wayyiqtol</td><td>Past</td><td>Perfective</td><td>Indicative</td></tr>
<tr><td>qatal</td><td>Past</td><td>Perfective</td><td>Indicative</td></tr>
<tr><td>weqatal</td><td>Unspecified</td><td>Unspecified</td><td>Unreal (conditional, imperative, etc.)</td></tr>
<tr><td>yiqtol</td><td>Future</td><td>Imperfective</td><td>Indicative</td></tr>
<tr><td>Participle</td><td>Present</td><td>Imperfective</td><td>Indicative</td></tr>
<tr><td>Imperative</td><td>Unspecified</td><td>Unspecified</td><td>Imperative</td></tr>
<tr><td>Verbless clauses (nominal sentences)</td><td>Present</td><td>Stative</td><td>Indicative</td></tr>
<tr><td colspan="4"></td></tr>
<tr><td colspan="5">Step 3. Reassess your analysis</td></tr>
<tr><td>Two steps of reassessment</td><td colspan="4">1. Revise relationships in light of the whole discourse
2. Determine boundaries of larger sections</td></tr>
<tr><td>Criteria for a compelling discourse relationship</td><td colspan="4">A good proposal for a discourse relationship usually will:

1. Not contravene the typical uses of discourse markers, verbal sequences, or word order.
2. Account for all elements of a clause, including the usual meanings of each individual word.
3. Fit sensibly with the surrounding context.</td></tr>
</table>

PART 2

Working with Biblical Hebrew Poetry

Frederic C. Putnam

Expanded Table of Contents

— Chapter 1 —

Introduction

A section that addresses the discourse analysis of biblical poems implies that there is a difference between poetry and prose and that this difference is far more fundamental than mere layout—how words are arranged on the page. It also recognizes the ubiquity of poetry in the Hebrew Bible, nearly one-half of which consists of poems.

Poetry and prose share the resources of a language—its vocabulary, grammar, syntax, culture, figurative language, etc.—but tend to use them so differently that poetry has been called the "other use of language." The lexicon of biblical poems, for example, includes a far higher number of words that occur only in poetry or are uncommon in the Hebrew Bible;[1] clausal syntax is more varied; verbal conjugations function less consistently in poetry than in prose; and its discourse structures not only differ from but are far less predictable—even within the overarching genre of "poetry"—than those of prose genres.

Poems can also organize or present their content in ways that are unlike prose. Biblical prose is more or less linear, moving from one event to the next,[2] or from one step to the next through a set of instructions,[3] or from a "case" ("if/when A occurs") to its legal resolution ("then do B"),[4] each with its own fairly predictable discourse structure. It is often difficult

1. This is true in all biblical genres and books; nearly every book has vocabulary that is unique to it, even books as short as Joel, Obadiah, and Jonah. Even a "frequent" word may be limited, as, for example, the word קֶרֶשׁ, "plank," which occurs fifty-one times in the Bible but only twice outside the book of Exodus.

2. This typifies all narrative, not just biblical stories (as do occasional flashbacks to past events and descriptions of "parallel" or simultaneous events). In Hebrew a series of *wayyiqtol*s forms the "backbone" of the story.

3. In Hebrew a series of *weqatal*s forms the "backbone" of a set of instructions, as in Exod 25–31.

4. See Exod 21–23.

to determine whether or not a poem describes a sequence of any kind; even poems that describe historical events rarely follow the sequence of events as they are described in the prose account (cf., e.g., Pss 104, 105, 106).

Poems are also instances of compressed language—saying as much as possible in as few words as possible. They tend to communicate much more compactly than prose, and poems can be so elliptical that their sense is ambiguous. This approach to the discourse analysis of biblical poems assumes that biblical poems are truly poems, examples of the "other use of language," and that they therefore need to be read through an "other" lens than that used to read prose. Further, this approach to the discourse analysis of biblical poetry demonstrates that biblical poems are often artistic in ways that disappear in translation but become obvious when we study the Hebrew text. The degree to which vocabulary, morphosyntax[5] (which is a factor in compression), inter-linear relationships, and the verbal artistry of a poem's content are *aspects of* its content show its poetic nature.

Writers of both biblical poetry and prose thus used the same linguistic resources[6] to write two types of discourse that differ much more from each other than, say, stories differ from instruction. They therefore require fundamentally different approaches to their discourse analysis, which means that we ask different questions and different *kinds* of questions about poems than we do about prose.

Many have been taught that to read a poem is to solve a riddle or decode a hidden message, but studying a poem does not mean asking, "What does it (the poem) mean?" This question merely encourages us to look for or expect to find something hidden "beyond" or "behind" the poem, or to view the poem as a secret that needs to be "unlocked" or "figured out"—it keeps us from reading the poem itself since we are really not reading it but merely looking for some real meaning "behind" or "beyond" the text.[7]

---

5. The term "morphosyntax" refers to both parsing and sentence structure; it combines the *shape* (Greek *morfe*, μορφή) or forms of words (their "grammar" or how they are inflected to indicate number, gender, state, conjugation, etc.) with their *arrangement* (Greek *syntaxis*, συντάξις < σύν + τάσσω) in phrases, clauses, sentences, paragraphs, etc.

6. The phrase "linguistic resources" is intended to forestall thinking about "language" primarily in terms of lexical items or word choice.

7. Reading poetry is a skill that can be learned, but it must be *learned* and strengthened through practice. The best place to begin is with the language of one's own culture. Studying

We do not therefore read or interpret biblical poems as though they were (really) just prose "in other words" or "reconfigured." Nor is our goal to figure out how to reduce the poem to a one-sentence summary of its content ("This poem means . . .")—a poet who wanted to communicate a single sentence chose to compose a poem.

I. BASIC ASSUMPTIONS

Poems are prime examples of the "poetic function" of language,[8] composed with a "focus on the language for its own sake."[9] Their study entails several fundamental convictions:

1. That they are poems;
2. That the goal is not to "condense" or "summarize" the poem in a prose statement (e.g., "This poem means . . ." or " . . . says . . .");[10]
3. That study requires contemplation—a patient receptivity rather than an insistent probing;
4. That the poem's text is the primary witness to the poem, not its proposed history (i.e., the details of the poet's life, or when or why it was composed);
5. That the poet wrote with concentration focused on every nuance of the linguistic resources at his or her command; and
6. That we cannot know what the biblical poet was thinking when composing a line or poem or choosing a particular word or verbal form.

---

poems in English does not, of course, directly translate into studying poems in Hebrew (just as reading Egyptian love poems does not directly improve our ability to read the Song of Songs). Nevertheless, reading poems composed in English (or one's own language) *does* help us read biblical poems because we learn to attend more closely to the nuances of vocabulary, syntax, and form. Two excellent resources for learning to read poems are Greg Johnson & Thomas R. Arp, *Perrine's Sound and Sense* (Boston, MA: Thomson Heinle, 2013) and John Frederick Nims, *Western Wind* (New York: Random House, 2005).

8. Jakobson identified six functions of language: referential, emotive (affective, expressive), conative, phatic, metalingual (metalinguistic, reflexive), and poetic. For a helpful summary, see Roman Jakobson, "Linguistics and Poetry," in *Style and Language*, ed. T. A. Sebeok (Cambridge, MA: MIT Press, 1960), 350–77.

9. Jakobson does not confine this function to poetry, but in poems the poetic function of language comes to the fore.

10. Cleanth Brooks calls this the "heresy of paraphrase," in the essay with that title (1970, 192–214).

We read biblical poems with the further conviction that each poem is a word from God, which leads us to expect that the poem will discuss or suggest some aspect of God and his relationship with what he has made, is redeeming, and sustains, and which we will want therefore to hear and understand. And this makes us even more diligent students of the text.

The poetic function of language suggests that noticing the details of the poet's language ought to strengthen our ability to appreciate the fruit of the poet's labors *and* that our ability to appreciate the poet's creativity is a *necessary* part of a genuine poetic encounter—the aesthetic appreciation that rewards close study is also an aspect of understanding.

II. THE PROCESS OF DISCOURSE ANALYSIS

Poets choose words not only because of their meaning or grammatical function but for their sound, shape, connotations, allusions, and other cultural and literary factors. They also choose words based on how they relate in sound, shape, and meaning to other words in the poem, often to those in immediately adjacent lines. And vocabulary can be used to organize biblical poems, as we shall see in the case of Psalm 121.

Discourse analysis, however, looks beyond vocabulary, assuming that just as phrases, clauses, and sentences can be analyzed and diagrammed, there is also grammar that functions above the level of the sentence—the grammar of paragraphs, stories, poems, and so forth.

Also fundamental to discourse analysis is the conviction that there are no unmotivated linguistic choices.[11] This means that we must attend to every aspect of a poem—the length and syntax of its lines, the morphology of its predicates, its lexical choices, participant tracking, relationships between lines, etc., all the while attempting to balance analysis and appreciation. How a text is organized by its grammar and syntax is thus a key aspect of discourse analysis.

Why do we want to know how a poet structured the poem? Primarily because understanding alone is rarely the goal of study. Study's real

---

11. From Robert E. Longacre, *Joseph. A Story of Divine Providence. A Text Theoretical and Textlinguistic Analysis of Genesis 37 and 39–48* (Winona Lake, IN: Eisenbrauns, 2003), xv. "Variation in a text is not random but motivated."

goal is understanding *in order to explain* the text (either to ourselves or to someone else). A poem's structure being inherent to what it is about, the poem should be explained in light of its own organization, because our real goal is to help others understand the text as it was meant to be read and not to impose our own logic or structure on it.[12]

III. DISCOURSE ANALYSIS OF BIBLICAL POEMS

English poems use meter, rhyme, stanzas, punctuation (comma, period, colon, etc.), line breaks, and the distinction between sentences and their lines to communicate. Hebrew prose uses genre-specific grammatical signals, such as *wayyiqtol*, disjunctive clauses, various conjunctions, *weqatal*, etc. Biblical poems use interlinear relationships, word choice (sound, form, denotation, connotation), verbal form/structure (stem, conjugation), length of line (number of words), word order (e.g., chiasms), syntax, participant tracking (via nouns and pronouns), ellipsis (leaving out one word or more), and other linguistic resources.

Biblical poets organize their poems not only by their choice of vocabulary but also by using various linguistic resources to create either continuity or discontinuity. Cohesive devices create *continuity*, which binds line together in larger units. *Discontinuity* is created by semantic and morphosyntactic choices that separate a line from the preceding line, creating a "seam" between two sections of the poem.[13] Seams in biblical poems are marked by changes in established patterns, including the length or syntax of the poem's lines, verbal morphology (stem, conjugation, person, gender, number), participant reference, and other linguistic devices.[14]

---

12. Far too often poetic texts are explained by reorganizing their content into a form that seems logical to the one doing the explaining. For example, the first point "comes from" v. 4, point two comes from v. 2, and point three comes from v. 12 (often ignoring the rest of the poem). The outline may be logical, but its logic is not the poet's.

13. In Hebrew narrative, for example, onset—the start of a new section—is mainly signaled by a change in the main character(s), location, time, or genre (or any combination of these), as when the genealogy of Esau (Gen 36) is followed by Joseph's story (Gen 37). Onset tends to be more clearly marked than its end ("closure"), apart from stereotypical statements such as "and they lived happily ever after."

14. "Parallelism," a term often heard in discussions of biblical poetry, is neither unique nor necessary to biblical poetry. It is a cohesive feature of biblical poems, a linguistic resource that helps to make biblical poems examples of *patterned language*.

Word choice and the morphosyntactic choices that create continuity and discontinuity are *mutually reinforcing* and interdependent; together they shape the poem. Seeing them, making them visible, is the goal of discourse analysis.

The process described in this book entails the following "steps":[15]

1. *Gloss* the text, creating a rough "translation" with which to work without repeatedly looking up unfamiliar vocabulary;
2. *Parse* the verbal forms;
3. *Lineate* the text, setting it out in lines, one clause per line;
4. *Describe* each line:
    a. its *syntax*—how the words function together to create the clause; this includes identifying each line's subject, object(s), predicate (whether that is a verbal form, noun, adjective, or prepositional phrase), and other parts;[16]
    b. the *grammar* of its predicates—whether or not any patterns appear and how they relate to its content;
    c. its *semantics*—how the content of each line relates to the preceding line; and
    d. its *type* (defined below) and its *logical* relationship to the preceding lines.

This process will at first seem laborious. Does it yield something other than what can be found out by studying the English text alone or by "regular" exegesis? We shall see that it does. Step after step offers insights of a kind that are rarely noticed (or are, at least, rarely commented upon). One of my favourite memories is of a student who assured me that he "hated poetry" (he had a graduate degree in mathematics) who, on seeing me in the seminary library, said "I get it! These really *are* poems!" And my experience with students assures that this process works.

After discourse analysis uncovers the "what" and "how" of a text, exegesis addresses the "why" by asking the questions that are appropriate

15. These are not discrete but overlap and even merge, especially as you become increasingly proficient with them.

16. There is a subtle distinction between "predicate" and "comment": the comment is everything apart from the topic (subject) of the clause or sentence, whereas the predicate is an individual verb, noun, adjective, or prepositional phrase.

for all poems. The goal is to help ourselves and others think about what it says, which makes four questions especially helpful:[17]

1. What do you notice? (What strikes you? What catches your attention?)
2. What is the poem about? (What sort of situation does it describe? What question does it address?)
3. What does the poem say about its subject?
4. How does the poet use his or her linguistic resources so that the poem says what it does?

We can summarize all of this by saying that poetic discourse analysis studies the morphosyntax of entire poems in order to understand *how* they say *what* they say, with two primary goals: (1) to discern how the poet used his or her linguistic resources to organize the poem by identifying its parts, relating them to the whole, and thus revealing the nature and progress of the poem's thought; and (2) to understand how each line relates to the preceding line within that larger structure, in order to see how the poet developed the "argument" of the poem.

In other words, discourse analysis seeks to understand the poem as a discourse and to both define its parts and the organization that makes them a whole.

IV. A NOTE TO TEACHERS

When teaching courses on biblical poetry, I would assign papers to be submitted in two "editions." Students first wrote an expository "inductive" essay on the poem produced using only this method and linguistic tools (e.g., lexicons, wordbooks, reference grammars). After getting a response to this paper, they were then free to use any materials that they liked (e.g., commentaries, articles, monographs) for their "research" edition.

---

17. Note that the goal is *not* to condense or summarize the poem or to come up with its "meaning"—the poet chose to write a poem, not a prose sentence or paragraph.

— *Chapter 2* —

Glossing and Parsing the Poem[1]

I. PSALM 117

We will begin by looking at Psalm 117, the shortest poem in the Psalter, which will also be the first example in each of the following chapters. In BHS the poem looks more or less like this:[2]

117 קיז	1	הַלְלוּ אֶת־יהוה כָּל־גּוֹיִם	שַׁבְּחוּהוּ כָּל־הָאֻמִּים׃
	2	כִּי גָבַר עָלֵינוּ חַסְדּוֹ	וֶאֱמֶת־יהוה לְעוֹלָם
			הַלְלוּ־יָהּ׃

The first step involves two evaluations: (1) determining poetic lines and (2) glossing[3] the Hebrew text. (For an expanded description of glossing, see Appendix 2, below.)

Poems are written in lines, which means that the numbered verses of the Hebrew Bible are *not* the primary units of biblical poems. We should therefore ignore the verse "boundaries" as later additions to the text.

---

1. Our first responsibility is to try to understand the poem that we find in the text before us; rather than base our analysis on a theory of how biblical poetry ought to work so that we adjust the text to fit that theory, this study is based on the MT as found in *BHS/BHQ*. That does not allow us to ignore either the *masora marginalis* or textual variants found in the footnotes when they are textually based and not merely conjectural emendations.

2. The gaps are exaggerated and some of the accents are left out. Also note that the divine name is not pointed out of respect (יהוה, יה), nor is it supplied with vowels in the English below (YHWH, YH).

3. Glosses are *not* polished translations, but rather word-for-word renditions of the Hebrew text as a point of reference.

This has three implications: (1) a verse of biblical poetry may consist of one or more poetic lines; (2) a line relates primarily to the preceding and following lines, whether or not they are in the same verse; and (3) lines may vary greatly in length.

For now, arrange the text by making each clause its own line, and then label each line with verse number and a letter corresponding to the order of the lines within the verse (1a, 1b, etc.).[4] At this point, these lines are "best guesses," and may need to be modified as as you continue to study the poem, but establishing smaller blocks of biblical text is beneficial at this early stage.

(2) The second step is to gloss the Hebrew text.

Key to Glossing		
"-" (hyphen)	links two or more English words that represent a *single Hebrew word*	כָּל־, "all-of"
obj	object marker	
"I", "you", "he", "she", "we", "they"	indicates the person and number of the verbal form	
"you/ms" **"you/fs"** **"you/mp"** **"you/fp"**	second person masculine singular second person feminine singular second person masculine plural second person feminine plural	see example in #4, below
simple past tense	all *qatal* and *wayyiqtol*	גָּבַר, "he-was-strong"
simple present tense	all *yiqtol* and *weqatal*	יֶהְגּוּ, "they/m-mutter"
"!"	imperative, cohortative, jussive	הַלְלוּ, "you/mp-praise!"
w-	conjunction *waw*	

Note: *These are suggested guidelines; you may prefer other symbols to record the same sort of information, and as you continue, you will modify whatever system you use. However, it is best to use a specific system and then modify it as you advance in your studies.*

4. The numeral is the verse number, of course, but this is a necessary concession.

Psalm 117: Lines and Gloss

L.	BHS	Gloss
1a	הַלְלוּ אֶת־יהוה כָּל־גּוֹיִם	you/mp-praise! obj-YHWH all-of nations
1b	שַׁבְּחוּהוּ כָּל־הָאֻמִּים׃	you/mp-laud!-him all-of peoples
2a	כִּי גָבַר עָלֵינוּ חַסְדּוֹ	for he-was-strong over-us his-lovingkindness
2b	וֶאֱמֶת־יהוה לְעוֹלָם	*w*-truth-of YHWH to-long-time
2c	הַלְלוּ־יָהּ׃	you/mp-praise! YH

II. NOUNS AND VERBS

Nouns tell us what a poem is about, *verbs* say something about the nouns.[5] List the nouns in the poem in order, keeping construct chains and prepositional phrases together. Psalm 117 has seven nouns, three of which begin construct chains.

Ps 117: Glossing Nouns[6]

L.	BHS	Gloss
1a	יהוה	YHWH
	כָּל־גּוֹיִם	all-of nations
1b	כָּל־הָאֻמִּים	all-of peoples[7]
2a	חַסְדּוֹ[8]	his-lovingkindness
2b	וֶאֱמֶת־יהוה	and-truth/faithfulness-of YHWH
	לְעוֹלָם	for-long-time[9]
2c	יָהּ	YH

Two of the nouns in Psalm 117 refer to humanity (כָּל־גּוֹיִם ,כָּל־הָאֻמִּים), four to YHWH (יהוה ,יָהּ) or his attributes (אֱמֶת־יהוה ,חַסְדּוֹ), and one to time (עוֹלָם). The first and last references to YHWH (1a, 2c) form an *inclusio*, a discourse-level cohesive device that helps tie the entire poem together (more on cohesion later). These observations suggest that Psalm 117 is *about* the relationships among YHWH, his attributes, and humanity.

5. You should know how to distinguish verbs, nouns, conjunctions, prepositions, construct chains, clauses, etc.

6. The charts are not the goal—handwritten notes will do just as well (preferably in pencil to allow changes).

7. This reads כָּל־הָאֻמִּים as כָּל־לְאֻמִּים, following LXX.

8. A noun with a pronominal suffix is "in construct to" its suffix, even if the noun does not have its usual construct form; cf. נַפְשִׁי, "my soul/soul of mine", with vs. נֶפֶשׁ, "soul"

9. On this rendering, see the discussion below.

After listing and glossing the nouns, list and gloss the verbs in sequence, parsing each form. Use the following chart to help you.

KEY TO PARSING

Person:	1, 2, 3		
Stem:	Q (qal); D (piel); Dp (pual="passive of D"); H (hiphil); Hp (hophal="passive of H"); N (niphal); Dt (hithpael)		
Number:	s (singular); p (plural)		
Gender:	m (masculine); f (feminine); c (common)		
Conjugation (and "other"):	C	**C**ohortative	
	F	*yiqtol*	(traditionally "imper**F**ect" or "**F**uture")
	J	**J**ussive	
	NA	i**N**finitive **A**bsolute	
	NC	i**N**finitive **C**onstruct	
	P	*qatal*	(traditionally "**P**erfect")
	pp	**p**repositional **p**hrase	
	Pr	*wayyiqtol*	"**Pr**eterite" = "past [narrative]"
	Ptc	**P**ar**t**i**c**iple	
	V	imperati**V**e	

PARSING EXPLANATION

Parsing verbs assures us that we know why we read the text as we do. There is no "correct" way to parse verbs; the most important consideration is consistency. For example, consistently parsing verbs by identifying their person, gender, number, stem, and conjugation *in that order* has two benefits: (1) we are much less likely to overlook some aspect of its parsing; and (2) the process of parsing gradually becomes more natural.

Note: Just as there is no universally "correct" way to parse a verb, there is no "correct" set of terms, abbreviations, or symbols for parsing. Those used here: (1) are short (to save space); and (2) make patterns more visible than do the traditional names (see, e.g., the discussion of Ps 113 below). You should use those which you find most helpful.

This table shows the result of applying these guidelines for glossing and parsing to the verbs in Psalm 117:

Psalm 117: Parsing and Glossing Verbs

L.	BHS	Parsing	Gloss
1a	הַלְלוּ	2mp Piel Imv	you/mp-praise!
1b	שַׁבְּחוּהוּ	2mp Piel Imv	you/mp-laud-him!
2a	גָבַר	3ms Qal Pf	it/he-is-strong
2b	[Since there is no verb in this line, it is left blank.]		
2c	הַלְלוּ	2mp Piel Imv	you/mp-praise!

Verbs tell us what the poem says *about* the subject identified by the nouns. Three verbs in Psalm 117 are *piel* imperative, describing worship or praise (הַלְלוּ [1a, 2c],[10] שַׁבְּחוּהוּ [1b]). The fourth verb is *qal* (גָבַר), describing a divine attribute (2a). The *inclusio*[11] suggested by the nouns יהוה (1a) and יָה (2c), noted in the table of above, is reinforced by the repeated verbal form (הַלְלוּ) in 1a and 2c.

Now we can combine the parsing with the gloss—the parsing ensures the validity of our gloss:

10. The repeated verbal predicate in the first and last lines is called an *inclusio* or "envelope" because the same form "envelops" a section of text. That this is more than a mere bordering device will become apparent (below).

It is tempting to dismiss terms like *inclusio* as jargon. Some terms may be. But they are used in commentaries and other resources without being explained—readers should know them. Just like the technical vocabulary with which we discuss a piece of music or a ballgame, technical terms function as shorthand. The difference between "identical beginning and end" (on the one hand) and "envelope" or *inclusio* (on the other) is one of efficiency and can be useful *as long as we remember* that the shorthand (the jargon) is *ours*, not the biblical authors' (which is not to deny that they may have had a name for this). Technical terms also let us refer to and compare different occurrences of the same types of things, even when they do not look the same at first glance. *Inclusio*, for example, is not uncommon in biblical poetry, but can have different forms.

11. When the last line of a poem or poetic section repeats its first line, this is called *inclusio* or "envelope," the final line including or enveloping everything between the two lines, as in Ps 117:1a and 2c (הַלְלוּ אֶת־יהוה and הַלְלוּ־יָהּ), in Ps 103 (בָּרְכִי נַפְשִׁי אֶת־יהוה, "Bless YHWH, my soul!"), or the "Hallelujah" psalms, all of which begin and end with הַלְלוּ־יָהּ (Pss 146–150). Repeated lines can also serve as a sort of refrain, which may mark a poem's sections, as in Ps 107: יוֹדוּ לַיהוה חַסְדּוֹ וְנִפְלְאוֹתָיו לִבְנֵי אָדָם׃, "They should thank YHWH [for] his lovingkindness, and [for] his marvels for the sons of men" (Ps 107:8, 15, 21, 31).

Psalm 117: Parsing and Gloss

L.	MT/BHS	Parsing	Gloss
1a	הַלְלוּ אֶת־יהוה כָּל־גּוֹיִם	2mp DV	[you-all-]praise! obj-YHWH all-of nations
1b	שַׁבְּחוּהוּ כָּל־הָאֻמִּים׃	2mp DV	[you-all]-laud!-him all-of peoples
2a	כִּי גָבַר עָלֵינוּ חַסְדּוֹ	3ms QP	for he-is-strong over-us his-lovingkindness
2b	וֶאֱמֶת־יהוה לְעוֹלָם		*w*-truth-of YHWH to-long-time
2c	הַלְלוּ־יָהּ׃	2mp DV	[you-all-]praise! YH

As noted above, your gloss is a tool—a working sketch that may well change with study—not a translation. What follows assumes that you have a working draft of the poem in both Hebrew (where it looks like a poem) and English (where it may not look or sound like much), that you can identify its nouns, verbs, construct chains, etc., and that you have a good idea of what each line is about. This will be the basis of the next steps, but you should feel free to revise your renderings as you work.

The next stages of the discourse analysis of a biblical poem may seem tedious at first, but with practice the rewards become increasingly significant and come earlier in the process. The predicates in Psalm 117—two *piel* imperatives (1a–b); a *qatal* in *qal* (2a); and a verbless line (2b); followed by a return to the *piel* imperative (2c)—already imply a three-part structure.

Chapter 3

Poetic Lines and Structure

Unlike English poetry, Hebrew poems do not use rhyme or meter as structuring devices.[1] Line length, on the other hand, is a discourse-level device that the biblical poets used to organize their poems.

Discourse analysis of a biblical poem means asking, line by line throughout the poem, how each line relates to the preceding line, which means that we must identify its lines. The importance of the interlinear relationships and the significance of line length to structure poems (below) mean that the first step in reading a biblical poem is to determine where lines begin and end. This section depends on and refers back to the discussion on lines under "glossing and parsing" (above).

LINES IN HEBREW POETRY

We said above that a poetic line consists of a single clause: one clause per line and one line per clause.[2] A clause consists of a subject (or Topic) and predicate (or Comment about the Topic). A clause's Topic may be a single word ("the righteous") or a noun phrase ("YHWH our God"); its Comment often includes a verb but can also be a prepositional phrase, a noun, or an adjective. Not all clauses are created equal, however, and the poet could vary the number of words in a clause (or line) so that the

1. See Appendix 1 on The Question of Meter.

2. An obvious exception to this is an introductory hortatory verb, such as לְכוּ נְרַנְּנָה ליהוה, "Come! Let us shout to YHWH" (Ps 95:1), where the opening "Come!" functions as "part of" the following volitional form.

length of different lines (i.e., the number of words in each line) was coordinated with, and thus supports, the poem's content.

There are a few simple rules for counting line length:

In counting the number of words, as in glossing the text, a "word" in Biblical Hebrew is *any form preceded or followed* (*or both*) *by a blank space.* This means, for example, that the conjunction *waw* is never counted, since it is always a prefix. It also means that inseparable prepositions and pronominal suffixes are not counted—they are considered part of the word to which they are attached. Words joined by *maqqef* remain separate words; the *maqqef* binds them into a single accentual. Let's consider a few examples.[3]

I. PSALM 117

Psalm 117: Topic, Comment, Line Length

L.	BHS	Topic	Comment	Number of Words		
1a	הַלְלוּ אֶת־יהוה כָּל־גּוֹיִם	nations	praise	4		
1b	שַׁבְּחוּהוּ כָּל־הָאֻמִּים׃	peoples	praise		3	
2a	כִּי גָבַר עָלֵינוּ חַסְדּוֹ	*hesed*	strong	4		
2b	וֶאֱמֶת־יהוה לְעוֹלָם	truth	long-lasting(?)		3	
2c	הַלְלוּ־יָהּ׃	[you]	praise			2

Even in short poems, the length of each line can signal sections of text. Here and in a few following examples, each word count is given its own column to make the differences more visible. The first line of text determines the number of words in the first column (4 in this poem); each new number adds one column to the right in order to show the progression of line length, as well as their relative length, as here. Note that for the

3. This is a pragmatic decision that lets us study the text without dividing lines at random, assuming the validity of the English versions, or burying ourselves in theories of Hebrew prosody. Counting the syllables in each "line" (which is one approach to identifying lines of Hebrew poetry), e.g., assumes that we know how Hebrew was pronounced centuries before the Masoretes pointed the text. It is linguistically inconceivable that there was no change in pronunciation over that period of time. Without access to the manuscripts used by the biblical poets, we cannot know how they intended their poems to appear and can therefore only apply some artificial rule in determining where lines open and close. (This contrasts with modern poems, which are typeset and published in collaboration with the poet, so that we know where the line breaks occur.)

sake of space, only the verbal portion of the predicate/comment is listed; the comment technically, however, comprises everything in the clause apart from the subject.

When considering the length of the poems' lines, the fifth line, 2c, stands out by being shorter than the first four lines and by breaking the 4–3–4–3 pattern. Discontinuities of any type often reveal seams and show how discourses are organized. This discontinuity is slight but significant—as in many biblical poems, the discontinuity signals the end of a section or poem.

II. PSALM 2:1–6

Psalm 2:1–6: Gloss

L.	BHS	Gloss
1a	לָמָּה רָגְשׁוּ גוֹיִם	for-what? they/c-raged nations
1b	וּלְאֻמִּים יֶהְגּוּ־רִיק׃	*w*-peoples they/m-mutter empty-one/m
2a	יִתְיַצְּבוּ מַלְכֵי־אֶרֶץ	they/m-take-their-stand kings-of earth
2b	וְרוֹזְנִים נוֹסְדוּ־יָחַד עַל־יהוה וְעַל־מְשִׁיחוֹ׃	*w*-rulers they/c-consulted together against YHWH *w*-against his-anointed-one
3a	נְנַתְּקָה אֶת־מוֹסְרוֹתֵימוֹ	we-will-tear-off their-bonds
3b	וְנַשְׁלִיכָה מִמֶּנּוּ עֲבֹתֵימוֹ׃	*w*-we-will-throw-off from-us their-cords
4a	יוֹשֵׁב בַּשָּׁמַיִם יִשְׂחָק	sitting-one in-heaven he-laughs
4b	אֲדֹנָי יִלְעַג־לָמוֹ׃	Lord he-derides [to-]them
5a	אָז יְדַבֵּר אֵלֵימוֹ בְאַפּוֹ	then he-speaks to-them in-his-anger
5b	וּבַחֲרוֹנוֹ יְבַהֲלֵמוֹ׃	*w*-in-his-wrath he-confounds-them
6	וַאֲנִי נָסַכְתִּי מַלְכִּי עַל־צִיּוֹן הַר־קָדְשִׁי׃	*w*-I I-set-up my-king on Zion hill-of my-holiness

Now that you have lineated and glossed them, you can count the number of words in each line and identify their Topic and Comments.

Psalm 2:1–6: Topic, Comment, Line Length

L.	BHS	Topic	Comment[1]	Number of Words
1a	לָמָּה רָגְשׁוּ גוֹיִם	nations	rage	3
1b	וּלְאֻמִּים יֶהְגּוּ־רִיק׃	peoples	ponder emptiness	3
2a	יִתְיַצְּבוּ מַלְכֵי־אֶרֶץ	kings of earth	station themselves	3
2b	וְרוֹזְנִים נוֹסְדוּ־יָחַד עַל־יהוה וְעַל־מְשִׁיחוֹ׃	rulers	counsel each other . . .	7
3a	נְנַתְּקָה אֶת־מוֹסְרוֹתֵימוֹ	we	will break . . .	3
3b	וְנַשְׁלִיכָה מִמֶּנּוּ עֲבֹתֵימוֹ׃	we	will throw off . . .	3
4a	יוֹשֵׁב בַּשָּׁמַיִם יִשְׂחָק	he who sits . . .	laughs	3
4b	אֲדֹנָי יִלְעַג־לָמוֹ׃	Lord	mocks them	3
5a	אָז יְדַבֵּר אֵלֵימוֹ בְאַפּוֹ	he	speaks to them . . .	3
5b	וּבַחֲרוֹנוֹ יְבַהֲלֵמוֹ׃	he	confounds them	2
6	וַאֲנִי נָסַכְתִּי מַלְכִּי עַל־צִיּוֹן הַר־קָדְשִׁי׃	I	installed my king . . .	7

The first eleven lines of Psalm 2 range in length from two to seven words; all but three lines consist of three words. The longest lines, 2b and 6 (shaded above), each have seven words, and each ends a section of the poem: the introduction of the human rulers (1a–2b) and the introduction of YHWH (3a–6). It is not the number of words per se in these lines that suggests this ending function (there is nothing special about a line's consisting of seven words), but rather the *contrast* between the pattern in the preceding lines. In this case, line 6 presents an even greater contrast than 2b, since 5b is the shortest line in the poem's second section.

III. PROVERBS 3:1–12

Proverbs 3:1–12 contains a single poem of twenty-four clauses (lines). First, let's delineate its lines and gloss it:

Proverbs 3:1–12: Gloss

L.	BHS	Gloss
1a	בְּנִי תּוֹרָתִי אַל־תִּשְׁכָּח	my-son my-teaching not you/ms-forget
1b	וּמִצְוֺתַי יִצֹּר לִבֶּךָ׃	*w*-my-commands he-guards your/ms-heart
2	כִּי אֹרֶךְ יָמִים וּשְׁנוֹת חַיִּים וְשָׁלוֹם יוֹסִיפוּ לָךְ׃	for length-of days *w*-years-of life *w*-peace they-add to you/ms
3a	חֶסֶד וֶאֱמֶת אַל־יַעַזְבֻךָ	kindness *w*-truth not they-abandon-you/ms
3b	קָשְׁרֵם עַל־גַּרְגְּרוֹתֶיךָ	you-/ms-tie-them on your/ms-throat
3c	כָּתְבֵם עַל־לוּחַ לִבֶּךָ׃	you/ms-write-them! on tablet-of your/ms-heart
4	וּמְצָא־חֵן וְשֵׂכֶל־טוֹב בְּעֵינֵי אֱלֹהִים וְאָדָם׃	*w*-you/ms-find favor *w*-success good in-eyes-of God *w*-humanity
5a	בְּטַח אֶל־יהוה בְּכָל־לִבֶּךָ	you/ms-trust! to YHWH with-all-of your/ms—heart
5b	וְאֶל־בִּינָתְךָ אַל־תִּשָּׁעֵן׃	*w*-to your/ms-discernment not you/ms-lean
6a	בְּכָל־דְּרָכֶיךָ דָעֵהוּ	in-all-of your/ms-ways you/ms-know-him!
6b	וְהוּא יְיַשֵּׁר אֹרְחֹתֶיךָ׃	*w*-he he-straightens your/ms-paths
7a	אַל־תְּהִי חָכָם בְּעֵינֶיךָ	not you/ms-be! wise-one in-your/ms-eyes
7b	יְרָא אֶת־יהוה	you/ms-fear! YHWH
7c	וְסוּר מֵרָע׃	*w*-you/ms-turn from-wickedness
8a	רִפְאוּת תְּהִי לְשָׁרֶּךָ	healing she-is to-your/ms-navel
8b	וְשִׁקּוּי לְעַצְמוֹתֶיךָ׃	*w*-drink to-your/ms-bones
9a	כַּבֵּד אֶת־יהוה מֵהוֹנֶךָ	you/ms-honor! YHWH from-your/ms-wealth
9b	וּמֵרֵאשִׁית כָּל־תְּבוּאָתֶךָ׃	*w*-from-beginning-of all-of your/ms-produce
10a	וְיִמָּלְאוּ אֲסָמֶיךָ שָׂבָע	*w*-they-are-filled your/ms-storehouses [with] plenty
10b	וְתִירוֹשׁ יְקָבֶיךָ יִפְרֹצוּ׃	*w*-new-wine your/ms-vats they-burst
11a	מוּסַר יהוה בְּנִי אַל־תִּמְאָס	discipline-of YHWH my-son not you/ms-despise
11b	וְאַל־תָּקֹץ בְּתוֹכַחְתּוֹ׃	*w*-not you/ms-abhor in-his-rebuke
12a	כִּי אֶת אֲשֶׁר יֶאֱהַב יהוה יוֹכִיחַ	for whom he-loves YHWH he-rebukes
12b	וּכְאָב אֶת־בֵּן יִרְצֶה׃	*w*-like-father son he-delights

Now we can consider the Topics and Comments and count the words in each line of this poem; as we count, we can also mark (by shading) lines that stand out as longer or shorter than what is normal in this poem.

Proverbs 3:1–12

L.	BHS	Topic	Comment	Number of Words
1a	בְּנִי תּוֹרָתִי אַל־תִּשְׁכָּח	my son	forget not	4
1b	וּמִצְוֹתַי יִצֹּר לִבֶּךָ׃	your heart	guard	3
2	כִּי אֹרֶךְ יָמִים וּשְׁנוֹת חַיִּים וְשָׁלוֹם יוֹסִיפוּ לָךְ׃	they	will add	8
3a	חֶסֶד וֶאֱמֶת אַל־יַעַזְבֻךָ	kindness & truth	must not abandon	4
3b	קָשְׁרֵם עַל־גַּרְגְּרוֹתֶיךָ	you	bind	3
3c	כָּתְבֵם עַל־לוּחַ לִבֶּךָ׃	you	write	4
4	וּמְצָא־חֵן וְשֵׂכֶל־טוֹב בְּעֵינֵי אֱלֹהִים וְאָדָם׃	you	will find	7
5a	בְּטַח אֶל־יהוה בְּכָל־לִבֶּךָ	you	trust	5
5b	וְאֶל־בִּינָתְךָ אַל־תִּשָּׁעֵן׃	you	do not lean	4
6a	בְּכָל־דְּרָכֶיךָ דָעֵהוּ	you	recognize	3
6b	וְהוּא יְיַשֵּׁר אֹרְחֹתֶיךָ׃	he	straightens	3
7a	אַל־תְּהִי חָכָם בְּעֵינֶיךָ	you	be not wise	4
7b	יְרָא אֶת־יהוה	you	fear	3
7c	וְסוּר מֵרָע׃	you	turn aside	2
8a	רִפְאוּת תְּהִי לְשָׁרֶּךָ	it	will be healing	3
8b	וְשִׁקּוּי לְעַצְמוֹתֶיךָ׃	{it}[4]	{will be} drink	2
9a	כַּבֵּד אֶת־יהוה מֵהוֹנֶךָ	you	honor	3
9b	וּמֵרֵאשִׁית כָּל־תְּבוּאָתֶךָ׃	{you}	{honor}	3
10a	וְיִמָּלְאוּ אֲסָמֶיךָ שָׂבָע	your storehouses	will be full	3
10b	וְתִירוֹשׁ יְקָבֶיךָ יִפְרֹצוּ׃	your vats	will burst	3
11a	מוּסַר יהוה בְּנִי אַל־תִּמְאָס	you	despise not	5
11b	וְאַל־תָּקֹץ בְּתוֹכַחְתּוֹ׃	you	abhor not	3
12a	כִּי אֶת אֲשֶׁר יֶאֱהַב יהוה יוֹכִיחַ	YHWH	corrects	5
12b	וּכְאָב אֶת־בֵּן יִרְצֶה׃	father	delights	3

4. Words in curly brackets { } are supplied from the preceding line(s); *ellipsis* will be discussed further below. The primary requirement is that an ellipsis must be "filled" by supplying the form used in the preceding line (only gender can differ).

This poem consists of six sets of commands or prohibitions, each followed by a "motive"—a statement promising a favorable outcome that is intended to motivate readers to obey the command. The dotted lines separate these sets of command/prohibition-and-motive. When we divide the poem this way, based on its content, we see that each of the two longest lines (2 and 4) signals the end of its "section," and the third (5a–6b) and final sections (11a–12b) are marked by the slightly longer length of their first lines. Even 7a (with only four words) stands out in its section, which has the only two-word lines in the poem. This suggests that the biblical poets had various means of signaling organization or structure and felt free to use them.

This passage illustrates another aspect of biblical poetry: *aperture* and *closure*, or the beginning and ending of a poem or section of a poem. With a few exceptions, it is obvious where most psalms begin and end, but in the poetic sections of other books, such as Proverbs 1–9, Job 3–41, Song of Songs, much of Isaiah, etc., we need other clues to know where one poem begins and the next ends.

Just as the contrast between Proverbs 2:22b and 3:1a shows that 3:1a opens a new poem, it is obvious that this poem ends in 3:12b because 3:13a begins a new poem or section. This is not because of a change in line length or subject matter, but because 3:13a and the following lines do not follow the patterns found in 3:1–12, as the table below highlights:

Proverbs 3:13a–14b: Topic and Comment

L.	BHS	Topic—Comment
11a	מוּסַר יהוה בְּנִי אַל־תִּמְאָס	discipline-of YHWH **my-son** *not you-despise*
11b	וְאַל־תָּקֹץ בְּתוֹכַחְתּוֹ׃	*w*-not **you**-*abhor* his-rebuke
12a	כִּי אֶת אֲשֶׁר יֶאֱהַב יהוה יוֹכִיחַ	for whom he-loves YHWH *he-disciplines*
12b	וּכְאָב אֶת־בֵּן יִרְצֶה׃	*w*-like-**father** son *he-delights*
13a	אַשְׁרֵי אָדָם מָצָא חָכְמָה	*happinesses-of* **man** he-finds wisdom
13b	וְאָדָם יָפִיק תְּבוּנָה׃	*w*-**man** *he-promotes discernment*
14a	כִּי טוֹב סַחְרָהּ מִסְּחַר־כָּסֶף	for *good-one* **her-worth** *from-income-of silver*
14b	וּמֵחָרוּץ תְּבוּאָתָהּ׃	*w-from-gold* **her-profit**

There are three major changes in these lines: (1) no second-person verbs; (2) no commands; and (3) the command/prohibition-and-motivation pattern of 3:1–12 has disappeared (the next command is in 3:21a.). Line 13a begins a new poem.

IV. PROVERBS 7:7–11, 14–20

Rather than analyzing the entire poem in Prov 7, this section illustrates the function of line length by focusing on two passages: Prov 7:7a–11c and 14a–20b. First we will establish the lines and gloss of 7:7a–11c, and then we'll consider the Topic, Comment, and Number of Words.

Proverbs 7:7a–11c: Gloss

L.	BHS	Gloss
7a	וָאֵרֶא בַפְּתָאיִם	*w*-I-saw in-the-simple-ones
7b	אָבִינָה בַבָּנִים נַעַר חֲסַר־לֵב׃	I-discern in-the-sons youth lack-of heart
8a	עֹבֵר בַּשּׁוּק אֵצֶל פִּנָּהּ	passing-by-one in-the-street near her-corner
8b	וְדֶרֶךְ בֵּיתָהּ יִצְעָד׃	*w*-way-of her-house he-walks
9a	בְּנֶשֶׁף־בְּעֶרֶב יוֹם	in-twilight in-evening-of day
9b	בְּאִישׁוֹן לַיְלָה וַאֲפֵלָה׃	in-middle ("apple")-of night *w*-darkness
10	וְהִנֵּה אִשָּׁה לִקְרָאתוֹ שִׁית זוֹנָה וּנְצֻרַת לֵב׃	*w*-behold! woman to-meet-him garment-of prostitute *w*-guarded-of heart
11a	הֹמִיָּה הִיא	boisterous-one she
11b	וְסֹרָרֶת בְּבֵיתָהּ	*w*-rebellious-one in-her-house
11c	לֹא־יִשְׁכְּנוּ רַגְלֶיהָ׃	not they-settled her-feet

Two lines stand out right away for their length: one long line in v. 10 and one short line in v. 15c. The discourse analysis of stories[5] always notes how characters are brought "on stage"; the longest line in this poem introduces the seductress (10). At seven words, line 10 stands in contrast to the lines immediately before and after it. Notice again how aligning word counts with their own column makes changes/differences more visible:

5. Stories are told in poems and prose, although their discourse devices differ.

Proverbs 7:7a–11c: Topic, Comment, Line Length

L.	BHS	Topic	Comment	Number of Words
7a	וָאֵרֶא בַפְּתָאִים	I	saw	2
7b	אָבִינָה בַבָּנִים נַעַר חֲסַר־לֵב׃	I	discerned	5
8a	עֹבֵר בַּשּׁוּק אֵצֶל פִּנָּהּ	[one passing]	in the street	4
8b	וְדֶרֶךְ בֵּיתָהּ יִצְעָד׃	he	walked	3
9a	בְּנֶשֶׁף־בְּעֶרֶב יוֹם	[time]		3
9b	בְּאִישׁוֹן לַיְלָה וַאֲפֵלָה׃	[time]		3
10	וְהִנֵּה אִשָּׁה לִקְרָאתוֹ שִׁית זוֹנָה וּנְצֻרַת לֵב׃	a woman	there was	7
11a	הֹמִיָּה הִיא	she	loud	2
11b	וְסֹרָרֶת בְּבֵיתָהּ	[she]	rebellious	2
11c	לֹא־יִשְׁכְּנוּ רַגְלֶיהָ׃	her feet	did not stay	3

We might first shade line 10 because of its length, but then notice that it not only begins with the only occurrence of הִנֵּה in the poem[6] but is preceded by three lines of the same length, 8b–9b, and followed by two lines of only two words, 11a–b. This contrast with its immediate context—not its length alone—makes it stand out from surrounding lines. Supported by הִנֵּה, the length of line 10 suggests that this "loud woman" (10, 11a)—the seductress—will play a significant role in the rest of the story.

The other line notable for its length comes at roughly the center of the poem (15c), so now let's consider the lines and gloss of 7:14a–20b.

Proverbs 7:14a–20b: Gloss

L.	BHS	Gloss
14a	זִבְחֵי שְׁלָמִים עָלָי	sacrifices-of peace on-me
14b	הַיּוֹם שִׁלַּמְתִּי נְדָרָי׃	the-day I-repay my-vows
15a	עַל־כֵּן יָצָאתִי לִקְרָאתֶךָ	on-thus I-come-out to-meet-you
15b	לְשַׁחֵר פָּנֶיךָ	to-seek your-face

(cont.)

6. The word הִנֵּה (traditionally, "behold!") is relatively rare in poetic texts; it occurs only three times in Proverbs (1.23; 7.10; 24.31). וְהִנֵּה (with *waw*) tends to occur in situations of seeing, as it does here (7a–b).

L.	BHS	Gloss
15c	וָאֶמְצָאֶךָּ׃	*w*-I-found-you
16	מַרְבַדִּים רָבַדְתִּי עַרְשִׂי חֲטֻבוֹת אֵטוּן מִצְרָיִם׃	coverlets I-cover my-bed colored-ones thread-of Egypt
17	נַפְתִּי מִשְׁכָּבִי מֹר אֲהָלִים וְקִנָּמוֹן׃	I-sprinkle my-bed myrrh aloes *w*-cinnamon
18a	לְכָה נִרְוֶה דֹדִים עַד־הַבֹּקֶר	[you-]come! we-will-be-saturated [with] loves until the-morning
18b	נִתְעַלְּסָה בָּאֳהָבִים׃	we-will-delight-ourselves with-loves
19a	כִּי אֵין הָאִישׁ בְּבֵיתוֹ	for there-is-not the-man in-his-house
19b	הָלַךְ בְּדֶרֶךְ מֵרָחוֹק׃	he-went on-road from-afar
20a	צְרוֹר־הַכֶּסֶף לָקַח בְּיָדוֹ	pouch-of the-silver he-took in-his-hand
20b	לְיוֹם הַכֵּסֶא יָבֹא בֵיתוֹ׃	for-the-day-of the-full-moon he-comes his-house

Now we can list its Topics, Comments, and count the words per line, which yields this:

Proverbs 7:14a–20b: Topic, Comment, Line Length

L.	BHS	Topic	Comment	Number of Words
14a	זִבְחֵי שְׁלָמִים עָלָי	peace offerings	with me	3
14b	הַיּוֹם שִׁלַּמְתִּי נְדָרָי׃	I	repaid my vows	3
15a	עַל־כֵּן יָצָאתִי לִקְרָאתֶךָ	I	went out to meet you	4
15b	לְשַׁחֵר פָּנֶיךָ	[I]	[went out] to seek	2
15c	וָאֶמְצָאֶךָּ׃	I	found you	1
16	מַרְבַדִּים רָבַדְתִּי עַרְשִׂי חֲטֻבוֹת אֵטוּן מִצְרָיִם׃	I	spread my couch	6
17	נַפְתִּי מִשְׁכָּבִי מֹר אֲהָלִים וְקִנָּמוֹן׃	I	sprinkled my bed	5
18a	לְכָה נִרְוֶה דֹדִים עַד־הַבֹּקֶר	we	saturate our selves	5
18b	נִתְעַלְּסָה בָּאֳהָבִים׃	we	delight our selves	2
19a	כִּי אֵין הָאִישׁ בְּבֵיתוֹ	the man	is not at home	4
19b	הָלַךְ בְּדֶרֶךְ מֵרָחוֹק׃	he	went	3
20a	צְרוֹר־הַכֶּסֶף לָקַח בְּיָדוֹ	he	took	4
20b	לְיוֹם הַכֵּסֶא יָבֹא בֵיתוֹ׃	he	will come	4

Lines 14a–15c stand out due to their length, which decreases from four words (15a) to two (15b) to the one-word line וָאֶמְצָאֶךָּ (15c)—"And I found you!" is the dramatic climax of her speech and implies that the hope of finding him was her (only) reason for going out. As above, giving each word count its own column makes the differences more obvious:

L.	BHS	Gloss	Number of Words		
15a	עַל־כֵּן יָצָאתִי לִקְרָאתֶךָ	On-thus I-went-out to-meet-you	4		
15b	לְשַׁחֵר פָּנֶיךָ	To-seek your-face		2	
15c	וָאֶמְצָאֶךָּ׃	And-I-found-you!			1

The brevity of this one-word line (15c) also stands out because of the following cluster of longer lines in which she describes her preparations, ending with the two longest clauses in her speech to that point, lines 16–17. The next line is also longer (18a; five words) and begins her invitation, lines 18a–20b. Here again the poet varied the length of the lines in order to highlight the poem's dramatic center (also its moral center): the moment at which this "naive youth" is confronted with the choice between wisdom and folly that is the message of the poem.

The "hallelujah" psalms (Pss 146–150) can seem straightforward and relatively unsophisticated—rather like one long, loud trumpet blast. When we gloss Ps 146, however, and list its Topics and Comments, and count its words per line, we find that its composer used the length of its lines to create its message.

V. PSALM 146

Psalm 146: Gloss

L.	BHS	Gloss
1a	הַלְלִי נַפְשִׁי אֶת־יְהוָה׃	you/mp-praise! my-soul YHWH
2a	אֲהַלְלָה יְהוָה בְּחַיָּי	I-praise! YHWH in-my-life
2b	אֲזַמְּרָה לֵאלֹהַי בְּעוֹדִי׃	I-sing! to-my-god while-I-still [am]
3a	אַל־תִּבְטְחוּ בִנְדִיבִים	not you/mp-trust in-nobles
3b	בְּבֶן־אָדָם שֶׁאֵין לוֹ תְשׁוּעָה׃	in-son-of humanity who-there-is-not for-him salvation
4a	תֵּצֵא רוּחוֹ	she-goes-out his-breath
4b	יָשֻׁב לְאַדְמָתוֹ	he-returns to-his-ground
4c	בַּיּוֹם הַהוּא אָבְדוּ עֶשְׁתֹּנֹתָיו׃	in-the-day the-that they-perished his-thoughts
5a	אַשְׁרֵי שֶׁאֵל יַעֲקֹב בְּעֶזְרוֹ	happinesses-of who-god-of Jacob in-his-help
5b	שִׂבְרוֹ עַל־יְהוָה אֱלֹהָיו׃	his-hope on YHWH his-god
6a	עֹשֶׂה שָׁמַיִם וָאָרֶץ אֶת־הַיָּם וְאֶת־כָּל־אֲשֶׁר־בָּם	making-one-of heaven *w*-earth the-sea *w*-all-of-which in-them
6b	הַשֹּׁמֵר אֱמֶת לְעוֹלָם׃	the-keeping-one-of truth for long-time
7a	עֹשֶׂה מִשְׁפָּט לָעֲשׁוּקִים	making-one-of justice for-the-oppressed-ones
7b	נֹתֵן לֶחֶם לָרְעֵבִים	giving-one-of bread to-the-hungry-ones
7c	יְהוָה מַתִּיר אֲסוּרִים׃	YHWH freeing-one-of bound-ones
8a	יְהוָה פֹּקֵחַ עִוְרִים	YHWH opening-one-of blind [eyes]
8b	יְהוָה זֹקֵף כְּפוּפִים	YHWH raising-one-of bowed-down-ones
8c	יְהוָה אֹהֵב צַדִּיקִים׃	YHWH loving-one-of righteous-ones
9a	יְהוָה שֹׁמֵר אֶת־גֵּרִים	YHWH watching-one-of sojourning-ones
9b	יָתוֹם וְאַלְמָנָה יְעוֹדֵד	fatherless-one *w*-widow he-restores
9c	וְדֶרֶךְ רְשָׁעִים יְעַוֵּת׃	*w*-way-of wicked-ones he-twists
10a	יִמְלֹךְ יְהוָה לְעוֹלָם	he-is-king YHWH for-long-time
10b	אֱלֹהַיִךְ צִיּוֹן לְדֹר וָדֹר	your-god Zion for-generation *w*-generation
10c	הַלְלוּ־יָהּ׃	you/mp-praise! YH

Psalm 146: Topic, Comment, Line Length

L.	BHS	Topic	Comment	Number of Words				
1a	הַלְלִי נַפְשִׁי אֶת־יהוה׃	my soul	praise!	3				
2a	אֲהַלְלָה יהוה בְּחַיָּי	I	praise!	3				
2b	אֲזַמְּרָה לֵאלֹהַי בְּעוֹדִי׃	I	sing!	3				
3a	אַל־תִּבְטְחוּ בִנְדִיבִים	you	not trust	3				
3b	בְּבֶן־אָדָם שֶׁאֵין לוֹ תְשׁוּעָה׃	[you]	[not trust]		5			
4a	תֵּצֵא רוּחוֹ	his spirit	leaves			2		
4b	יָשׁוּב לְאַדְמָתוֹ	he	returns			2		
4c	בַּיּוֹם הַהוּא אָבְדוּ עֶשְׁתֹּנוֹתָיו׃	his plans	perish				4	
5a	אַשְׁרֵי שֶׁאֵל יַעֲקֹב בְּעֶזְרוֹ	[he]	has				4	
5b	שִׂבְרוֹ עַל־יהוה אֱלֹהָיו׃	his hope	on YHWH				4	
6a	עֹשֶׂה שָׁמַיִם וָאָרֶץ אֶת־הַיָּם וְאֶת־כָּל־אֲשֶׁר־בָּם	[YHWH]	made					7
6b	הַשֹּׁמֵר אֱמֶת לְעוֹלָם׃	[YHWH]	guards	3				
7a	עֹשֶׂה מִשְׁפָּט לָעֲשׁוּקִים	[YHWH]	makes	3				
7b	נֹתֵן לֶחֶם לָרְעֵבִים	[YHWH]	gives	3				
7c	יהוה מַתִּיר אֲסוּרִים׃	YHWH	frees	3				
8a	יהוה פֹּקֵחַ עִוְרִים	YHWH	opens	3				
8b	יהוה זֹקֵף כְּפוּפִים	YHWH	comforts	3				
8c	יהוה אֹהֵב צַדִּיקִים׃	YHWH	loves	3				
9a	יהוה שֹׁמֵר אֶת־גֵּרִים	YHWH	guards	3				
9b	יָתוֹם וְאַלְמָנָה יְעוֹדֵד	[YHWH]	restore	3				
9c	וְדֶרֶךְ רְשָׁעִים יְעַוֵּת׃	[YHWH]	bends	3				
10a	יִמְלֹךְ יהוה לְעוֹלָם	YHWH	rules	3				
10b	אֱלֹהַיִךְ צִיּוֹן לְדֹר וָדֹר	your god	[rules]				4	
10c	הַלְלוּ־יָהּ׃	[you]	praise!			2		

Most of the lines in Psalm 146 consist of two to four words, so lines 3b and 6a stand out. Line 3b is nearly in the center of the first ten lines; its contrasting length supports its denial that human beings are capable of תְּשׁוּעָה ("salvation"). It is also the first line in the poem without a verbal predicate; if we fill in the ellipsis by supplying אַל־תִּבְטְחוּ, "do not trust" (from 3a), line 3b becomes the same length as 6a.

At seven words, line 6a is the longest line in the poem and opens a list of eleven three-word lines that describe divine actions (6b–10a); the first eight participles describe YHWH (6b–9a),[7] the last three use *yiqtol* (9b–10a). The final two lines—four and two words, respectively (10b–c)—break the pattern and end the poem. Once again, by varying the length of its lines, the poet organizes the poem.

VI. SUMMARY

The above analysis of determining a poem's lines, glossing the text, delineating the length of the lines, and providing information regarding its content (Topic and Comment) demonstrates the value of close attention to detail that is crucial in understanding any text. Next, we will closely address verbal forms and their morphology as they are found in the poetry of Psalm 117.

This process demonstrates the value of close attention to detail that is crucial to understanding any text. Note that not all cases are as clear as the examples offered above, nor is line length always significant of itself, nor is it the only—or even the primary—device in biblical poetry. It is, however, the easiest device to see once the text is set out in lines.

Next, we shall see how an equally close examination of verbal forms and their morphology reveals how the biblical poets could creatively use even such a mundane matter as grammar in composing their poems.

7. Line 6a also follows two nonverbal lines (nominal clauses); see on the use (and non-use) of verbal conjugation below.

Chapter 4

Verbal Forms

The function of verbal conjugations is far less predictable in Hebrew poetry than in prose. In narrative prose, for example, a series of *wayyiqtol*s forms the story's "backbone," so that to mark its *wayyiqtol*s "outlines" the story (even if it consists only of "and he said . . . and he said . . ."). In the same way, a series of *weqatal*s outlines the main steps in a set of instructions.[1]

This is not the case in poetry; verbal conjugations occur unpredictably. They are unpredictable, but they are not random—a biblical poet will sometimes use the conjugation and stem of verbal predicates to structure a poem.[2] Psalm 117 is again a good example of this.

I. PSALM 117

Notice how the morphology of the verbal predicates in Psalm 117 supports the poem's structure:

Psalm 117[3]: Parsing

L.	BHS	Parsing
1a	הַלְלוּ	2mp DV
1b	שַׁבְּחוּהוּ	2mp DV

(cont.)

1. This distinction is obvious when the directions for building and furnishing the tabernacle (Exod 25–31) are compared with the narrative of their construction (Exod 35–39); where the instructions use *weqatals*, the corresponding narrative uses *wayyiqtol*. Disjunctive clauses are less frequent in poetry than in prose (of any type)—the ancillary information that they add to prose materials is much less common in biblical poems.

2. Person and number also vary, but these depend directly on the poem's content; this is not a common discourse-level device.

3. The columns in this chart will vary in number and order from poem to poem. The

L.	BHS	Parsing
2a	גָּבַר	3ms QP
2b	לְעוֹלָם	pp?[4]
2c	הַלְלוּ	2mp DV

This table is immediately suggestive, but it is even more helpful to assign each aspect of parsing to its own column. Consider the table below, where the person, gender, number, stem, and conjugation are identified.[5] If the form does not fall into these categories, the final column may be utilized to identify the text.

Psalm 117: Predicate Morphology

L.	BHS	Person		Gender	Number		Stem		Conjugation		
1a	הַלְלוּ	2		m	p		D		V		
1b	שַׁבְּחוּהוּ	2		m	p		D		V		
2a	גָּבַר		3	m		s		Q		P	
2b	לְעוֹלָם										pp
2c	הַלְלוּ	2		m	p		D		V		

Verbal morphology distinguishes the third and fourth lines (2a–b) from the other three (1a–b, 2c), each of which has a *piel* (D) verb. The morphology of line 2a differs in all but gender from the other three verbal lines, and line 2b differs even more, being the poem's only nonverbal line.[6] The morphology of its predicates helps shape the poem.[7]

---

order in which morphological choice is listed (from left to right) is determined by the text of the poem—if the first verb is *piel* (as here), the first column under "stem" is D (*piel*), not by some assumed order of priority (e.g., *qal* over *piel*, masculine over feminine, singular over plural). It also means that only those aspects that actually occur are assigned a column. Since the verbs in Ps 117, for example, are all masculine in gender, there is only one column under gender. In longer poems this chart can be more elaborate.

4. Until we investigate this line further (below), its predicate is not obvious, but may be the prepositional phrase.

5. The order in which these elements are listed is not important, although it will be helpful to always list them in the same order; after a while this will become automatic, ensuring that you do not overlook some aspect of parsing (e.g., gender). See the note on parsing (above).

6. A quick glance shows that English versions of this line differ but in almost every case supply some verb.

7. From this point on, a gloss is provided when a poem is introduced, but preliminary and intermediary tables are assumed.

II. PSALM 113

Diagramming the predicates of Psalm 113 reveals the poem's organization. First let's consider the division of lines and gloss:

Psalm 113: Gloss

L.	BHS	Gloss
1a	הַלְלוּ יָהּ	[you-all]-praise! YH
1b	הַלְלוּ עַבְדֵי יְהוָה	[you-all]-praise! servants-of YHWH
1c	הַלְלוּ אֶת־שֵׁם יְהוָה׃	[you-all]-praise! name-of YHWH
2	יְהִי שֵׁם יְהוָה מְבֹרָךְ מֵעַתָּה וְעַד־עוֹלָם׃	it-shall-be name-of YHWH blessed-one from-now *w*-until long-time
3	מִמִּזְרַח־שֶׁמֶשׁ עַד־מְבוֹאוֹ מְהֻלָּל שֵׁם יְהוָה׃	from-dawn-of sun until its-going-in praised-one name-of YHWH
4a	רָם עַל־כָּל־גּוֹיִם יְהוָה	exalted-one on all-of nations YHWH
4b	עַל הַשָּׁמַיִם כְּבוֹדוֹ׃	on the-heaven his-glory
5	מִי כַּיהוָה אֱלֹהֵינוּ הַמַּגְבִּיהִי לָשָׁבֶת׃	who like-YHWH our-god the- making-high-one to-sit
6	הַמַּשְׁפִּילִי לִרְאוֹת בַּשָּׁמַיִם וּבָאָרֶץ׃	the-making-low-one to-see in-the-heaven *w*-in-the-earth
7a	מְקִימִי מֵעָפָר דָּל	raising-one from-dust poor-one
7b	מֵאַשְׁפֹּת יָרִים אֶבְיוֹן׃	from-ash-heaps he-exalts impoverished-one
8a	לְהוֹשִׁיבִי עִם־נְדִיבִים	to-seat[-him] with rulers
8b	עִם נְדִיבֵי עַמּוֹ׃	with rulers-of his-people
9a	מוֹשִׁיבִי עֲקֶרֶת הַבַּיִת אֵם־הַבָּנִים שְׂמֵחָה	seating-one barren-one-of the-house mother-of the-sons joyous-one
9b	הַלְלוּ־יָהּ׃	[you-all-] praise! YH

Now we are ready to address verbal morphology.

Psalm 113: Predicate Morphology

L.	BHS	Person		Gender	Number		Stem				Conjugation				
1a	הַלְלוּ	2		m	p		D				V				
1b	הַלְלוּ	2		m	p		D				V				
1c	הַלְלוּ	2		m	p		D				V				
2	יְהִי...מְבֹרָךְ		[3]	m		s		Dp				Ptc			[Q J][8]
3	מְהֻלָּל			m		s		Dp				Ptc			
4a	רָם			m		s			Q			Ptc			
4b															
5	לָשָׁבֶת... הַמַּגְבִּיהִי			m		s				H		Ptc			[Q C]
6	הַמַּשְׁפִּילִי לִרְאוֹת			m		s				H		Ptc			[Q NC]
7a	מְקִימִי			m		s				H		Ptc			
7b	יָרִים		3	m		s				H			F		
8a	לְהוֹשִׁיבִי			m		s				H				NC	
8b															
9a	מוֹשִׁיבִי			m		s				H		Ptc			
9b	הַלְלוּ	2		m	p		D				V				

This table makes the patterns more obvious; a vertical string of symbols in any column (or in several columns) makes continuity visible (1a–c, 2–3, 5–8a), whereas a break in the vertical string shows a discontiuity (2, 5, 9b). A diagonal "line" of symbols, as under "stem" in lines 3–5, for example, shows that each line uses a different stem (with an ellipsis in 4b). The composer of the poem used the number of the subject (plural or singular) as well as verbal stems and conjugations to "outline" Psalm 113 along the seams suggested by the dotted lines. Psalm 113 is thus divided by verbal stem into three primary sections (lines 1a–3, 2–9a, 9b) and by conjugation and number into three slightly different but overlapping sections (lines 1a–c, 2–9a, 9b):

8. The square brackets [ ] show that this form is not the main predicate but secondary in the clause.

Psalm 113: Summary of Predicates

<table>
<tr><th>L.</th><th>Stem</th><th>Conjugation</th><th>Number</th></tr>
<tr><td>1a–c</td><td rowspan="2">piel/pual[9]</td><td>V</td><td>p</td></tr>
<tr><td>2–3</td><td rowspan="2">Ptc[10]</td><td rowspan="2">s</td></tr>
<tr><td>4–9a</td><td>hiphil</td></tr>
<tr><td>9b</td><td>piel</td><td>V</td><td>p</td></tr>
</table>

Piel and *pual*, both being stems with a doubled middle radical (D stems), link 1a–3 (as does the repeated הלל), just as *hiphil* verbs link the next nine lines (4–9a); the final *piel* (9b) and imperative return to 1a. The stems of the main verbs in each line divide the poem into three main sections, as do their conjugations—but not into quite the same grouping, since the participles begin in line 2 and proceed through 9a. Lines 2–3 thus function as a sort of "hinge" on which the entire poem swings, from calls to praise to reasons for praise, from *piel* to *hiphil*, from imperative to participle, from plural to singular.

The last line (9b) is identical to the first (1a). The last line of an *inclusio* never merely repeats the opening line, even when they are verbally identical, since what it says is enriched by what lies between them—in this case, a number of reasons for the call to praise. In other words, an opening "Praise YH!" raises questions, such as "Who is he?" "What has he done?" "Praise him for what?"; having read the poem's list (catalog) of YHWH's good deeds, we read the renewed command to worship as a command now replete with answers to the implicit questions "Why?" and "For what?"

The *inclusio* also reminds readers of the initial reason for the catalog—the list in 4–9a is not a mere theological treatise or argument but intended to motivate the praise demanded by both halves of the *inclusio*. The threefold division of Psalm 113 by verbal stems and conjugations reveals that parsing is not just an academic exercise—it is a tool of poetic composition revealed by discourse analysis.

9. The *qal* jussive (2) is auxiliary to the *pual* participles and is subsumed by the imperatives.

10. Primarily—the imperfect (7b), infinitive construct (8a), and nonverbal line (8b) interrupt the string of participles, but the *hiphil* participle in 9a suggests that 7b–8b are contained within an overarching participial sequence (2–9a).

III. PSALM 1

Let's turn now to an analysis of the very familiar poem of Psalm 1.

Psalm 1: Gloss

L.	BHS	Gloss
1a	אַשְׁרֵי־הָאִישׁ	happinesses-of the-man
1b	אֲשֶׁר לֹא הָלַךְ בַּעֲצַת רְשָׁעִים	who not he-walked in-advice-of wicked-ones
1c	וּבְדֶרֶךְ חַטָּאִים לֹא עָמָד	*w*-in-path-of sinners not he-stood
1d	וּבְמוֹשַׁב לֵצִים לֹא יָשָׁב׃	*w*-in-settlement-of scoffers not-he-settled
2a	כִּי אִם בְּתוֹרַת יהוה חֶפְצוֹ	but (for if)[11] in-teaching-of YHWH his-delight
2b	וּבְתוֹרָתוֹ יֶהְגֶּה יוֹמָם וָלָיְלָה׃	*w*-in-his-teaching he-mutters by-day *w*-night
3a	וְהָיָה כְּעֵץ שָׁתוּל עַל־פַּלְגֵי מָיִם	*w*-he-is like-tree transplanted-one on ditches-of water
3b	אֲשֶׁר פִּרְיוֹ יִתֵּן בְּעִתּוֹ	which his-fruit he-gives in-his-time
3c	וְעָלֵהוּ לֹא־יִבּוֹל	*w*-his-leaf not he-fades
3d	וְכֹל אֲשֶׁר־יַעֲשֶׂה יַצְלִיחַ׃	*w*-all-of which he-does he-succeeds
4a	לֹא־כֵן הָרְשָׁעִים	not thus the-wicked-ones
4b	כִּי אִם־כַּמֹּץ אֲשֶׁר־תִּדְּפֶנּוּ רוּחַ׃	but (for if) like-the-chaff which it-drives-it-away wind
5a	עַל־כֵּן לֹא־יָקֻמוּ רְשָׁעִים בַּמִּשְׁפָּט	on thus not they-rise wicked-ones in-the-judgment
5b	וְחַטָּאִים בַּעֲדַת צַדִּיקִים׃	*w*-sinners in-congregation-of righteous-ones
6a	כִּי־יוֹדֵעַ יהוה דֶּרֶךְ צַדִּיקִים	for knowing-one YHWH path-of righteous-ones
6b	וְדֶרֶךְ רְשָׁעִים תֹּאבֵד׃	*w*-path-of wicked-ones it-perishes

Diagramming the predicates of even a poem as familiar as Psalm 1 can yield unexpected rewards:

11. The compound conjunction כִּי אִם is a strong adversative, "but."

Psalm 1: Predicate Morphology

L.	BHS	Person	Gender	Number	Stem	Conjugation
1a						
1b	הָלַךְ	3	m	s	Q	P
1c	עָמָד	3	m	s	Q	P
1d	יָשָׁב	3	m	s	Q	P
2a	בְּתוֹרַת					pp
2b	יֶהְגֶּה	3	m	s	Q	F
3a	וְהָיָה	3	m	s	Q	*w*+P
3b	יִתֵּן	3	m	s	Q	F
3c	יִבּוֹל	3	m	s	Q	F
3d	יַעֲשֶׂה	[3	m	s	Q	F]
	יַצְלִיחַ	3	m	s	H	F
4a	לֹא־כֵן					adv
4b	תִּדְּפֶנּוּ	3	f	s	Q	F
5a	יָקֻמוּ	3	m	p	Q	F
5b						
6a	יוֹדֵעַ		m	s	Q	Ptc
6b	תֹּאבֵד	3	f	s	Q	F

This table reveals several discourse-level devices that structure Psalm 1:

1. The initial cluster of three parallel *qatal*s (1b–d)[12] is followed by a verbless line (2a) and a line with *yiqtol* (2b); the changes from verbal to nonverbal and then to a different conjugation parallel the change in content, which moves from what does not characterize the happy man (1a–d) to what does (2a–b). This consistency divides these lines even more sharply from the rest of the poem

12. These are negated; the negation could be included in this analysis, whereas in line 4a, the negative לֹא must be included because it *is* the predicate.

because the *weqatal* in 3a functions more or less like the *yiqtols* that characterize the rest of the psalm.[13]

2. All of the verbal forms in Psalm 1 are *qal* except the *hiphil* יַצְלִיחַ (3e). This might seem normal, since more than two-thirds of all verbs in the Hebrew Bible are *qal*, and *hiphil* is the next most common stem. The *hiphil* in 1:3e, however, not only stands in contrast to the consistent *qals* in the rest of the poem[14] but also concludes its first main section, the "happy man" (1a–3e).
3. Lines 2a and 4a are nonverbal. The predicate of 2a is a prepositional phrase (בְּתוֹרַת־יהוה); the predicate of 4a is an adverb (לֹא־כֵן); each of these lines begins a new section of the poem: what the happy man does (3a–e) and the fate of the wicked (4a–5b).
4. Finally, the only non-finite predicate in the poem is the participle יוֹדֵעַ (6a).[15] Since the six verbal predicates in lines 3b–6a are *yiqtols*, it seems highly probable that the poet used a participle here for either or both of these reasons (at least):
    a. to mark the shift from the description of the wicked to the summary statement that closes the poem[16] and maintains the "righteous . . . wicked" pattern of the body of the poem (6a–b);
    b. to match the vowel pattern of the final verb תֹּאבֵד (6b) so that the repeated sound *o-e* both opens and closes the syntactic chiasm of 6a–b.

The predicates in Psalm 1 reveal that the poet chose their forms in order to reinforce what the poem "says"—its semantic content.

Now let's turn to another familiar psalm, Psalm 121.

---

13. The parsing of these verbs is discourse level because their form functions above the level of the clause as a cohesive device that identifies these first three lines as a group.

14. When a poem's verbs consist of only one stem with a single exception, as here, we might call that unique form a morphological orphan or isolate. Psalm 121, in which an orphan *hiphil* is surrounded by *qals* seems to be the only other psalm like this. (See on 121:6, below.)

15. The participle in 3a is attributive ("a tree [that has been] transplanted").

16. This shift is also marked by the elision of the verb in 5b. (See on ellipsis, chapter 7.)

IV. PSALM 121

Psalm 121: Gloss

L.	BHS	Gloss
1a	שִׁיר לַמַּעֲלוֹת	chant for-the-steps
1b	אֶשָּׂא עֵינַי אֶל־הֶהָרִים	I-lift my-eyes to the-mountains
1c	מֵאַיִן יָבֹא עֶזְרִי׃	from-where he-comes my-help
2	עֶזְרִי מֵעִם יהוה עֹשֵׂה שָׁמַיִם וָאָרֶץ׃	my-help from-with YHWH making-one-of sky *w*-earth
3a	אַל־יִתֵּן לַמּוֹט רַגְלֶךָ	not he-gives to-stumble your-foot
3b	אַל־יָנוּם שֹׁמְרֶךָ׃	not he-slumbers your-watchman
4a	הִנֵּה לֹא־יָנוּם	behold not he-slumbers
4b	וְלֹא־יִישָׁן שׁוֹמֵר יִשְׂרָאֵל׃	*w*-not he-sleeps watchman-of Israel
5a	יהוה שֹׁמְרֶךָ	YHWH your-watchman
5b	יהוה צִלְּךָ עַל־יַד יְמִינֶךָ	YHWH your-shade on hand your-right
6a	יוֹמָם הַשֶּׁמֶשׁ לֹא־יַכֶּכָּה	by-day the-sun not he-strikes-you
6b	וְיָרֵחַ בַּלָּיְלָה׃	*w*-moon in-the-night
7a	יהוה יִשְׁמָרְךָ מִכָּל־רָע	YHWH he-guards-you from-all-of evil
7b	יִשְׁמֹר אֶת־נַפְשֶׁךָ׃	he-guards your-soul
8	יהוה יִשְׁמָר־צֵאתְךָ וּבוֹאֶךָ מֵעַתָּה וְעַד־עוֹלָם׃	YHWH he-guards your-leaving *w*-your-coming from-now *w*-until long-time

L.	BHS	Person	Gender	Number	Stem	Conjugation
1a	אֶשָּׂא	1	c	s	Q	F
1b	יָבֹא	3	m	s	Q	F
2						
3a	יִתֵּן	3	m	s	Q	F
3b	יָנוּם	3	m	s	Q	F
4a	יָנוּם	3	m	s	Q	F
4b	יִישָׁן	3	m	s	Q	F
5a	שֹׁמְרֶךָ		m	s	Q	Ptc

(cont.)

L.	BHS	Person	Gender	Number	Stem	Conjugation
5b	צִלְּךָ		m	s		noun
6a	יַכֶּכָּה	3	m	s	H	F
6b						
7a	יִשְׁמָרְךָ	3	m	s	Q	F
7b	יִשְׁמֹר	3	m	s	Q	F
8	יִשְׁמָר	3	m	s	Q	F

One of many striking features of Psalm 121—a poem structured in extreme detail—is the sole *hiphil* (6a) in a poem that otherwise uses only *qal* forms. This *hiphil* is the central term in the only chiasm in Psalm 121 (which is why 6b lacks a verbal predicate), which calls attention to this line's structural position as a sort of hinge between lines containing three substantive *qal* participles of שׁמר (3a–5b) and three *yiqtol*s of שׁמר (also in *qal*) in lines 7a–8. An exegete will try to determine the difference in meaning between the three participles and *yiqtol*s of שׁמר; the discourse analyst is more likely to see these as structurally motivated. The structure and verbal morphology of line 6 make the line itself stand out and also divides the two sets of שׁמר.

The equally distinctive substantive predicates in 5a–b (the final occurrence of the substantive/nominal participle שֹׁמְרֶךָ, "[your] watchman," and צִלְּךָ, "your shade") mark the end of the poem's second major section (3a–5b).[17] They also remind us that not all predicates are verbs.

Psalm 98 is another example of a poem that is structured by the morphology of its verbs.

17. Two features separate lines 1a–2 from the rest of the poem: (1) the first person verb (אֶשָּׂא, "I lift") and pronominal suffixes (עֶזְרִי, "my help") versus the consistent second person singular suffixes (ךָ-, "your") in lines 3a–8; and (2) the noun עֵזֶר, "help," a rather generic term that does not occur in 3a–8, but which the root שׁמר, "watch, guard, keep" explains by answering the question "What kind of help?" (3b-8).

V. PSALM 98

Psalm 98: Gloss

L.	BHS	Gloss
1a	שִׁירוּ לְיהוה שִׁיר חָדָשׁ	you/mp-sing! to-YHWH song new-one
1b	כִּי־נִפְלָאוֹת עָשָׂה	for wonderful-things he-did
1c	הוֹשִׁיעָה־לּוֹ יְמִינוֹ וּזְרוֹעַ קָדְשׁוֹ׃	he-saved for-him his-right [hand] *w*-arm-of his-holiness
2a	הוֹדִיעַ יהוה יְשׁוּעָתוֹ	he-made-known YHWH his-victory
2b	לְעֵינֵי הַגּוֹיִם גִּלָּה צִדְקָתוֹ׃	to-eyes-of the-nations he-uncovered his-righteousness
3a	זָכַר חַסְדּוֹ וֶאֱמוּנָתוֹ לְבֵית יִשְׂרָאֵל	he-remembered his-lovingkindness *w*-his-truthfulness to-house-of Israel
3b	רָאוּ כָל־אַפְסֵי־אָרֶץ אֵת יְשׁוּעַת אֱלֹהֵינוּ׃	they-saw all-of ends-of earth victory-of our-god
4a	הָרִיעוּ לְיהוה כָּל־הָאָרֶץ	you/mp-shout-out! to-YHWH all-of the-earth
4b	פִּצְחוּ	you/mp-break-forth!
4c	וְרַנְּנוּ	*w*-you/mp-shout-aloud!
4d	וְזַמֵּרוּ׃	*w*-you/mp-sing!
5a	זַמְּרוּ לְיהוה בְּכִנּוֹר	you/mp-sing! to-YHWH with-lyre
5b	בְּכִנּוֹר וְקוֹל זִמְרָה׃	with-lyre *w*-sound-of song
6a	בַּחֲצֹצְרוֹת וְקוֹל שׁוֹפָר	with-trumpets *w*-sound-of ram's-horn
6b	הָרִיעוּ לִפְנֵי הַמֶּלֶךְ יהוה׃	you/mp-shout-out! before the-king YHWH
7a	יִרְעַם הַיָּם וּמְלֹאוֹ	he-thunders the-sea *w*-its-fulness
7b	תֵּבֵל וְיֹשְׁבֵי בָהּ׃	world *w*-dwelling-ones in-it
8a	נְהָרוֹת יִמְחֲאוּ־כָף	rivers they/m-clap palm
8b	יַחַד הָרִים יְרַנֵּנוּ׃	together mountains they/m-shout
9a	לִפְנֵי־יהוה כִּי בָא לִשְׁפֹּט הָאָרֶץ	before YHWH for he-comes to-judge the-earth
9b	יִשְׁפֹּט־תֵּבֵל בְּצֶדֶק	he-judges world with-righteousness
9c	וְעַמִּים בְּמֵישָׁרִים׃	*w*-peoples with-uprightness

Psalm 98: Predicate Morphology

L.	BHS	Person		Gender		Number		Stem			Conjugation				
1a	שִׁירוּ	2		m		p		Q			V				
1b	עָשָׂה		3	m			s	Q				P			
1c	הוֹשִׁיעָה		3		f		s		H			P			
2a	הוֹדִיעַ		3	m			s		H			P			
2b	גִּלָּה		3	m			s			D		P			
3a	זָכַר		3	m			s	Q				P			
3b	רָאוּ		3	m		p		Q				P			
4a	הָרִיעוּ	2		m		p			H		V				
4b	פִּצְחוּ	2		m		p		Q			V				
4c	וְרַנְּנוּ	2		m		p				D	V				
4d	וְזַמֵּרוּ׃	2		m		p				D	V				
5a	זַמְּרוּ	2		m		p				D	V				
5b															
6a															
6b	הָרִיעוּ	2		m		p			H		V				
7a	יִרְעַם		3	m			s	Q					F		
7b															
8a	יִמְחֲאוּ		3	m		p		Q					F		
8b	יְרַנֵּנוּ׃		3	m		p				D			F		
9a	בָא			m			s	Q						Ptc	
9b	לִשְׁפֹּט							Q							NC
9c	יִשְׁפֹּט		3	m			s	Q					F		

The poet has used verbal morphology to reinforce the poem's content:

1. After the opening second-person imperative (1a), the *subject* alternates from third person (1b–3b) to second (4a–6b) and back to third (7a–9c).
2. After the initial imperative (1a) the verbal conjugations shift from *qatal* (1b–3b) to imperative (4a–6b) to *yiqtol* (7a–9c).

3. The series of *yiqtols* in 7a–9c is disrupted by a participle and infinitive construct (9a–b), which differ so radically from the rest of the poem that they create a "zone of turbulence," a discourse-level function that often signals the peak of a discourse.[18] This peak is the climax toward which the discourse has been building. In Psalm 98 it is the promise that YHWH's coming will bring with it consummatory justice for the entire created order; hence that entire order is summoned to rejoice.

The confluence of these factors divides the poem into three main parts: past (1b–3b), present (4a–6b), and present/future (7a–8b),[19] with the last three lines as a sort of coda (9a–c). The patterns in Psalm 98 can be summarized:

Psalm 98: Predicate Summary

<table>
<tr><th>L.</th><th>Conjugation</th><th>Number</th></tr>
<tr><td>1a</td><td>imperative</td><td>plural</td></tr>
<tr><td>1b–3b</td><td>qatal</td><td>singular[20]</td></tr>
<tr><td>4a–6b</td><td>imperative</td><td rowspan="2">plural</td></tr>
<tr><td>7a–9c</td><td>yiqtol/jussive</td></tr>
</table>

The[20] poem's structure, in which the poet (1) recalls YHWH's history with Israel (1b–3b); (2) summons [Israel?] to worship YHWH as king (4a–6b);[21] and (3) calls on the created order to celebrate YHWH's coming

---

18. A "zone of turbulence" (the term is from Robert Longacre, *Joseph: A Story of Divine Providence: A Text Theoretical and Textlinguistic Analysis of Genesis 37 and 39–48*. 2nd ed. [Winona Lake, IN: Eisenbrauns, 2003], 38–48) is a stretch of discourse in which patterns established to that point are disrupted *in some way*. In Ps 98 that disruption happens to be realized by changes in verbal conjugation, but it can also be accomplished by a change in the length of lines, in verbal stem, or by *any linguistic resource* available to an author or speaker. Zones of turbulence are not found in every discourse, nor are they limited by genre (Longacre's examples are all prose)—cf., e.g., slow motion in a movie or a shift to the historic present when telling a story. Their form depends on linguistic culture, genre, author (and audience), and the features of the individual discourse.

19. Imperatives are spoken in the present, but refer to an anticipated (future) action.

20. This refers to 1b–3a; the predicate in 3b is plural, creating a morphological overlap similar to that in Ps 113 (above).

21. We will look more closely at the extremely elaborate patterning of this section (below).

justice (7a–9c), is marked and reinforced by the morphology of its verbal predicates.[22]

VI. PSALM 119:25–32

Psalm 119 is famous for its twenty-two stanzas, each of which consists of eight lines that begin with the same letter of the Hebrew alphabet. We do not know if its poet thought of it as twenty-two individual poems or as a single work, but when we examine the "*dalet*-stanza" (Ps 119:25–32), we find that some interesting patterns in the predicate morphology of these lines .

Psalm 119:25–32: Gloss

L.	BHS	Gloss
25a	דָּבְקָה לֶעָפָר נַפְשִׁי	it-cleaves to-dust my-soul
25b	חַיֵּנִי כִּדְבָרֶךָ׃	[you-]make-me-live! like-your-word
26a	דְּרָכַי סִפַּרְתִּי	my-ways I-recount
26b	וַתַּעֲנֵנִי	*w*-you-answer-me
26c	לַמְּדֵנִי חֻקֶּיךָ׃	[you-]teach-me! your-statutes
27a	דֶּרֶךְ־פִּקּוּדֶיךָ הֲבִינֵנִי	way-of your-precepts [you-]make-me-discern!
27b	וְאָשִׂיחָה בְּנִפְלְאוֹתֶיךָ׃	*w*-I-muse in-your-wonders
28a	דָּלְפָה נַפְשִׁי מִתּוּגָה	it-drops my-soul from-grief
28b	קַיְּמֵנִי כִּדְבָרֶךָ׃	[you-]make-me-stand! like-your-word
29a	דֶּרֶךְ־שֶׁקֶר הָסֵר מִמֶּנִּי	way-of lie [you-]remove! from-me
29b	וְתוֹרָתְךָ חָנֵּנִי׃	*w*-your-teaching [you-]be-gracious-to-me!
30a	דֶּרֶךְ־אֱמוּנָה בָחָרְתִּי	way-of truthfulness I-chose
30b	מִשְׁפָּטֶיךָ שִׁוִּיתִי׃	your-judgments I-reckon-suitable(?)
31a	דָּבַקְתִּי בְעֵדְוֹתֶיךָ יהוה	I-cleaved in-your-testimonies YHWH
31b	אַל־תְּבִישֵׁנִי׃	not you-shame-me
32a	דֶּרֶךְ־מִצְוֹתֶיךָ אָרוּץ	way-of your-commands I-run
32b	כִּי תַרְחִיב לִבִּי׃	for it-enlarges my-heart

22. Unlike Ps 113, however, verbal stem is not a discourse-level feature of Ps 98—it does not contribute to the poem's structure.

Psalm 119:25–32: Predicate Morphology

L.	BHS	Person	Gender	Number	Stem	Conjugation
25a	דָּבְקָה	3	f	s	Q	P
25b	חַיֵּנִי	2	m	s	D	V
26a	סִפַּרְתִּי	1	c	s	D	P
26b	וַתַּעֲנֵנִי	2	m	s	Q	Pr
26c	לַמְּדֵנִי	2	m	s	D	V
27a	הֲבִינֵנִי	2	m	s	H	V
27b	וְאָשִׂיחָה	1	c	s	Q	C
28a	דָּלְפָה	3	f	s	Q	P
28b	קַיְּמֵנִי	2	m	s	D	V
29a	הָסֵר	2	m	s	H	V
29b	חָנֵּנִי	2	m	s	D	V
30a	בָחָרְתִּי	1	c	s	Q	P
30b	שִׁוִּיתִי	1	c	s	D	P
31a	דָּבַקְתִּי	1	c	s	Q	P
31b	תְּבִישֵׁנִי	2	m	s	H	F
32a	אָרוּץ	1	c	s	Q	F
32b	תַּרְחִיב	2	m	s	H	F

We can make a few observations about this stanza:

1. Every verbal root that begins with *dalet* is both first in its line and a *qatal* in *qal*, and its subject is the speaker (either "my soul" [25a, 28a] or "I" [31a]);
2. Every third-person verb is feminine (25a, 28a), referring to "my soul";
3. Every second-person verb is masculine (25b, 26b–27a, 28b–29b, 31b, 32b), referring to God/YHWH;
4. Every first-person verb (26a, 27b, 30a–31a, 32a) refers to the speaker;[23]
5. Lines 31b–32b all have *yiqtol*, the only *yiqtols* in these lines.

23. *Yiqtols* occur throughout Ps 119; what is unusual here is the use of *yiqtol* only at the stanza's end, and that is unusual only in light of the preceding lines of the *dalet* section of the poem—another example of turbulence.

As in Psalm 98 (above), what is unusual (for this poem, at least) marks an ending.

VII. PSALM 13

The morphologically defined "sections" of Psalm 13 map perfectly its content, suggesting that the poet composed it so that its grammar (invisible in translation) would support the poem's treatment of its subject.

Psalm 13: Gloss

Line	BHS	Gloss
2a	עַד־אָנָה יהוה	until when YHWH
2b	תִּשְׁכָּחֵנִי נֶצַח	you-forget-me ever
2c	עַד־אָנָה תַּסְתִּיר אֶת־פָּנֶיךָ מִמֶּנִּי	until when you-hide your-face from-me
3a	עַד־אָנָה אָשִׁית עֵצוֹת בְּנַפְשִׁי	until when I-put counsels in-my-soul
3b?	יָגוֹן בִּלְבָבִי יוֹמָם	griefs in-my-heart by-day
3c	עַד־אָנָה יָרוּם אֹיְבִי עָלָי׃	until when he-exalts my-foe on-me
4a	הַבִּיטָה	you/ms-pay-attention!
4b	עֲנֵנִי יהוה אֱלֹהָי	you/ms-answer-me! YHWH my god
4c	הָאִירָה עֵינַי	you/ms-light-up! my-eyes
4d	פֶּן־אִישַׁן הַמָּוֶת׃	lest I-sleep the-death
5a	פֶּן־יֹאמַר אֹיְבִי	lest he-say my-foe
5b?	יְכָלְתִּיו	I-overcame-him
5c	צָרַי יָגִילוּ	my-enemies they-rejoice
5d	כִּי אֶמּוֹט׃	for I-stumble
6a	וַאֲנִי בְּחַסְדְּךָ בָטַחְתִּי	*w*-I in-your-lovingkindness I-trusted
6b	יָגֵל לִבִּי בִּישׁוּעָתֶךָ	he-rejoices! my-heart in-your-salvation
6c	אָשִׁירָה לַיהוה	I-sing! to-YHWH
6d	כִּי גָמַל עָלָי׃	for he-did-good on-me

Psalm 13: Predicate Morphology

L.	BHS	Person	Gender	Number	Stem	Conjugation
2a						
2b	תִּשְׁכָּחֵנִי	2	m	s	Q	F
2c	תַּסְתִּיר	2	m	s	H	F
3a	אָשִׁית	1	c	s	Q	F
3b						
3c	יָרוּם	3	m	s	Q	F
4a	הַבִּיטָה	2	m	s	H	V
4b	עֲנֵנִי	2	m	s	Q	V
4c	הָאִירָה	2	m	s	H	V
4d	אִישַׁן	1	c	s	Q	F
5a	יֹאמַר	3	m	s	Q	F
5b	יְכָלְתִּיו	1	c	s	Q	P
5c	יָגִילוּ	3	m	p	Q	F
5d	אֶמּוֹט	1	c	s	N	F
6a	בָטַחְתִּי	1	c	s	Q	P
6b	יָגֵל	3	m	s	Q	J
6c	אָשִׁירָה	1	c	s	Q	C
6d	גָמַל	3	m	s	Q	P

In the predicate morphology of this brief psalm, several things stand out:

1. The poem opens with a patterned set of five lines in which two nonverbal lines (2a, 3b) flank a *qal-hiphil-qal* trio of *yiqtols* (2b–3a);
2. Three consecutive imperatives (4a–c) delineate its second section;
3. A second set of five lines in lines 4d–5d (two *yiqtols*–*qatal*–two *yiqtols*), which also alternate in person and gender (1c–3m–1c–3m–1c);
4. A zone of turbulence using two unique verbal forms (jussive and cohortative) framed by *qatals* ends the poem (6a–d). Since the only other *qatal* in Psalm 13 occurs within a quotation (5b), the *qatals* in 6a and d contribute to this morphological turbulence.

By this point it should be apparent that verbal predicate morphology is a powerful tool in the hands of a skilled poet, one that can be varied at will to support the poem's content in any of a number of ways. We now turn to a slightly different use of the same information, the analysis of types of clauses.

Chapter 5

Type of Clause

I. PSALMS 29 AND 13

Another way to use verbal morphology is to group a poem's lines according to their type of clause, which can be revealed by verbal conjugation, as in Psalm 29. First, begin by delineating the text's lines and creating a gloss.

Psalm 29: Gloss

L.	BHS	Gloss
1b	הָבוּ לְיהוה בְּנֵי אֵלִים	[you-]ascribe! to-YHWH sons-of gods
1c	הָבוּ לְיהוה כָּבוֹד וָעֹז׃	[you-]ascribe! to-YHWH glory and strength
2a	הָבוּ לְיהוה כְּבוֹד שְׁמוֹ	[you-]ascribe! to-YHWH glory-of his-name
2b	הִשְׁתַּחֲווּ לַיהוָה בְּהַדְרַת־קֹדֶשׁ׃	[you-]worship! YHWH in-splendor-of holiness
3a	קוֹל יהוה עַל־הַמָּיִם	voice-of YHWH over the-waters
3b	אֵל־הַכָּבוֹד הִרְעִים	god-of the-glory he-thundered
3c	יהוה[1] עַל־מַיִם רַבִּים׃	YHWH [he-thundered] over waters mighty-ones
4a	קוֹל־יהוה בַּכֹּחַ	voice-of YHWH in-strength
4b	קוֹל יהוה בֶּהָדָר׃	voice-of YHWH in splendor
5a	קוֹל יהוה שֹׁבֵר אֲרָזִים	voice-of YHWH shattering-one cedars
5b	וַיְשַׁבֵּר יהוה אֶת־אַרְזֵי הַלְּבָנוֹן׃	*w*-he-shattered YHWH cedars-of the-Lebanon

(cont.)

1. This assumes an ellipsis of the verb in this line (below).

L.	BHS	Gloss
6a	וַיַּרְקִידֵם כְּמוֹ־עֵגֶל לְבָנוֹן	*w*-he-made-skip like calf Lebanon
6b	וְשִׂרְיֹן כְּמוֹ בֶן־רְאֵמִים׃	*w*-Sirion like son-of wild oxen
7	קוֹל־יהוה חֹצֵב לַהֲבוֹת אֵשׁ׃	voice-of YHWH splitting-one flames-of fire
8a	קוֹל יהוה יָחִיל מִדְבָּר	voice-of YHWH he-makes-writhe wilderness
8b	יָחִיל יהוה מִדְבַּר קָדֵשׁ׃	he-makes-writhe YHWH wilderness-of Qadeš
9a	קוֹל יהוה יְחוֹלֵל אַיָּלוֹת	voice-of YHWH he-makes-give-birth does
9b	וַיֶּחֱשֹׂף יְעָרוֹת	*w*-he-strips-bare forests
9c	וּבְהֵיכָלוֹ כֻּלּוֹ אֹמֵר כָּבוֹד׃	*w*-in-his-temple all-of-it saying-one glory
10a	יהוה לַמַּבּוּל יָשָׁב	YHWH to-the-flood he-sat
10b	וַיֵּשֶׁב יהוה מֶלֶךְ לְעוֹלָם׃	*w*-he-sat YHWH king for-long-time
11a	יהוה עֹז לְעַמּוֹ יִתֵּן	YHWH strength to-his-people he-gives
11b	יהוה יְבָרֵךְ אֶת־עַמּוֹ בַשָּׁלוֹם׃	YHWH he-blesses his-people with-peace

In charting by type of clause, each conjugation is given its own column (as are verbless lines), but these are listed according to their order of occurrence in the poem, since each poem may use this kind of information in its own way. The clause type of the first line forms the first column (on the right); when the type of clause changes, a new column is added to the left of the previous column (e.g., 3a). A line that is the same clause type as a preceding line is listed in that column (e.g., 4a and b are under 3a). In Psalm 29, lines 1b–2b are all commands (imperatives), but these are the only imperatives in the poem.[2]

2. The title is the first line in the Hebrew text, but not included in analysis; 1b begins the poem proper.

Psalm 29: Type of Clause

L.	*yiqtol*	*wayyiqtol*	Participle	*qatal*	Verbless	Imperative
1b						הָבוּ לַיהוה בְּנֵי אֵלִים
1c						הָבוּ לַיהוה כָּבוֹד וָעֹז׃
2a						הָבוּ לַיהוה כְּבוֹד שְׁמוֹ
2b						הִשְׁתַּחֲווּ לַיהוָה בְּהַדְרַת־קֹדֶשׁ׃
3a					קוֹל יהוה עַל־הַמָּיִם	
3b				אֵל־הַכָּבוֹד הִרְעִים		
3c				יהוה עַל־מַיִם רַבִּים׃		
4a					קוֹל־יהוה בַּכֹּחַ	
4b					קוֹל יהוה בֶּהָדָר׃	
5a			קוֹל יהוה שֹׁבֵר אֲרָזִים			
5b		וַיְשַׁבֵּר יהוה אֶת־אַרְזֵי הַלְּבָנוֹן׃				
6a		וַיַּרְקִידֵם כְּמוֹ־עֵגֶל לְבָנוֹן				
6b		וְשִׂרְיֹן כְּמוֹ בֶן־רְאֵמִים׃				
7			קוֹל־יהוה חֹצֵב לַהֲבוֹת אֵשׁ׃			
8a	קוֹל יהוה יָחִיל מִדְבָּר					
8b	יָחִיל יהוה מִדְבַּר קָדֵשׁ׃					
9a	קוֹל יהוה יְחוֹלֵל אַיָּלוֹת					
9b		וַיֶּחֱשֹׂף יְעָרוֹת				
9c			וּבְהֵיכָלוֹ כֻּלּוֹ אֹמֵר כָּבוֹד׃			
10a				יהוה לַמַּבּוּל יָשָׁב		
10b		וַיֵּשֶׁב יהוה מֶלֶךְ לְעוֹלָם׃				
11a	יהוה עֹז לְעַמּוֹ יִתֵּן					
11b	יהוה יְבָרֵךְ אֶת־עַמּוֹ בַשָּׁלוֹם׃					

In order to make a poem's patterning more obvious, each clause type can be assigned a letter (a, b, c, etc.—any letter or symbol will do). When the clauses of Psalm 29 are arranged by letter, the poem's four sections become clear: an introductory set of imperatives followed by three parallel patterns:

Psalm 29: Type of Clause (Summary)

L.	*yiqtol*	*wayyiqtol*	Participle	*qatal*	Verbless	Imperative
1a						
1b						a
1c						a
2a						a
2b						a
3a					b	
3b				c		
3c				c		
4a					b	
4b					b	
5a			d			
5b		e				
6a		e				
6b		e				
7			d			
8a	f					
8b	f					
9a	f					
9b		e				
9c			d			
10a				c		
10b		e				
11a	f					
11b	f					

The initial imperatives (1b–2b) are followed by two blocks of lines, each of which uses two conjugations/clause types: (1) verbless clauses and *qatal*s (3a–4b); and (2) participial clauses and *wayyiqtol* clauses (5a–7). In 3a–4b the clause types are nearly chiastic (b–c–c–b–b), in 5a–7 they form a perfect chiasm (d–e–e–e–d). These are followed by a more elaborate near-chiasm (8a–11b) in which 9c–10a stand out as the only unique forms within their section, thus breaking the pattern of two types per section (3a–7) and interrupting the *yiqtol–wayyiqtol–yiqtol* pattern of these lines. This interruption suggests that this is the zone of turbulence that marks the poem's peak. Simplifying this even further makes the pattern more clear (though less precise):

Psalm 29: Type of Clause (Abstract)

L.	*yiqtol*	*wayyiqtol*	Participle	*qatal*	Verbless	Imperative
1b–2b						a
3a					b	
3b–c				c		
4a–b					b	
5a			d			
5b–6b		e				
7			d			
8a–9a	f					
9b		e				
9c			d			
10a				c		
10b		e				
11a–b	f					

This diagram reveals a progression in Psalm 29 from the opening commands to the promise of future blessing. Applied to Psalm 13 (see Gloss above) the same process reveals a different, but no less striking, pattern. The categories for Psalm 13 are different, and in a different order, because the list of categories and the order in which they are listed depends on the order of the occurrence of particular features in each poem. Psalm 13 moves from verbless to *yiqtol* to imperative to *qatal* to volitional, whereas in Psalm 29 the first verbal predicate was imperative, the next clause was verbless, etc.[3]

Psalm 13: Type of Clause (Abstract)

L.	Volitional[4]	*qatal*	Imperative	*yiqtol*	Verbless
2a					a
2b				b	
2c				b	
3a				b	
3b				[b]	
3c				b	
4a			c		
4b			c		
4c			c		
4d				b	
5a				b	
5b		d			
5c				b	
5d				b	
6a		d			
6b	e				
6c	e				
6d		d			

After the initial nonverbal clause, the next eight lines fall into two blocks: five *yiqtol*s (2b–3c) followed by three imperatives (4a–c). The rest of the poem (4d–6d) is much more complex and can be analyzed in two different ways: (1) as two chaisms (b–b–d–b–b [4d–5d] and d–e–e–d [6a–d]=solid

3. This contrasts with the recommendation that you always parse verbal forms in the same order: person, gender, number, stem, conjugation.

4. The verbs in this column are volitional—jussive (יָגֵל) and cohortative (אָשִׁירָה). Listing them as *yiqtol* would create an even more striking pattern.

lines); or (2) as three pair of *yitqol* forms (4d–5a, 5c–d, 6b–c) each followed by a *qatal* (5b, 6a, 6d), as shown by the dotted lines. The overall pattern is b–*d*–b–*d*–e–*d* in 2–1–2–1–2–1 lines. In both patterns, line 6a marks the transition between the body of the poem (2a–5d) and its conclusion (6a–d).

II. CLAUSE-INITIAL *W* + PRONOUN

One final aspect of Psalm 13:6a—one not directly concerned with verbal morphology—supports its pivotal role in the psalm: it begins with *waw* plus a pronoun (וַאֲנִי). In the Psalter, *waw* + pronoun signals a shift in primary reference from one character to another. For example, whenever a poetic line begins with וַאֲנִי, the poem turns away from the enemies to the poet (as here): "But as for me . . ." It may also turn from the situation to or from YHWH, either in contrast ("But . . .") or merely as a change of topic ("Now as for me/you/them . . .").[5] In Psalm 55:22a–24c, for example, four of ten consecutive lines begin with *waw* + pronoun (this is illustrative—these lines do not constitute an entire discourse). First, we delineate and gloss the lines:

Psalm 55:22a–24c: Gloss

L.	BHS	Gloss
22a	חָלְקוּ מַחְמָאֹת פִּיו	they-are-smooth butters his-mouth
22b	וּקֲרָב־לִבּוֹ	*w*-battle [is] his-heart
22c	רַכּוּ דְבָרָיו מִשֶּׁמֶן	they-are-soft his-words than-oil
22d	וְהֵמָּה פְתִחוֹת׃	*w*-they [are] drawn-swords
23a	הַשְׁלֵךְ עַל־יהוה יְהָבְךָ	you/ms-throw! on YHWH your-portion (lot)
23b	וְהוּא יְכַלְכְּלֶךָ	*w*-he he-sustains-you
23c	לֹא־יִתֵּן לְעוֹלָם מוֹט לַצַּדִּיק׃	not he-gives for-long-time stumbling to-the-righteous
24a	וְאַתָּה אֱלֹהִים תּוֹרִדֵם לִבְאֵר שַׁחַת	*w*-you God you-bring-them-down to-well-of pit
24b	אַנְשֵׁי דָמִים וּמִרְמָה לֹא־יֶחֱצוּ[6] יְמֵיהֶם	men-of blood *w*-deceit not they-see-half [of] their-days
24c	וַאֲנִי אֶבְטַח־בָּךְ׃	*w*-I I-trust in-you

5. Initial *w* + pronoun occurs about seventy-five times in the Psalter.
6. Usually interpreted as "they shall not live out half of their (normally allotted) days" (the root is חצה, apparently "be half [of]").

When we examine the content of these lines and their function within the poem we see that each line that begins with *w* + pronoun changes the Topic from the preceding line(s). This table is custom-designed to help us examine these lines more closely in order to see how the lines beginning with *w* + pronoun are functioning.

Psalm 55:22a–24c: Clause Opening and Function

L.	BHS	Clause Opening	Function
22a	חָלְקוּ מַחְמָאֹת פִּיו	verb	description (appearance)
22b	וּקֲרָב־לִבּוֹ	*w* + noun	contrast with preceding line (reality)
22c	רַכּוּ דְבָרָיו מִשֶּׁמֶן	verb	description (appearance)
22d	וְהֵמָּה פְתִחוֹת׃	*w* + pronoun	contrast with preceding line (reality)
23a	הַשְׁלֵךְ עַל־יהוה יְהָבְךָ	verb	command (to the reader)
23b	וְהוּא יְכַלְכְּלֶךָ	*w* + pronoun	change of topic/character to יהוה what he will do for one who trusts him
23c	לֹא־יִתֵּן לְעוֹלָם מוֹט לַצַּדִּיק׃	verb	negative description: what will not happen
24a	וְאַתָּה אֱלֹהִים תּוֹרִדֵם לִבְאֵר שַׁחַת	*w* + pronoun	change of topic/character to יהוה what he will do to his enemies
24b	אַנְשֵׁי דָמִים וּמִרְמָה לֹא־יֶחֱצוּ יְמֵיהֶם	noun	description (parallels 24a)
24c	וַאֲנִי אֶבְטַח־בָּךְ׃	*w* + pronoun	change of topic/character to the voice in the poem[7]

We often "sense" a change in the content of biblical poems without being quite sure what changed or when. One sure signal of a change is that a line begins with *w* + pronoun. In these ten lines from Psalm 55, each of four occurrences of *waw* + pronoun signals a change in perspective:

7. Readers of a poem must distinguish the poet's voice from the voice or *persona* of the poem; the use of the first person does not imply that a poem describes the poet's own experience, feeling, situation, etc.—the poem may be a work of the imagination. It is therefore always more helpful (and safer) to refer to what "the poem/text says" or to say "the poet wrote" rather than "the poet says/said."

1. From the sound of the enemies' words (22a, c) to their real nature (22d);
2. After mentioning YHWH as the object of a preposition (23a), he becomes the Topic of the line that describes what he will do for "you" (23b);
3. The poet then switches from speaking about YHWH (23c) to addressing him directly, but now as "God" (24a); and
4. The last *w* + pronoun (24c), contrasts the voice in the poem with the fate of the wicked (24b).[8]

III. PREDICATE MORPHOLOGY AND STRUCTURE

Parsing the poem's predicates and charting or diagramming their sequence often reveals poetic "seams" or "discontinuities," changes in some aspect of the verbal form—person, number, gender, stem, or conjugation (or any combination thereof)—that indicate the main breaks in the poem, even if, as in Ps 119:31b–32b, they primarily reveal poetic closure in a poem in which the lines are relatively consistent.

As with the length of poetic lines, not all cases are equally clear, nor is parsing always the means (or even a means) by which the poem is structured. It can be, however, used in ways that are extremely sophisticated, as the opening lines of Psalm 2 illustrate (see Gloss above):

Several factors come together in these lines:

1. The *verbal conjugations* in 1a–2b form chiasms of both gender and conjugation.
2. The *person* of the subject in 1a–5b is chiastic (3–1–3)—four third-person verbs forming the extremes (the beginning and end of the chiasm) and two first-person verbs forming the mean (the center).
3. The *verbal stem* suggests a pattern in that the only *hiphil* verbs (3a–b) are also the only cohortatives, and quote the kings, rulers, et al. that are the subjects of 1a–2b.

---

8. Readers of a poem must distinguish the poet's voice from the voice or persona of the poem; the use of the first person does not imply that a poem describes the poet's own experience, feeling, situation, etc.—the poem may be a work of the imagination. It is therefore always more helpful (and safer) to refer to what "the poem/text says" or to say, "the poet wrote" rather than "the poet says/said."

4. The two *longest lines* mark changes of subject (and each has a *qatal* predicate following two or four lines with *yiqtol*): 2b ends the description or the rulers' activities and is followed by their exclamations (3a–b), and 6 contains YHWH's declaration.
5. These lines end with another morphological *chiasm*: the verbal stems are *qal–piel–piel–qal* (4b–6). Person, stem, conjugation, line length, and chiastic predicates function together to shape the first half of this poem.

Psalm 2:1a–6

L.	BHS	Words	Person	Gender	Number	Stem	Conjugation
1a	רָגְשׁוּ	3	3	c	p	Q	P
1b	יֶהְגּוּ	3	3	m	p	Q	F
2a	יִתְיַצְּבוּ	3	3	m	p	Dt	F
2b	נוֹסְדוּ	7	3	c	p	N	P
3a	נְנַתְּקָה	3	1	c	p	H	Co
3b	וְנַשְׁלִיכָה	3	1	c	p	H	Co
4a	יִשְׂחָק	3	3	m	s	Q	F
4b	יִלְעַג	3	3	m	s	Q	F
5a	יְדַבֵּר	4	3	m	s	D	F
5b	יְבַהֲלֵמוֹ	2	3	m	s	D	F
6	נָסַכְתִּי	7	1	c	s	Q	P

Chapter 6

Syntax

By now it should be obvious that discourse analysis entails paying extremely close attention to aspects of language that are often treated as something to be gotten out of the way before moving on to the "real" work of interpretation. And in reading a poem, discourse analysis involves examining each text from every angle, since we *cannot predict in advance* which linguistic tool(s) or combination thereof the poet will use.

Having lineated the poem, counted the words in each line, and parsed their predicates, we now turn to syntax, or how the words work together to make the line say what it does. This entails identifying each line's functional units and labeling them as either subject, predicate, object, prepositional phrase, etc.

As with verbal conjugations, word order is much less consistent in Hebrew poetry than in prose; the usual verb–subject–object (VSO) structure of the main clauses in a narrative, for example, occurs much less frequently and rarely reflects the form of the verbal predicate (apart from relatively few *wayyiqtol*s in poems) or clause. Word order occasionally functions above the level of the clause but almost always relates a line to its immediately adjacent lines.

I. PSALM 117

Begin by identifying the Topic and Comment of each line (above, chapter 3), maintaining the order of the Hebrew words; this may require some creativity in orering the columns. In Psalm 117 (below), it seems worthwhile to identify Comments as, e.g., either Pre-Topic or Post-Topic. Then identify what is "left over," labeling and assigning a column to each part. There is *no right way* to do this, nor is there any guarantee that doing it in a particular way will yield useful results.

Doing this for Psalm 117 yields something like this:

Psalm 117: Topics & Comments

L.	Comment (Post-Topic)	Topic	Comment (Pre-Topic)	Conjunction
1a		כָּל־גּוֹיִם	הַלְלוּ אֶת־יהוה	
1b		כָּל־הָאֻמִּים׃	שַׁבְּחוּהוּ	
2a		חַסְדּוֹ	גָּבַר עָלֵינוּ	כִּי
2b	לְעוֹלָם	וֶאֱמֶת־יהוה		
2c			הַלְלוּ יָהּ׃	

Note: *The "Comment (Post-Topic)" column is on the left and the "Conjunction" column is on the right in order to keep the words of each line in their Hebrew order.*

In order to see what each word or group of words is doing in its clause, we can diagram the line's syntax using abbreviations and symbols to identify their function. It is also useful to include the number of words per line, because this gives us a rough idea (to be refined later) of how compact the syntax is. Here are abbreviations and symbols that we can use to describe the syntax of the lines:

Key to Syntactical Symbols

cj	conjunction (other than *waw*)
O	object (direct/ indirect)
P	predicate
pp	prepositional phrase
qv	Quasiverbal[1]
S	subject (= topic)
v	finite verb

voc	vocative
w	*waw*
–	separates words
+	elements combined in one word
/	consists of
&	both combined in one form[2]

1. The term "quasiverbal" refers to a small group of words: אַיֵּה, "where is/are?," אַיִן/אֵין, "there is/are/not," הִנֵּה, "there is/are," יֵשׁ, "there is/are," עוֹד, "remains," "is still." Although nonverbal, these words often have a verbal function—they are therefore quasiverbal.

2. This symbol almost always describes a participle when it functions substantivally (as a noun) but also has an object within is own clause, as in, e.g., Prov 15:32a–b: פּוֹרֵעַ מוּסָר מוֹאֵס נַפְשׁוֹ, "Whoever neglects discipline despises his [own] soul," in which both participles are substantive, one serving as subject, the other as predicate nominative, and both have objects of their own (see further, below).

You may be wondering why we use labels (letters or symbols) rather than the Hebrew text itself. We label things rather than simply using the Hebrew text because labels condense a great deal of information and make continuities and discontinuities more obvious. Their clarity makes them both helpful and dangerous—helpful because they simplify the process of comparison and analysis, showing relationships at a glance; dangerous because the labels are made up or invented and are not the same as the Hebrew text but merely a convenient way of referring to it as we study.

Here is how this applies to Psalm 117:

Psalm 117

L.	BHS	Function	Symbol
1a	הַלְלוּ	Predicate, consisting of a verb	P/v
	אֶת־יהוה	Object	O
	כָּל־גּוֹיִם	Subject/vocative	S/voc
1b	שַׁבְּחוּהוּ	Predicate, consisting of a verb+Object	P/v+O
	כָּל־הָאֻמִּים׃	Subject, which here is vocative	S/voc
2a	כִּי	conjunction	cj
	גָבַר	Predicate, consisting of a verb	P/v
	עָלֵינוּ	prepositional phrase	pp
	חַסְדּוֹ	Subject	S
2b	וֶאֱמֶת־יהוה	*waw*+Subject	w+S
	לְעוֹלָם	?prepositional phrase	pp
		?Predicate, consisting of a prepositional phrase	P/pp
2c	הַלְלוּ־	Predicate, consisting of a verb	P/v
	יָהּ׃	Object	O

Psalm 117

L.	BHS	Words	Syntax
1a	הַלְלוּ אֶת־יהוה כָּל־גּוֹיִם	4	P/v—O—S/voc
1b	שַׁבְּחוּהוּ כָּל־הָאֻמִּים׃	3	P/v + O—S/voc
2a	כִּי גָבַר עָלֵינוּ חַסְדּוֹ	4	cj—P/v—pp—S
2b	וֶאֱמֶת־יהוה לְעוֹלָם	3	w + S—P/pp(?)
2c	הַלְלוּ־יָהּ׃	2	P/v—O

The first word in line 1a is a verbal predicate and so is labeled P/v (= predicate, consisting of a verb); the second word is the object (O); and the last two words are the subject (S), which is a vocative (/v); the speaker is talking directly to "all nations," since the predicate is an imperative.[3] The abbreviation pp is a neutral description of the grammatical form of the two prepositional phrases (עָלֵינוּ, "over us" [2a], and לְעוֹלָם, "for a long time" [2b]); it does not assign them a function. Construct chains are single syntactical units, since only the first word in the chain has a clause-level function (subject, object, etc.)—the rest of the chain merely modifies that word.[4]

Each of the last two lines lacks an element (predicate [2b], topic [2c]). The final line thus falls outside the pattern of the first four lines in length, lacks a topic, and is set off formally by the ellipsis in 2b. This step thus raises questions about poetic structure and alerts us to pay further attention to these lines.[5]

This step shows which lines are parallel in structure and which lines break established patterns. In Psalm 117, the first two lines are completely parallel in structure (1a–b), even though the suffixed object in 1b obscures this at first glance. Line 2b stands out not only because it is the only line that does not begin with its predicate (the conjunction כִּי in 2a will be reckoned as part of the predicate), but because it lacks a predicate; both factors help it mark the end of the poem's body, coming as it does just before the last line (2c), which, as the shortest line in the poem, disrupts the 4–3–4–3 pattern of the first four lines—another case of a marked ending, as in Psalms 146, 150 (above).

---

3. As in English, the subject of a Hebrew imperative can be implicit, as in "Come here!" (= "You to whom I am speaking, come here!") or explicit, as in Ps 117:1a ("All nations, praise YHWH!")

4. In the English, "The red book fell off the wooden table," the words "red" and "wooden" and in fact the entire phrase "off the wooden table" can be removed without changing the core of the sentence: "The book fell." This core offers so little information that seems hardly worth stating out of context. Information added by the adjectives identifies the book as *red* (not green) and the table as *wooden* (not plastic or steel). The word "John's" in the sentence "John's book fell off the grey table" functions just like the words "red" and "wooden"—it modifies and limits the potential range of the word "book" but does not affect its syntactical function.

5. The length of Ps 117 makes this less pressing—it is hard not to notice what is going on in a span of five lines. In longer poems, however, this becomes crucial.

II. ECCLESIASTES 3:1–8

The poem that opens Ecclesiastes 3 is entirely unlike anything in the Psalter, consisting almost entirely of two-word lines, with no finite verbal forms. Begin by delineating and glossing the text on your own.

Ecclesiastes 3:1–8: Gloss

L.	BHS	Gloss
1a	לַכֹּל זְמָן	to-the-each appointed-time
1b	וְעֵת לְכָל־חֵפֶץ תַּחַת הַשָּׁמָיִם׃	*w*-time to-each delight under the-sky
2a	עֵת לָלֶדֶת	time to-give-birth
2b	וְעֵת לָמוּת	*w*-time to-die
2c	עֵת לָטַעַת	time to-plant
2d	וְעֵת לַעֲקוֹר נָטוּעַ׃	*w*-time to-uproot planted-one
3a	עֵת לַהֲרוֹג	time to-kill
3b	וְעֵת לִרְפּוֹא	*w*-time to-heal
3c	עֵת לִפְרוֹץ	time to-make-a-breach
3d	וְעֵת לִבְנוֹת׃	w-time to-build
4a	עֵת לִבְכּוֹת	time to-weep
4b	וְעֵת לִשְׂחוֹק	*w*-time to-laugh
4c	עֵת סְפוֹד	time to-mourn
4d	וְעֵת רְקוֹד׃	*w*-time to-dance
5a	עֵת לְהַשְׁלִיךְ אֲבָנִים	time to-throw stones
5b	עֵת כְּנוֹס אֲבָנִים	*w*-time to-gather stones
5c	עֵת לַחֲבוֹק	time to-embrace
5d	וְעֵת לִרְחֹק מֵחַבֵּק׃	*w*-time to-be-far from-embracing
6a	עֵת לְבַקֵּשׁ	time to-seek
6b	וְעֵת לְאַבֵּד	*w*-time to-destroy
6c	עֵת לִשְׁמוֹר	time to-keep
6d	וְעֵת לְהַשְׁלִיךְ׃	*w*-time to-throw
7a	עֵת לִקְרוֹעַ	time to-tear (in grief/anguish)
7b	וְעֵת לִתְפּוֹר	*w*-time to-mend
7c	עֵת לַחֲשׁוֹת	time to-be-silent
7d	וְעֵת לְדַבֵּר׃	*w*-time to-speak
8a	עֵת לֶאֱהֹב	time to-love
8b	וְעֵת לִשְׂנֹא	*w*-time to-hate
8c	עֵת מִלְחָמָה	time-of war
8d	וְעֵת שָׁלוֹם׃	*w*-time-of peace

Ecclesiastes 3:1–8: Analysis

L.	BHS	Words	Syntax	Parsing
1a	לַכֹּל זְמָן	2	P/pp—S	pp
1b	וְעֵת לְכָל־חֵפֶץ תַּחַת הַשָּׁמָיִם׃	5	w + S—P/pp	pp
2a	עֵת לָלֶדֶת	2	S—P/v	QNC
2b	וְעֵת לָמוּת	2	w + S—P/v	QNC
2c	עֵת לָטַעַת	2	S—P/v	QNC
2d	וְעֵת לַעֲקוֹר נָטוּעַ׃	3	w + S—P/v—O	QNC
3a	עֵת לַהֲרוֹג	2	S—P/v	QNC
3b	וְעֵת לִרְפּוֹא	2	w + S—P/v	QNC
3c	עֵת לִפְרוֹץ	2	S—P/v	QNC
3d	וְעֵת לִבְנוֹת׃	2	w + S—P/v	QNC
4a	עֵת לִבְכּוֹת	2	S—P/v	QNC
4b	וְעֵת לִשְׂחוֹק	2	w + S—P/v	QNC
4c	עֵת סְפוֹד	2	S—P/v	QNC
4d	וְעֵת רְקוֹד׃	2	w + S—P/v	QNC
5a	עֵת לְהַשְׁלִיךְ אֲבָנִים	3	S—P/v—O	HNC
5b	עֵת כְּנוֹס אֲבָנִים	3	S—P/v—O	QNC
5c	עֵת לַחֲבוֹק	2	S—P/v	QNC
5d	וְעֵת לִרְחֹק מֵחַבֵּק׃	3	w + S—P/v—pp	QNC
6a	עֵת לְבַקֵּשׁ	2	S—P/v	DNC
6b	וְעֵת לְאַבֵּד	2	w + S—P/v	DNC
6c	עֵת לִשְׁמוֹר	2	S—P/v	QNC
6d	וְעֵת לְהַשְׁלִיךְ׃	2	w + S—P/v	HNC
7a	עֵת לִקְרוֹעַ	2	S—P/v	QNC
7b	וְעֵת לִתְפּוֹר	2	w + S—P/v	QNC
7c	עֵת לַחֲשׁוֹת	2	S—P/v	QNC
7d	וְעֵת לְדַבֵּר׃	2	w + S—P/v	DNC
8a	עֵת לֶאֱהֹב	2	S—P/v	QNC
8b	וְעֵת לִשְׂנֹא	2	w + S—P/v	QNC
8c	עֵת מִלְחָמָה	2	S	
8d	וְעֵת שָׁלוֹם׃	2	w + S	

What is most striking about this poem is its lack of finite verbal forms—the only verbs are infinitives construct. Nor do the length of the lines or verbal stems offer any help.[6] The final two lines are shaded because they differ from the rest of the lines in the poem in syntax—both are construct chains without a predicate. Here the syntax shows that the poem is precisely what it appears to be—a carefully constructed catalog (or list) that is so intentionally uniform that no one part stands out until the syntax of the final two lines draws attention to their content ("war" and "peace") and marks the poem's end—a subtle zone of turbulence.

III. SUMMARY

The biblical poets used the full range of linguistic devices to structure their poems, ranging from the length of the poetic line to verbal conjugation and stem, devices most of which are lost in translation. Because these devices function at such a basic level of language—the choice of verbal root may determine the choice of verbal stem, as in the *piel* stem for הלל and בָּרַךְ in Psalm 113:1a–3, or a chiasm of verbal conjugations, as in Psalm 2:1a–b. How many choices were unconscious and how many are the result of deliberate choice? This question is unanswerable—the text does not describe its own composition.

---

6. The two *piel* verbs in 6a–b mark these lines as "different," but the significance of that difference (if any) is obscure, nor do the two *hiphil* verbs (5a, 6d) have any apparent structural function; this is the only repeated form in the poem. As for line length, 5a–b are notable in that they are the only consecutive lines of more than two words. Some conjunction of these factors—if the only *piel* verbs occcurred in the only consecutive longer lines, for example—would encourage a closer look at why these two lines stand out.

Chapter 7

Semantic Cohesion

Discourse analysis asks (among other things) how a discourse is structured or, in other words, how it can be *divided* into its constituent parts. This is the goal of analysis, which is why to this point the main question has been "How is this poem organized?" so that we can follow its structure when discussing and explaing it rather than impose some imagined external outline on the text.

Discourse analysis also asks what makes a discourse work *as a whole*? This entails studying cohesive devices, those linguistic resources that unite a discourse. To answer this question, analysts talk about "cohesion" and "cohesive devices." Semantic cohesion refers to different words (lexical items) within a discourse that refer to the same person, idea, or thing, as in this paragraph:[1]

> My sister has a new sweater. **It** is *red*—her *favorite color.* She wears **it** nearly every day, so I know that she likes ***it***. I am not all that fond of *red*, so I'll be relieved when she stops wearing **it**. But I love my sister, so I'm glad ***it*** makes her happy.

The five occurrences of "it" (in **bold**) refer to the red sweater. In each case the reader must remember what is being referred to and mentally supply "red sweater" or "sweater" when encountering the word "it." The words in *italics*, refer to the color red; the third and fifth occurrences of "it" are bold and italic, since it is not altogether clear which is being referred to—the sweater, its color, or both. By making readers remember

---

1. Semantics is the study of meaning—what words, sentences, paragraphs, speeches, etc. mean, and why.

who or what was previously mentioned, pronouns ("it," "she," "her") and repeated words unify the passage.[2]

In Biblical Hebrew prose, verb-initial clauses are the main structuring device: in narrative a series of *wayyiqtol*s forms the backbone of the story—marking or listing the *wayyiqtol*s in a narrative outlines the story. Stories in English tend to be told in the past tense; *wayyiqtol*s bind a story together by naming the sequence of events, just as *weqatal*s outline the main steps of instructions, e.g., building and furnishing the tabernacle (Exodus 25–31) or offering a sacrifice (Leviticus 1–5).

There is nothing comparable to this in biblical poetry. Biblical poets did not use particular conjugations or clause types to trace their basic line of thought. This means that poems cannot be studied by assuming that noting a particular type of clause or verb will reveal their basic structure—no single linguistic resource creates cohesion throughout biblical poetry.

Cohesion in biblical poems depends primarily on two factors, either of which may be more or less important in a given poem: (1) *semantic cohesion*—repeated and varied references to the same idea or thing; and (2) *participant reference* (a specific type of semantic cohesion)—repeated references to characters and objects mentioned in the poem. Semantic cohesion can be as simple as synonyms or antonyms used in parallel, as in Prov 10:1b–c:

Proverbs 10:1b–c

L.	MT/BHS	Gloss
1b	בֵּן חָכָם יְשַׂמַּח־אָב	son wise-one he-makes-happy father
1c	וּבֵן כְּסִיל תּוּגַת אִמּוֹ׃	*w*-son foolish-one grief-of his-mother

The parallel terms rendered "wise/foolish," "father/mother," and "makes happy/[is] grief" and the repeated "son" link these lines together, implicitly reminding us that 10:1b–c form a single unit that is meant to

2. Pronouns are often said to "take the place of" nouns and to be used for "variety" in order to avoid the boredom or tedium of repeating the same word(s) over and over. Although this may be one of their effects, at the level of discourse they unify and bind together the passage. (And in this little paragraph the consistently present-tense verbs are a grammatical cohesive device, telling us that the entire "story" is occurring as it is being told.)

be read and understood together. Seeing these connections is the goal of the semantic analysis described in the next section.

I. PSALM 117

In biblical poems, semantic cohesion links a line to the immediately preceding line or lines and relates directly to syntactic analysis (above). It entails assigning a symbol (like consecutive letters of the alphabet) to each functional unit in a line and then repeating those symbols when the same thing is referred to in following lines. To identify semantic units and their relationships to units in other poetic lines we can align units that correspond in meaning or reference in columns and label each column consecutively:

Psalm 117

L.	f/c	e/b	d/a	c	b	a
1a				כָּל־גּוֹיִם	אֶת־יהוה	הַלְלוּ
1b				כָּל־הָאֻמִּים׃		שַׁבְּחוּהוּ
2a	חַסְדּוֹ	עָלֵינוּ	כִּי גָבַר			
2b	וֶאֱמֶת־יהוה					
			לְעוֹלָם			
2c					יָהּ׃	הַלְלוּ

Here are a few suggestions for labeling semantic units. You will notice that some of them overlap with both the rules for glossing and for labeling grammatical units (above).

1. Construct chains are labeled as a single unit.
2. Words "compounded" of more than one semantic referent, such as predicate plus (pronominal) object (שַׁבְּחוּהוּ, "praise him") are labeled according to their units but linked with "+."
3. Prepositional phrases are labeled as single units.
4. Conjunctions (e.g., כִּי, וְ-), negations (אַל, לֹא), the direct object marker (אֵת, אֶת־), and other "function words" are counted as part of the following content word.

Psalm 117

L.	BHS	Semantics			Morphosyntax[3]	
1a	הַלְלוּ אֶת־יהוה כָּל־גּוֹיִם	a.b.c	a.b.c	4:1.1.2[4]	P/v—O—S	2mp DV
1b	שַׁבְּחוּהוּ כָּל־הָאֻמִּים׃	$a^1+b^1.c^1$	$a^1+b^1.c^1$	3:1.2	P/v + O—S	2mp DV
2a	כִּי גָבַר עָלֵינוּ חַסְדּוֹ	a.b.c	d.e.f	4:2.1.1	cj—P/v—pp—S	3ms QP
2b	וֶאֱמֶת־יהוה לְעוֹלָם	$c^1.a^1$	$f^1.d^1$	3:2.1	w + S—pp	pp
2c	הַלְלוּ יָהּ׃	$a.b^1$	$a.b^1$	2:1.1	P/v—O—S	2mp DV

In Psalm 117:1a, the verbal predicate, הַלְלוּ, "praise," is the line's first semantic unit, which is therefore labeled "a"; the next unit in this line, אֶת־יהוה, "YHWH," is labeled "b," and כָּל־גּוֹיִם is labeled "c." They are labeled in the order order that they occur in the Hebrew text.

In line 1b the first word, שַׁבְּחוּהוּ, refers to both the action and its object, combining the "a" and "b" of 1a; a "plus" sign (+) therefore joins them: "a + b." Since, however, they are not exactly the same (different roots and different forms of the object), each letter receives a superscript number "1" (for "first variant"): "a^1+b^1." כָּל־הַלְאֻמִּים (1b, following LXX) has the same referent as כָּל־גּוֹיִם, and so both are labeled "c," but since כָּל־הַלְאֻמִּים is not exactly the same, it is labeled "c^1."

The referents in line 2a are not the same as those in 1a–b—there is no mention of praise, of the nations, or of YHWH, except within construct chains: חַסְדּוֹ and אֱמֶת־יהוה. A change of referent can be indicated in two ways: (1) a horizontal dotted line is inserted, the first word in the next line is labeled "a," and the process of labeling begins again; or (2) the next letter in the alphabet—in this case "d"—begins the line. The diagram above shows both possibilities for Psalm 117. In a very short poem the

3. Note that the columns of Syntax and Predicate Morphology have been combined under "Morphosyntax," a standard term in grammatical and discourse studies. You may find it more helpful to keep them separate.

4. After labeling the semantic units, we divide the total number of words in the line among its semantic units. The first numeral is the number of words in the line; after the colon each numeral shows the number of words in each unit. The elements of 1a are הַלְלוּ (1 word), אֶת־יהוה (1 word), and כָּל־גּוֹיִם (2 words), hence 4:1.1.2. Function words are included in the word count, although the object marker is not (as above). Counting the words per unit provides a further check on the earlier work of semantic analysis because it requires deciding what each word is doing in its line, what it refers to relative to the preceding line(s), and helps determine whether or not parallel semantic units (a/a^1, for example) have the same syntactical function. It also ensures that nothing has been overlooked, as the column of numbers can easily be correlated to the Hebrew text.

latter method, called "through-analysis," can work well; in longer poems through-analysis quickly becomes confusing because there are simply too many letters to keep track of.

Line 2b has only two semantic units, both of which parallel elements in 2a. The construct chain אֱמֶת־יהוה corresponds to חַסְדּוֹ, and לְעוֹלָם parallels גָּבַר.[5]

Line 2c also consists of two units, but these reflect the semantic units in line 1a and not 2b. Because the opening and closing lines of this poem are (nearly) identical, they form an *inclusio*.

Because Psalm 117 is so short and because of its high degree of repetition, through-analysis (the second column of letters) does not offer a great deal of added information, apart from pointing out the difference between 2a–b and the other three lines[6] and making the *inclusio* more obvious (1a, 2c).

What is important about this step is not labels or symbols but instead the thought required to answer, "How does this line relate to the preceding line?" In Psalm 117, lines 1a–b address the topic of "praise/commendation"; the next two lines explain why this is right and good (2a–b); and the closing line 2c returns to the original subject.

To sum up, in Psalm 117 line 1b displays continuity of both form and referent with 1a—these two lines are parallel in both meaning (a.b.c/ $a^1.b^1.c^1$) and structure (P/v–O–S/voc). Line 2b has continuity with 2a, but 2a's referential/semantic and syntactical discontinuity with 1a–b sets off these two lines as a separate section;[7] finally, line 2c is discontinous with 2b, returning to the form and content of 1a–b, further distinguishing 2a–b from 1a–b and 2c.

Psalm 117, in other words, does not consist of five lines chosen at random from a variety of stock clauses. Nor is it "simple" because it is short. It is rather a carefully composed poetic whole in which every aspect—line length, syntax, predicate morphology, personal reference—contributes to moving readers from its opening call to praise to the act of worship itself.

---

5. This assumes that the third masculine singular pronominal suffix "his" refers to YHWH, the only masculine singular referent in the poem to this point.

6. In both tables the dotted lines that divide the text into sections fall in the same places.

7. The syntax of 2a–b also reflects the change of subject (from "nations . . . peoples" to "his . . .")—they are the only two lines in the poem that lack an object and that contain prepositional phrases.

When we turn to a longer poem, for example Psalm 113 (lineated and glossed in chapter 4, above), and lay out its line length, full semantic analysis, and morphosyntax, we see how all of these aspects of Hebrew can function together to structure a biblical poem.

II. PSALM 113

Psalm 113: Analysis

L.	BHS	Semantics		Morphosyntax	
1a	הַלְלוּ יָהּ	a.b	2:1.1	P/v—O	2mp DV
1b	הַלְלוּ עַבְדֵי יהוה	a.c	3:1.2	P/v—S/voc	2mp DV
1c	הַלְלוּ אֶת־שֵׁם יהוה׃	$a.b^1$	3:1.2	P/v—O	2mp DV
2	יְהִי שֵׁם יהוה מְבֹרָךְ מֵעַתָּה וְעַד־עוֹלָם׃	a.b.c	8:[1].2.1.3	S—P/Ptc— pp—w + pp	3ms QJ ms DpPtc
3	מִמִּזְרַח־שֶׁמֶשׁ עַד־מְבוֹאוֹ מְהֻלָּל שֵׁם יהוה׃	$c^1.b^1.a$	7:4.1.2	pp—pp—P/ Ptc—S	ms DpPtc
4a	רָם עַל־כָּל־גּוֹיִם יהוה	a.b.c	5:1.3.1	P/Ptc—pp—S	ms QPtc
4b	עַל הַשָּׁמַיִם כְּבוֹדוֹ׃	$b^1.c^1$	3:2.1	pp—S	
5	מִי כַּיהוה אֱלֹהֵינוּ הַמַּגְבִּיהִי לָשָׁבֶת׃	a.b.c.d	5:1.2.1.1	S—pp—PN	ms HPtc— Q NC
6	הַמַּשְׁפִּילִי לִרְאוֹת בַּשָּׁמַיִם וּבָאָרֶץ׃	$c^1.d^1$. e	4:1.1.2	S—P/NC—pp	ms HPtc— Q NC
7a	מְקִימִי מֵעָפָר דָּל	a.b.c	3:1.1.1	P/ Ptc—pp—O	ms HPtc
7b	מֵאַשְׁפֹּת יָרִים אֶבְיוֹן׃	$b^1.a^1.c^1$	3:1.1.1	pp—P/v—O	3ms HF
8a	לְהוֹשִׁיבִי עִם־נְדִיבִים	d.e	3:1.2	P/NC—pp	ms HPtc
8b	עִם נְדִיבֵי עַמּוֹ׃	e^1	3:3	pp	
9a	מוֹשִׁיבִי עֲקֶרֶת הַבַּיִת אֵם־הַבָּנִים שְׂמֵחָה	$a^2.c^2.f$	6:1.2.3	P/Ptc—O—O^2	ms HPtc
9b	הַלְלוּ־יָהּ׃	a.b	2:1.1	P/v—O	2mp DV

Psalm 113's combination of semantic and morphosyntactic analysis shows that consecutive lines may have the same number of words and even the same syntactic elements, but that these can be distributed differently and arranged in patterns, as in lines 1a–3. Consider the following table.

Psalm 113:1a–3 Semantics and Morphosyntax

L.	BHS	Semantics		Morphosyntax
1a	הַלְלוּ יָהּ	a.b	2:1.1	P/v—O
1b	הַלְלוּ עַבְדֵי יהוה	a.c	3:1.2	P/v—S/voc
1c	הַלְלוּ אֶת־שֵׁם יהוה׃	a.b[1]	3:1.2	P/v—O
2	יְהִי שֵׁם יהוה מְבֹרָךְ מֵעַתָּה וְעַד־עוֹלָם׃	a.b.c	8:[1].2.1.3	S—P/Ptc—pp—w + pp
3	מִמִּזְרַח־שֶׁמֶשׁ עַד־מְבוֹאוֹ מְהֻלָּל שֵׁם יהוה׃	c[1].b[1].a	7:4.1.2	pp—pp—P/Ptc—S

Lines 1b–c have three words each, the first of which is identical (הַלְלוּ, "Praise!"); 1c returns to the syntax of 1a (P/v—O), and only 1b has an explicit subject (עַבְדֵי יהוה, "YHWH's servants")—a two-word construct chain that makes the parallel word count possible. At the same time, eliding the object of praise in 1b ties all three lines together, since the object is explicit in 1a (יָהּ) and expanded upon in 1c (שֵׁם יהוה). This also makes these three lines somewhat chiastic: ab–ac–ab[1], which binds them even more tightly to each other.

Treating the initial *yiqtol* as "included in" the participle מְבֹרָךְ,[8] lines 2–3 form a chiasm with regard to the number of words, subject (שֵׁם יהוה), and stem (מְבֹרָךְ and מְהֻלָּל are both *pual*). And—as we noted when we parsed the verbs in these lines (chapter 4)—the main verbal predicates in the first five lines are either *piel* (1a–c) or *pual* (2–3) (all D stem forms), which also ties together this first section of the poem. Two such consecutive chiasms (1a–c and 2–3), created by a variety of linguistic means, cannnot be coincidental; they highlight the theme of praise and unify these lines.

III. PROVERBS 6:12–19

The third poem in Proverbs 6, following the "Warning Against Surety" (6:1a–5b) and "The Sloth and the Ant" (6:6a–11b), begins by announcing

8. The divided predicate in line 2, where the subject lies between the *yiqtol* predicate (יְהִי) and the participle that serves as a predicate adjective (מְבֹרָךְ, "blessed"), complicates the analysis of this line. The clause יְהִי שֵׁם יהוה מְבֹרָךְ, "Blessed be YHWH's name" also occurs in Job 1:21, which supports the idea that יְהִי is a function word in this clause.

its subject as "the man of Belial" (12a). After a one-line introduction, the main portion of the poem (12b–15c) is united semantically, syntactically, and morphologically:

Proverbs 6:12a–15c: Gloss

L.	BHS	Gloss
12a	אָדָם בְּלִיַּעַל אִישׁ אָוֶן	human-of Belial man-of wickedness
12b	הוֹלֵךְ עִקְּשׁוּת פֶּה׃	walking-one/m crookedness-of mouth
13a	קֹרֵץ בְּעֵינָיו	winking-one/m with-his-eyes
13b	מֹלֵל בְּרַגְלָו	scraping-one/m with-his-feet
13c	מֹרֶה בְּאֶצְבְּעֹתָיו	teaching(?)-one/m with-his-fingers
14a	תַּהְפֻּכוֹת בְּלִבּוֹ חֹרֵשׁ רָע	perversities in-his-heart devising-one/m evil
14b	בְּכָל־עֵת מְדָנִים יְשַׁלֵּחַ׃	in-all-of time strifes he-sends
15a	עַל־כֵּן פִּתְאֹם יָבוֹא אֵידוֹ	on thus suddenly he-comes his-distress
15b	פֶּתַע יִשָּׁבֵר	[with] suddenness he-is-broken
15c	וְאֵין מַרְפֵּא׃	w-there-is-no healing-one/m

Proverbs 6:12a–15c: Full Analysis

L.	BHS	Semantics		Morphosyntax	
12a	אָדָם בְּלִיַּעַל אִישׁ אָוֶן	$a.a^{1}$	4:2.2	S—P/n	ms n
or				P/n—S	
12b	הוֹלֵךְ עִקְּשׁוּת פֶּה׃	a.b	3:1.2	P/Ptc—O?	ms QPtc
13a	קֹרֵץ בְּעֵינָיו	$a^{1}.b^{1}$	2:1.1	P/Ptc—pp	ms QPtc
13b	מֹלֵל בְּרַגְלָו	$a^{2}.b^{2}$	2:1.1	P/Ptc—pp	ms QPtc
13c	מֹרֶה בְּאֶצְבְּעֹתָיו	$a^{3}.b^{3}$	2:1.1	P/Ptc—pp	ms QPtc
14a	תַּהְפֻּכוֹת בְּלִבּוֹ חֹרֵשׁ רָע	$c.b^{4}.d.e$	4:1.1.1.1	O—pp—P/Ptc—O	ms QPtc
14b	בְּכָל־עֵת מְדָנִים יְשַׁלֵּחַ׃	$b^{5}.e^{1}.d^{1}$	4:1.1	pp—O—P/v	3ms DF
15a	עַל־כֵּן פִּתְאֹם יָבוֹא אֵידוֹ	a.b.c	5:3.1.1	pp—adv—P/v—S	3ms QF
15b	פֶּתַע יִשָּׁבֵר	$a^{1}.(b+c)^{1}$	2:1.1	adv—P/v	3ms NF
15c	וְאֵין מַרְפֵּא׃	d.e	2:1.1	w + P/q—S	qv

The introduction (12a) is set off from the rest of the poem by its syntactical contrast with a series of substantive participles that catalog the vices of the אָדָם בְּלִיַּעַל (12b–14a). This listing ends in 14b with a *yiqtol* (יָבוֹא), which sets the verbal tone for the conclusion (15a–c). The last three lines are set off by the the length of its first line (15a), the inferential phrase עַל־כֵּן, "therefore" (15a), and the quasi-verbal predicate (וְאֵין) of the last line (15c), another small zone of turbulence.

The final line of the middle and last sections uses a predicate unique to that section: a string of participial predicates (12b–14a) ends with a *yiqtol* (14b); a string of *yiqtol*s ends with the quasi-verbal predicate וְאֵין (15c), more or less bookending its nonverbal opening line (12a), as its morphological chart shows:

Proverbs 6:12a–15c: Predicate Morphology

L.	BHS	Person	Gender	Number	Stem	Conjugation
12a *or*	אִישׁ אָדָם		m	s		n
12b	הוֹלֵךְ		m	s	Q	Ptc
13a	קֹרֵץ		m	s	Q	Ptc
13b	מֹלֵל		m	s	Q	Ptc
13c	מֹרֶה		m	s	Q	Ptc
14a	חֹרֵשׁ		m	s	Q	Ptc
14b	יְשַׁלֵּחַ	3	m	s	D	F
15a	יָבוֹא	3	m	s	Q	F
15b	יִשָּׁבֵר	3	m	s	N	F
15c	וְאֵין					qv

This wisdom poem combines line length, morphology, syntax, and semantic continuities and discontinuities to signal the shape of the poem and to raise questions in the minds of its readers, questions like these: Why do lines 14b–15b have finite verbal predicates? Even if the poet wanted to distinguish what will happen to him (15a–b) from the description of his behaviour, line 14b could have a participial predicate. That would strengthen the distinction by maintaining the pattern of the other five lines that describe what the "man of wickedness" does (12b–14a). Or is 14b a line of transition, still describing his behavior but leading into the description of his fate as an event rather than as a pattern of behavior?

Without close attention to the details of verbal morphology, we would not even know to raise these questions.

The next poem in this chapter of Proverbs, 6:16–19, is signaled by another introductory formula, "Six . . . / And seven . . ." This numerical formula announces that the following verses will identify things that YHWH hates because he considers them abominations (16a–b). Please lineate and gloss it before continuing:

Proverbs 6:16a–19b: Gloss

L.	BHS	Gloss
16a	שֶׁשׁ־הֵנָּה שָׂנֵא יהוה	six they he-hates YHWH
16b	וְשֶׁבַע תּוֹעֲבוֹת נַפְשׁוֹ׃	w-seven abominations-of his-soul
17a	עֵינַיִם רָמוֹת	eyes high-ones
17b	לְשׁוֹן שָׁקֶר	tongue-of lie
17c	וְיָדַיִם שֹׁפְכוֹת דָּם־נָקִי׃	w-hands shedding-ones/m blood innocent
18a	לֵב חֹרֵשׁ מַחְשְׁבוֹת אָוֶן	heart devising-one/m thoughts-of trouble
18b	רַגְלַיִם מְמַהֲרוֹת לָרוּץ לָרָעָה׃	feet hastening-ones/m to-run to-the-evil
19a	יָפִיחַ כְּזָבִים עֵד שָׁקֶר	he-breathes lies witness[-of?] lie
19b	וּמְשַׁלֵּחַ מְדָנִים בֵּין אַחִים׃	w-sending-one/m strifes between brothers

Proverbs 6:16a–19b: Full Analysis

L.	BHS	Semantics		Morphosyntax	
16a	שֶׁשׁ־הֵנָּה שָׂנֵא יהוה	a.b.c	4:2.1.1	O—P/v—S	3ms QP
16b	וְשֶׁבַע תּוֹעֲבוֹת נַפְשׁוֹ׃	$a^1.(b^1.c^1)$[9]	3:1.(1.1)	w + P/n—S	fs n
17a	עֵינַיִם רָמוֹת	a.b	2:1.1	S	
17b	לְשׁוֹן שָׁקֶר	$a^1.b^1$	2:1.1	S	
17c	וְיָדַיִם שֹׁפְכוֹת דָּם־נָקִי׃	$a^2.b^2.c$	4:1.1.2	w + S—P/v—O	fp QPtc
18a	לֵב חֹרֵשׁ מַחְשְׁבוֹת אָוֶן	$a^3.b^3.c^1$	4:1.1.2	S—P/v—O	ms QPtc
18b	רַגְלַיִם מְמַהֲרוֹת לָרוּץ לָרָעָה׃	$a^4.b^4.d.c^2$	4:1.1.1.1	S—P/v—O/v—pp	fp DPtc
19a	יָפִיחַ כְּזָבִים עֵד שָׁקֶר	a.b.c	4:1.1.2	P/v—O—S	3ms QF
19b	וּמְשַׁלֵּחַ מְדָנִים בֵּין אַחִים׃	$a^1.b^1.d$	4:1.1.2	w + P/v—O—pp	ms DPtc

9. The parentheses indicate that a construct chain is divided in order to show the parallelism between its parts and its parallels.

Here is the spreadsheet of its predicates:

Proverbs 6:16a–19b: Predicates

L.	BHS	Per.	Gen.	No.	Stem	Conjugation
16a	שֵׁשׁ־הֵנָּה שָׂנֵא יהוה	3	m	s	Q	P
16b	וְשֶׁבַע תּוֹעֲבוֹת נַפְשׁוֹ׃		f	s		n
17a	עֵינַיִם רָמוֹת					
17b	לְשׁוֹן שָׁקֶר					
17c	וְיָדַיִם שֹׁפְכוֹת דָּם־נָקִי׃		f	p	Q	Ptc
18a	לֵב חֹרֵשׁ מַחְשְׁבוֹת אָוֶן		m	s	Q	Ptc
18b	רַגְלַיִם מְמַהֲרוֹת לָרוּץ לָרָעָה׃		f	p	D	Ptc
19a	יָפִיחַ כְּזָבִים עֵד שָׁקֶר	3	m	s	Q	F
19b	וּמְשַׁלֵּחַ מְדָנִים בֵּין אַחִים׃		m	s	D	Ptc

As in Prov 6:12a–15c, the introduction (6:16a–b) is followed by a list of his misdeeds, but here the poem catalogs five body parts (17a–18b) before identifying the troublemaker as עֵד שָׁקֶר, a "lying witness" (19a). This delayed identification,[10] along with one change in morphology from participles to *yiqtol* and another in syntax (the verbal predicate is fronted in both lines, unlike any of the preceding lines) create a zone of turbulence that suggests that 19a–b are the poem's climax, pointing to the witness who disrupts society by breathing the lies (19a) that cause strife (19b).

Delaying identification of the culprit creates a conceptual *inclusio* spanning both of the poems addressed above—the lying witness (19b) parallels both אִישׁ אָוֶן and אָדָם בְּלִיַּעַל (12a)—and raises the question of whether lines 12–19 form one poem or two.

Now let's compare these two poems by listing their topics in order side-by-side:

10. "Delayed identification" is a cohesive device since readers have to wait to find out who is being described and so must hold the description in mind. See Ps 121:3–5a for a more compact example of delayed identification.

Comparing Proverbs 6:12a–15b and 6:16a–19b

L.	12–15	Topic	16–19	L.
12a	אָדָם בְּלִיַּעַל אִישׁ אָוֶן	"title"/ "introduction"	שֶׁשׁ־הֵנָּה שָׂנֵא יהוה	16a
			וְשֶׁבַע תּוֹעֲבוֹת נַפְשׁוֹ׃	16b
12b	הוֹלֵךְ עִקְּשׁוּת פֶּה׃	mouth [19a]		
13a	קֹרֵץ בְּעֵינָו	eyes	עֵינַיִם רָמוֹת	17a
		tongue	לְשׁוֹן שָׁקֶר	17b
13b	מֹלֵל בְּרַגְלָו	feet [18b]		
13c	מֹרֶה בְּאֶצְבְּעֹתָיו	hands/fingers	וְיָדַיִם שֹׁפְכוֹת דָּם־נָקִי׃	17c
14a	תַּהְפֻּכוֹת בְּלִבּוֹ חֹרֵשׁ רָע	heart	לֵב חֹרֵשׁ מַחְשְׁבוֹת אָוֶן	18a
		feet [13b]	רַגְלַיִם מְמַהֲרוֹת לָרוּץ לָרָעָה׃	18b
		mouth/lies [12b]	יָפִיחַ כְּזָבִים עֵד שָׁקֶר	19a
14b	בְּכָל־עֵת מְדָנִים יְשַׁלֵּחַ׃	sends strife	וּמְשַׁלֵּחַ מְדָנִים בֵּין אַחִים׃	19b
15a	עַל־כֵּן פִּתְאֹם יָבוֹא אֵידוֹ	"fate"/ "conclusion"		
15b	פֶּתַע יִשָּׁבֵר וְאֵין מַרְפֵּא׃			

Comparing them makes me wonder if there may be some semantic parallels—some semantic continuity between these two poems (or half-poems—which is what we are trying to discern). Listing a generic semantic range (e.g., "mouth" rather than "lips" or "tongue") lets us see if these elements are (1) repeated; (2) organized in a similar way; or (3) both (or neither).

Proverbs 6:12a–19b: Semantic Continuity

L.	man	mouth	eyes	feet	hands	heart	strife
12a	a						
12b		b					
13a			c				
13b				d			
13c					e		
14a						f	
14c							g
15a–b							
16a–b	a^1						
17a			c^1				
17b		b^1					
17c					e^1		
18a						f^1	
18b				d^1			
19a		b^2					
19b							g^1

Both poems list six characteristics of the wicked: his mouth, eyes, feet, hands, heart, and strife. The first (12–15) describes the doom of the wicked as sudden and irremediable (15); the second describes YHWH's hatred of the abominations that typify the lying witness but does not mention his fate.

The semantic correspondences between these two short poems may suggest that they were composed as complementary reflections on a similar type of person or that they were independent compositions that an editor organized so that they would be read in light of each other. They may also suggest that catalogs were, like numerical sayings, a type of Israelite wisdom literature.

On the other hand, placing the "fate" of the wicked at the center of the poems (15a–b) and using an *inclusio* to identify him (12a, 16a–b) suggests that if they were originally independent compositions—which the differences in syntax and verbal morphology may suggest, the editor of Proverbs set them in this order with the goal of using their semantic overlap to enhance their effect.

Whichever we decide, the detailed analysis has enabled us to raise and begin to answer questions that are invisible in translation and difficult to see when we are focused only on getting the "right" meaning for each word.

IV. PSALM 1

We have already looked at the verbal morphology of Psalm 1 (chapter 4), but now let's examine its semantic cohesion.

Psalm 1: Analysis

L.	BHS	Semantics		Morphosyntax	
1a	אַשְׁרֵי־הָאִישׁ	a	2:2	S	
1b	אֲשֶׁר לֹא הָלַךְ בַּעֲצַת רְשָׁעִים	a.b	5:3.2	rel—adv—P/v—pp	3ms QP
1c	וּבְדֶרֶךְ חַטָּאִים לֹא עָמָד	$b^1.a^1$	4:2.2	w + pp—adv—P/v	3ms QP
1d	וּבְמוֹשַׁב לֵצִים לֹא יָשָׁב׃	$b^2.a^2$	4:2.2	w + pp—adv—P/v	3ms QP
2a	כִּי אִם בְּתוֹרַת יהוה חֶפְצוֹ	$c.b^3a^3$	5:4.1	cj—P/pp—S	pp
2b	וּבְתוֹרָתוֹ יֶהְגֶּה יוֹמָם וָלָיְלָה׃	$b^4.a^4.d$	4:1.1.2	w + pp—P/v—adv	3ms QF
3a	וְהָיָה כְּעֵץ שָׁתוּל עַל־פַּלְגֵי מָיִם	a.b.c	6:2.1.3	w + P/v—pp—pp	3ms QP
3b	אֲשֶׁר פִּרְיוֹ יִתֵּן בְּעִתּוֹ	$a^1.d.e.f$	4:1.1.1.1	rel[O-P/v-pp]	3ms QF
3c	וְעָלֵהוּ לֹא־יִבּוֹל	$d^1.e^1$	3:1.2	w + O—adv—P/v	3ms QF
3d	וְכֹל אֲשֶׁר־יַעֲשֶׂה יַצְלִיחַ׃	$d.e^2$	4:3.1	w + S[O-rel-P/v]—P/v	[3ms QF] 3ms HF
4a	לֹא־כֵן הָרְשָׁעִים	a.b	3:2.1	P/adv—S	adv
4b	כִּי אִם־כַּמֹּץ אֲשֶׁר־תִּדְּפֶנּוּ רוּחַ׃	a^1c	6:3.3	cj—P/pp—rel [P/v+O—S]	3fs QF
5a	עַל־כֵּן לֹא־יָקֻמוּ רְשָׁעִים בַּמִּשְׁפָּט	a.b.c	6:4.1.1	cj—adv—P/v—S—pp	3mp QF
5b	וְחַטָּאִים בַּעֲדַת צַדִּיקִים׃	$b^1.c^1$	3:1.2	w + S—pp	
6a	כִּי־יוֹדֵעַ יהוה דֶּרֶךְ צַדִּיקִים	a.b.c	5:2.1.2	cj—P/v—S—O	ms QPtc
6b	וְדֶרֶךְ רְשָׁעִים תֹּאבֵד׃	$c^1.a^1$	3:2.1	w + S—P/v	3fs QF

The semantic analysis of these lines suggests that 1a functions primarily as a title—"The Happy Man," who is then the subject of the next nine lines (1b–3d) before the poet spends four lines describing the wicked (and "unhappy") (4a–5b), followed by a conclusion (6a–b). Analyzing the content also shows that the poem is arranged in the pattern a–b–a–b, highlighting the contrast between the righteous and wicked and implicitly identifying the righteous of 6a (and 5b) with the happy man of the poem's opening statements.

Psalm 1: Topics

L.			
1a	Title	a	
1b–3d	The Happy Man	a^1	
4a–5b	The Wicked		b
6a	The Righteous	a^2	
6b	The Wicked		b^1

We have seen that the vocabulary that a poet's chose to use is a key cohesive device in biblical poems, but cohesion can also be created in ways other than by the choice of vocabulary, all of which we have already seen—chiasm, ellipsis, participant reference, and inclusio. Now let's take a closer look each of these.

V. CHIASM

Chiasm is a two-part rhetorical figure in which the order of elements in the first part is reversed in the second. It can function across a number of lines but is most common between two parallel lines. Here are some examples of each from poems studied above:

A. PSALM 121:6

Psalm 121:6a–b

L.	BHS	Semantics		Morphysyntax	
6a	יוֹמָם הַשֶּׁמֶשׁ לֹא־יַכֶּכָּה	a.b.c	4:1.1.2	adv—S—adv—P/v	3ms HF
6b	וְיָרֵחַ בַּלָּיְלָה׃	$b^1.a^1$	2:1.1	w + S—pp	

The poet reversed the order of the syntactic elements in 6b that correspond to those in 6a so that this pair of lines begins and ends with "by day" and "by night," then (moving toward the center of the lines) he names the "sun" and "moon," which makes the center the single word יַכֶּכָּה, "it will not strike you," as this vertical diagram shows:

Psalm 121:6: Chiasm

c	b	a
		יוֹמָם
	הַשֶּׁמֶשׁ	
לֹא־יַכֶּכָּה		
	וְיָרֵחַ	
		בַּלָּיְלָה׃

The term chiasm is named for the Greek letter *chi* (X), because when the lines are arranged with the words above each other (as they are in the verse) and lines drawn to connect corresponding elements, the lines form the letter *chi.*

Psalm 121:6a–b: Chiasm

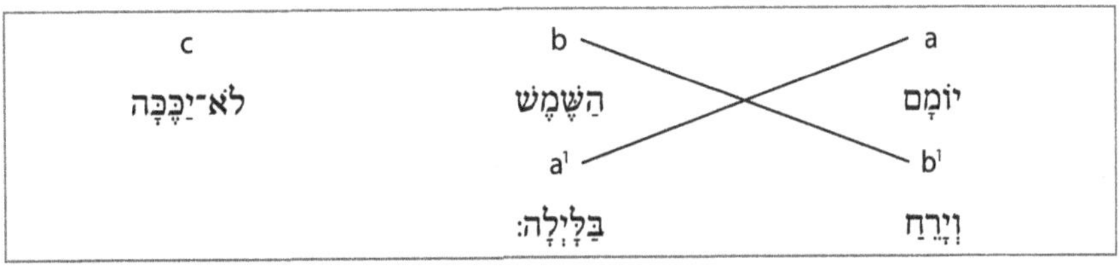

Since there is only one central term, which is also the verbal predicate, verse 6 could be read as a single line with a "double-duty" predicate with two subjects and adverbs, or as two lines with an elided verb in the second. Because the final element of 6a provides the predicate for both clauses, the two lines pivot around that element; this type of parallelism can also therefore be called a "pivot pattern." The perfect alignment of the elements (a–b–c–b^1–a^1), however, suggests that this should be read chiastically.

Furthermore, the chiastic arrangement of verse 6—the only chiastic verse in the psalm and the only line(s) with a non-*qal* predicate—separates the three substantive participles of שׁמר (3b–5b), describing *who* YHWH is (שֹׁמְרֶךָ), from its three *yiqtol* occurrences (7a–8), which identify *what* he *does* (יִשְׁמָרְךָ), changing the poem's tone without changing its lexicon.

B. PSALM 98:2

A non-chiastic pivot pattern occurs in Psalm 98:2; the prepositional phrase "to the eyes of the nations" may serve as the "indirect" object of both verbs in these lines. Consider the following tables:

Psalm 98:2a–b: Full Analysis

L.	BHS	Semantics		Morphosyntax	
2a	הוֹדִיעַ יהוה יְשׁוּעָתוֹ לְעֵינֵי הַגּוֹיִם	a.b.c.d	5:1.1.1.2	P/v—S—O—pp	3ms HP
2b	גִּלָּה צִדְקָתוֹ׃	a¹.c¹	2:1.1	pp—P/v—O	3ms DP

Psalm 98:2a–b: Pivot

2a	הוֹדִיעַ	a
	יהוה	b
	יְשׁוּעָתוֹ	c
2b	לְעֵינֵי הַגּוֹיִם	d
	גִּלָּה	a¹
	צִדְקָתוֹ׃	c¹

There is no chiasm in this verse—for that, the order of elements in 2b would have to be reversed; the position and potentially dual role of לְעֵינֵי הַגּוֹיִם nonetheless makes this a pivot that strengthens the cohesion between these lines (and implicitly equates יְשׁוּעָתוֹ and צִדְקָתוֹ). The pivot links the two lines into a conceptual whole.

C. PSALM 1:6

The last two lines of Ps 1:6 are chiastic; 6b reverses the order of the subject and predicate from 6a:

Psalm 1:6a–b: Chiasm

L.	BHS	Semantics		Morphosyntax	
6a	כִּי־יוֹדֵעַ יהוה דֶּרֶךְ צַדִּיקִים	a.b.c	5:2.1.2	cj—P/v—S—O	ms QPtc
6b	וְדֶרֶךְ רְשָׁעִים תֹּאבֵד׃	$c^1.a^1$	3:2.1	w+S—P/v	3fs QF

The syntax of these two lines is not symmetrical, mainly because the verb אבד does not govern an object in the *qal*, but the lack of a "b" element in the second line does not make this non-chiastic; incomplete chiasms are not uncommon.

Psalm 1:6: "Incomplete" Chiasm

L.			
	c	b	a
6a	דֶּרֶךְ צַדִּיקִים	יהוה	כִּי־יוֹדֵעַ
	a^1		c^1
6b	תֹּאבֵד׃		וְדֶרֶךְ רְשָׁעִים

D. PSALM 2:1–2

Chiasms need not be semantic only; they can be both semantic and morphological, as in the opening lines of Psalm 2, which we looked at above (chapters 3, 5):

Psalm 2:1a–2b: Chiasms (Semantic & Morphological)

L.	BHS	Semantics		Morphosyntax	
1a	לָמָּה רָגְשׁוּ גוֹיִם	a.b	3:2.1	adv—P/v—S	3cp Q**P**
1b	וּלְאֻמִּים יֶהְגּוּ־רִיק׃	$b^1.a^1$	3:1.2	w + S—P/v—O	3mp Q**F**
2a	יִתְיַצְּבוּ מַלְכֵי־אֶרֶץ	$a^2.b^2$	3:1.2	P/v—S	3mp Dt**F**
2b	וְרוֹזְנִים נוֹסְדוּ־יָחַד עַל־יהוה וְעַל־מְשִׁיחוֹ׃	$b^3.a^3.c$	7:1.2.4	w + S—P/v—adv—pp	3cp N**P**

The semantic chiasm in lines 1a–b only hints at a much more complex structure extending beyond the verse boundary and linking the first four lines semantically and morphosyntactically. First, and most obviously, the semantic structure through these four lines is in effect a double chiasm: a–b–b–a–a–b–b–a[–c]. Second, there is a double morphological chiasm of both verbal conjugation (*qatal–yiqtol–yiqtol–qatal*) and gender (common–masculine–masculine–common). Third, as noted above under the discussion of line length, the length of line 2b makes it a zone of turbulence and signals the end of the first section of the poem.[11]

This demarcation is even more striking in light of the following lines (2:3–4), each pair of which has the same semantic structure (a–b/a^1–b^1–c). Lines 3a–b share the same verbal conjugation—the first time in the poem that consecutive lines have the same conjugation.

Psalm 2:3a–4b: Non-Chiastic Discontinuity with 2:3a–4b

L.	BHS	Semantics		Morphosyntax	
3a	נְנַתְּקָה אֶת־מוֹסְרוֹתֵימוֹ	a.b	3:1.2	P/v—O	1cp DCo
3b	וְנַשְׁלִיכָה מִמֶּנּוּ עֲבֹתֵימוֹ׃	a^1.b^1.c	3:1.1.1	P/v—pp—O	1cp HCo
4a	יוֹשֵׁב בַּשָּׁמַיִם יִשְׂחָק	a.b	3:2.1	S—P/v	3ms QF
4b	אֲדֹנָי יִלְעַג־לָמוֹ׃	a^1.b^1.c	3:1.1.1	S—P/v—pp	3ms QF

The verbal predicates in 4a–b are *yiqtol*; these lines also front their subjects (יֹשֵׁב, אֲדֹנָי), in contrast to 3a–b. Both of these sets of lines avoid the complicated chiasms of 1a–2b.

E. PSALM 113:2–3

Chiasms also occur across verse "boundaries" (yet another reason for ignoring the verses), as in the chiasm in Psalm 113:2–3. It appears to be incomplete, but that is due to the limitations of the verbal predicate; *pual* volititional forms are so rare as to be non-existent, and so the poet used the *yiqtol* יְהִי in first position to "make" the *pual* of both lines volitional.[12]

11. One result of these compound cohesive factors is to imply that the opening interrogative לָמָּה, "Why . . . ?" is to be read across all four lines.

12. The volitional force of the initial יְהִי extends across both lines.

Psalm 113: 2–3: Chiasm (Semantic)

L.	BHS	Semantics		Morphosyntax	
2	יְהִי שֵׁם יהוה מְבֹרָךְ מֵעַתָּה וְעַד־עוֹלָם׃	a.b.c	7:[1] 2.1.3	S—P/v—- pp—w + pp	3ms QJ + ms DpPtc
3	מִמִּזְרַח־שֶׁמֶשׁ עַד־ מְבוֹאוֹ מְהֻלָּל שֵׁם יהוה׃	c'.b'.a	7:4.1.2	pp—pp—- P/v—S	ms DpPtc

This yields a lovely chiasm that becomes visible when we lay out its semantic units:

Psalm 113:2–3: Chiasm

2	יְהִי	
	שֵׁם יהוה	a
	מְבֹרָךְ	b
	מֵעַתָּה וְעַד־עוֹלָם׃	c
3	מִמִּזְרַח־שֶׁמֶשׁ עַד־מְבוֹאוֹ	c'
	מְהֻלָּל	b'
	שֵׁם יהוה׃	a'

These are the longest lines in Psalm 113, and chiasms of this length are unusual. In this case, the chiasm ends the "D-stem section" of the poem (1a–3). We do not know why biblical poets used chiasms—whether they draw attention to the extremes (the first and last elements), or to the means (the central elements), or were purely ornamental (or were a way to show one's creativity)—one effect of a chiasm is to link closely the lines in which it occurs. Like ellipses (below), chiasms rarely extend beyond a few lines, but they are a powerful cohesive device used by poets throughout the Hebrew Bible.

VI. ELLIPSIS

Perhaps the most powerful linguistic cohesive device is ellipsis—a syntactical "gap" that is the result of leaving out (eliding) one or more of the elements of a clause.[13] The cohesion is created by the reader's need to fill the gap by importing the missing term from the context; in biblical poetry this is usually supplied from the immediately preceding line.

Ellipsis is not cohesively powerful in the sense that it binds together long passages (although a well-designed series of ellipses could do this), but rather because, like a pronoun, an ellipsis makes the reader recall and supply the missing term(s) from the preceding line.

We noted the ellipsis in our "paradigm poem" (Ps 117) when we glossed it (chapter 1, above), but let's revisit it in light of its cohesive function.

A. PSALM 117

Psalm 117: Full Analysis

L.	BHS	Semantics		Morphosyntax	
1a	הַלְלוּ אֶת־יהוה כָּל־גּוֹיִם	a.b.c	4:1.1.2	P/v—O—S/voc	2mp DV
1b	שַׁבְּחוּהוּ כָּל־הָאֻמִּים׃	$a^1+b^1.c^1$	3:1.2	P/v+O—S/voc	2mp DV
2a	כִּי גָבַר עָלֵינוּ חַסְדּוֹ	a.b.c	4:2.1.1	cj—P/v—pp—S	3ms QP
2b	וֶאֱמֶת־יהוה לְעוֹלָם	$c^1.a^1$	3:2.1	w+S—pp	
2c	הַלְלוּ־יָהּ׃	a.b	2:1.1	P/v—O	2mp DV

Psalm 117:2b lacks a predicate. The line—"And YHWH's truth for a long time"—requires either an equation ("And YHWH's truth [*is*/*was*] for a long time") or a verb. If we supply גָבַר from 2a, the line would read "and YHWH's truth *prevails/is strong* for a long time."[14]

This illustrates the basic requirements of ellipses: (1) the syntax of the two lines must be parallel, if not identical;[15] and (2) the form that is borrowed in order to fill the ellipsis must be the same root (lexical item), stem, and conjugation as the form in the corresponding line. As here, it

13. Ellipsis is common in everyday language, as when someone asks "Would you like a cup of tea?" and the response is "Yes, thanks," which is shortened from "Yes, I would like a cup of tea. Thank you." This type of ellipsis is so normal that we rarely notice it.

14. The form supplied in this case would be גָּבְרָה rather than גָּבַר, since the subject of 2b (אֱמֶת) is feminine.

15. Here the broken chiasm (a–b–c/c^1–a^1) means that the word order of the two lines is not identical.

need not be the same person, gender, or number, since these refer to the subject of the elliptical line.[16]

Psalm 114 is a longer poem that is striking for its ellipses. Since we haven't looked at this before, we begin by lineating and glossing it.

B. PSALM 114

Psalm 114: Gloss

L.	BHS	Gloss
1a	בְּצֵאת יִשְׂרָאֵל מִמִּצְרָיִם	when-went-out Israel from-Egypt
1b	בֵּית יַעֲקֹב מֵעַם לֹעֵז׃	house-of Jacob from-people-of stammering-one
2a	הָיְתָה יְהוּדָה לְקָדְשׁוֹ	it-was Judah to-his-holy-place
2b	יִשְׂרָאֵל מַמְשְׁלוֹתָיו׃	Israel his-realm
3a	הַיָּם רָאָה	the-sea it-saw
3b	וַיָּנֹס	*w*-it-fled
3c	הַיַּרְדֵּן יִסֹּב לְאָחוֹר׃	the-Jordan it-turned-around to-behind
4a	הֶהָרִים רָקְדוּ כְאֵילִים	the-mountains they-shook like-rams
4b	גְּבָעוֹת כִּבְנֵי־צֹאן׃	hills like-sons-of flock
5a	מַה־לְּךָ הַיָּם	what to-you the-sea
5b	כִּי תָנוּס	that you-flee
5c	הַיַּרְדֵּן תִּסֹּב לְאָחוֹר׃	the-Jordan you-turn-around to-behind
6a	הֶהָרִים תִּרְקְדוּ כְאֵילִים	the-mountains you-shake like-rams
6b	גְּבָעוֹת כִּבְנֵי־צֹאן׃	hills like-sons-of flock
7a	מִלִּפְנֵי אָדוֹן חוּלִי אָרֶץ	from-presence-of Lord [you-]writhe! Earth
7b	מִלִּפְנֵי אֱלוֹהַּ יַעֲקֹב׃	from-presence-of god-of Jacob
8a	הַהֹפְכִי הַצּוּר אֲגַם־מָיִם	the-one-turning the-cliff pool-of water
8b	חַלָּמִישׁ לְמַעְיְנוֹ־מָיִם׃	flint to-springs-of water

Then, as usual, the next step is to create the table in which we analyze its line length, semantics, and morphosyntax.

16. The terms "supply," "fill," etc. do not mean that the verb is added to the line; it is supplied only in the reader's imagination.

Psalm 114: Full Analysis

L.	BHS	Semantics		Morphosyntax	
1a	בְּצֵאת יִשְׂרָאֵל מִמִּצְרָיִם	a.b.c	3:1.1.1	P/v—S—pp	Q NC
1b	בֵּית יַעֲקֹב מֵעַם לֹעֵז׃	$b^1.c^1$	4:2.2	S—pp	
2a	הָיְתָה יְהוּדָה לְקָדְשׁוֹ	a.b.c	3:1.1.1	P/v—S—pp	3fs QP
2b	יִשְׂרָאֵל מַמְשְׁלוֹתָיו׃	$b^1.c^1$	2:1.1	S—O	
3a	הַיָּם רָאָה	a.b	3:1.1	S—P/v	3ms QP
3b	וַיָּנֹס	c	1:1	w + P/v	3ms QPr
3c	הַיַּרְדֵּן יִסֹּב לְאָחוֹר׃	$a^1.c^1$	3:1.2	S—P/v—pp	3ms QF
4a	הֶהָרִים רָקְדוּ כְאֵילִים	$a^2.c^2.d$	3:1.1.1	S—P/v—pp	3cp QP
4b	גְּבָעוֹת כִּבְנֵי־צֹאן׃	$a^3.d^1$	3:1.2	S—pp	
5a	מַה־לְּךָ הַיָּם	e.a	5:2.1	pn-pp—S/voc—cj	
5b	כִּי תָנוּס	c^1	2:2	cj—P/v	2ms QF
5c	הַיַּרְדֵּן תִּסֹּב לְאָחוֹר׃	$a^1.c^2$	3:1.2	S/voc—P/v—pp	2ms QF
6a	הֶהָרִים תִּרְקְדוּ כְאֵילִים	$a^2.c^3.d$	3:1.1.1	S—P/v—pp	2mp QF
6b	גְּבָעוֹת כִּבְנֵי־צֹאן׃	$a^3.d^1$	3:1.2	S—pp	
7a	מִלִּפְנֵי אָדוֹן חוּלִי אָרֶץ	a.b.c	4:2.1.1	pp—P/v—S/voc	2fs QV[17]
7b	מִלִּפְנֵי אֱלוֹהַּ יַעֲקֹב׃	a^1	3:3	pp	
8a	הַהֹפְכִי הַצּוּר אֲגַם־מָיִם	$a^2.e.f$	4:1.1.2	S&P/v—O—O	ms QPtc
8b	חַלָּמִישׁ לְמַעְיְנוֹ־מָיִם׃	$e^1.f^1$	3:1.2	O—pp	

One-third of the lines in Psalm 114 are elliptical: 1b, 2b, 4b, 6b, 7b;[18] each lacks a verbal predicate, which must be supplied from the preceding line. Each of these will be addressed in turn. Consider, for example, that 1b does not make sense as a nonverbal predication ("Jacob's household [was] from a stammering people"):

Psalm 114:1a–b: Ellipsis

L.	BHS	Semantics		Morphosyntax	
1a	בְּצֵאת יִשְׂרָאֵל מִמִּצְרָיִם	a.b.c	3:1.1.1	P/v—S—pp	Q NC
1b	בֵּית יַעֲקֹב מֵעַם לֹעֵז׃	$b^1.c^1$	4:2.2	S—pp	

17. "QV" (both capitalized) = *qal* imperative; "qv" (both lower case) = "quasiverbal." There may be a better abbreviation.

18. On 8b, see below.

When we supply the predicate from 1a, 1b is read as though it was written:

1a	בְּצֵאת יִשְׂרָאֵל מִמִּצְרָיִם	When Israel left Egypt
1b	[בְּצֵאת] בֵּית יַעֲקֹב מֵעַם לֹעֵז׃	[When] Jacob's household [left] a stammering people

Unlike 1b, 2b *can* be understood nonverbally: "Israel [was] his dominion." This line is more complex than 1b because if the gap in 2b is the result of an ellipsis, the ellipsis has two parts: the verb itself (הָיְתָה) and the preposition לְ.[19]

Psalm 114:2a–b: Ellipsis

L.	BHS	Semantics		Morphosyntax	
2a	הָיְתָה יְהוּדָה לְקָדְשׁוֹ	a.b.c	3:1.1.1	P/v—S—pp	3fs QP
2b	יִשְׂרָאֵל מַמְשְׁלוֹתָיו׃	$b^1.c^1$	2:1.1	S—O	

Reading the line this way yields the following:

2a	הָיְתָה יְהוּדָה לְקָדְשׁוֹ	Judah became (הָיְתָה . . . לְ-) his holy place
2b	[הָיָה] מַמְשְׁלוֹתָיו׃ [לְ]יִשְׂרָאֵל	Israel [became] his dominion

On the other hand, since both readings—"Israel [was] his dominion" and "Israel [became] his dominion"—are reasonable and both make sense, both are possible. There is no way to determine which one the poet intended.

Line 4b also lacks a predicate:

Psalm 114:4a–b: Ellipsis

L.	BHS	Semantics		Morphosyntax	
4a	הֶהָרִים רָקְדוּ כְאֵילִים	$a^2.c^2.d$	3:1.1.1	S—P/v—pp	3cp QP
4b	גְּבָעוֹת כִּבְנֵי־צֹאן׃	$a^3.d^1$	3:1.2	S—pp	

19. The verb היה can be used with the preposition ל to show either possession ("his/her/etc.") or signal the idea of "becoming." Both can occur together, as in וַתְּהִי לִי לְאִשָּׁה, "and she became my wife" (Gen 20:12).

Reading 4b as a verbless clause—"Hills [are] like the young of the flock"—does not fit the context of the preceding three lines, each of which describes how an aspect of the created order responded to Israel's departure from Egypt: "The sea *saw* and *fled*; / The Jordan *turned back*; / The mountains *trembled* like rams." The verbal predicate from the preceding line fits both the meaning and the grammar; the supplied form would be identical, since the third plural *qatal* is not inflected for gender:

4a	הֶהָרִים רָקְדוּ כְאֵילִים	The mountains trembled like rams
4b	[רָקְדוּ] גְּבָעוֹת כִּבְנֵי־צֹאן׃	Hills [trembled] like sons of the flock

There is no ellipsis in 5a–b, since each line is syntactically complete. Lines 6a–b, however, are identical to 4a–b, apart from the conjugation of the verbal predicate in 6a, תִּרְקְדוּ, "you tremble" which is *yiqtol* rather than *qatal*.

Psalm 114:6: Ellipsis

L.	BHS	Semantics		Morphosyntax	
6a	הֶהָרִים תִּרְקְדוּ כְאֵילִים	a².c³.d	3:1.1.1	S—P/v—pp	2mp QF
6b	גְּבָעוֹת כִּבְנֵי־צֹאן׃	a³.d¹	3:1.2	S—pp	

The introductory מַה־לְּךָ in 5a governs the following three lines (5b–6b), so that 6a–b are also questions, which also means that 6b does not merely repeat 4b (to which it is identical). Because the subject of 6b is feminine plural, the supplied verbal form differs in gender from the verb in 6a, although the person, number, conjugation, and stem remain the same.

6a	[מַה־לְּךָ] הֶהָרִים תִּרְקְדוּ כְאֵילִים	[Why do you], mountains, tremble like rams?
6b	[מַה־לְּךָ] גְּבָעוֹת[20] [תִּרְקְדְנָה] כִּבְנֵי־צֹאן׃	[Why do you], hills [tremble] like sons of the flock?

20. The medial vowel cannot be determined, since the root רקד does not occur with a whole vowel in this position.

The prepositional phrase in 7a is fronted, which creates a discontinuity with 6b and separates the last four lines of the poem from those that precede them (see above).

Psalm 114:7a–b: Ellipsis

L.	BHS	Semantics		Morphosyntax	
7a	מִלִּפְנֵי אָדוֹן חוּלִי אָרֶץ	a.b.c	4:2.1.1	pp—P/v—S/voc	2fs QV
7b	מִלִּפְנֵי אֱלוֹהַּ יַעֲקֹב׃	a[1]	3:3	pp	

Here two elements are lacking, unlike the ellipses in verses 1b, 2b, and 4b. Line 7b consists of a single prepositional phrase, which corresponds to the first semantic unit of 7a: line 7b lacks both subject and predicate. If, as in 8b (below), the prepositional phrase ended line 7a, 7b could be read in apposition ("Earth, tremble *in the presence of* the Lord, [i.e.,] *in the presence of* Jacob's God"), rather than as an ellipsis. Since, however, the prepositional phrase מִלִּפְנֵי אָדוֹן begins 7a rather than ending it, 7b requires both a subject and a predicate,[21] neither of which can be known,[22] nor can the order of its parts, although it is usually interpreted as though it read:

7a	מִלִּפְנֵי אָדוֹן חוּלִי אָרֶץ	In the Lord's presence, tremble, Earth
7b	מִלִּפְנֵי אֱלוֹהַּ יַעֲקֹב [חוּלִי תֵּבֵל] ׃	In the presence of Jacob's god, [tremble, World]

This brings us to the special case of lines 8a–b:

Psalm 114:8a–b: Ellipsis

L.	BHS	Semantics		Morphosyntax	
8a	הַהֹפְכִי הַצּוּר אֲגַם־מָיִם	a[2].e.f	4:1.1.2	S&P/Ptc—O—O	ms QPtc
8b	חַלָּמִישׁ לְמַעְיְנוֹ־מָיִם׃	e[1].f[1]	3:1.2	O—pp	

21. Although the predicate is most commonly elided, any syntactical element can be left out to form an ellipsis.

22. Was the poet perhaps thinking of תֵּבֵל rather than אֶרֶץ (as often in the Psalter)?

Here the preposition is in the second line (contrast 2b), and the repeated vocabulary ends both lines (מָיִם) rather than beginning them (contrast 7a–b). Line 8b could be read as a nonverbal predication, if the preposition לְ is read as though it were part of the compound ל plus היה ("become"; cf. line 2b): "Flint [became] a pool of water." If, however, it is read as an ellipsis, with its subject and predicate supplied by 8a, it becomes [הַהֹפְכִי, "He who turns] flint . . ."[23]

In 8a one of two objects is being "changed into" the other, although the direction of the change is not immediately clear—does rock become water or vice versa?[24] If the syntax of the two lines is parallel, the preposition לְ (8b) implies that 8a reads "flint *into* springs of water."[25]

8a	הַהֹפְכִי הַצּוּר [לַ]אֲגַם־מָיִם	He who turns the crag [into] a pool of water
8b	[הַהֹפְכִי] חַלָּמִישׁ לְמַעְיְנוֹ־מָיִם׃	[He who turns] flint into springs of water

Line 8a thus supplies the main predicate for 8b, and 8b supplies the preposition that "completes" the predicate in 8a—the two lines must be read together in order for either to make complete sense.

C. PROVERBS 17:27–28

In Prov 17:27–28, ellipses raise the same questions as in Psalm 114, but without the advantage of repeated lines and the context of an obvious poetic unit, although these two sayings are linked by the themes of silence and wisdom. Since this is a first look at these verses, lineate and gloss them before going on.

23. Lines in which a participle identifies both the subject and predicate (8a) are not uncommon in biblical poems, but they complicate the line's analysis—the substantive aspect of the participle functions as the topic ("he who/the one who") and its verbal aspect as the predicate ("changes"). Or the participle can be interpreted as a "complex topic" that incorporates part of its own comment.

24. As noted above, we need to be cautious about assuming that the subject is mentioned first—that is a function of word order in English.

25. This is not the end of question. Perhaps, as in Psalm 107, these lines present contrasting divine works: he "turns a pool of water into a crag, [but] flint into springs of water." Perhaps the article (הַצּוּר) marks the first object (i.e., "that which becomes," not "that which something else turns into").

Proverbs 17:27a–28b: Ellipsis

L.	BHS	Gloss
27a	חוֹשֵׂךְ אֲמָרָיו יוֹדֵעַ דָּעַת	withholding-one/m his-sayings knowing-one-of/m knowledge
27b	וְקַר־רוּחַ אִישׁ תְּבוּנָה׃	w-cool-one-of/m spirit man-of discernment
28a	גַּם אֱוִיל מַחֲרִישׁ חָכָם יֵחָשֵׁב	also foolish-one/m being-silent-one/m wise-one/m he-is-reckoned
28b	אֹטֵם שְׂפָתָיו נָבוֹן׃	shutting-one/m his-lips discerning-one/m

Proverbs 17:27a–28b: Ellipsis

L.	BHS	Semantics		Morphosyntax	
27a	חוֹשֵׂךְ אֲמָרָיו יוֹדֵעַ דָּעַת	a.b.c	4:2.1.1	S[P/v—O]—P/v—O	ms QPtc
27b	וְקַר־רוּחַ אִישׁ תְּבוּנָה׃	$a^1.c^1$	4:2.2	w + S—P/n	ms n
or			4:2.2	w + P/n—S	ms a
28a	גַּם אֱוִיל מַחֲרִישׁ חָכָם יֵחָשֵׁב	$a^2.c^2$.d	5:3.1.1	cj—S—O—P/v	3ms NF
28b	אֹטֵם שְׂפָתָיו נָבוֹן׃	$a^3.c^3$	3:2.1	S[P/v-O]—P/a	ms a
or			3:1.1.1	P/v—O—S	ms QPtc

The syntax of 27a and 28a is straightforward; "Whoever holds back his words knows knowledge" (27a), "Even a silent fool is reckoned wise" (28a). Their second lines, however, lack a predicate: should 27b be supplied with יוֹדֵעַ, "knows," or should this line be read as an equation? In the same way, is יֵחָשֵׁב, "be reckoned," the implicit predicate of 28b, or is this line an equation: "whoever shuts his lips [is] [a] discerning [person]"? Reading the second line of each saying as a nonverbal clause (i.e., as though there were no ellipsis) yields this:

27a	חוֹשֵׂךְ אֲמָרָיו יוֹדֵעַ דָּעַת	Whoever withholds his words knows knowledge
27b	וְקַר־רוּחַ אִישׁ תְּבוּנָה׃	And a quiet spirit [is] a man of discernment
28a	גַּם אֱוִיל מַחֲרִישׁ חָכָם יֵחָשֵׁב	Even a silent fool is reckoned wise
28b	אֹטֵם שְׂפָתָיו נָבוֹן׃	Whoever shuts his lips [is] discerning

Reading them as ellipses, however, yields this:

27a	חוֹשֵׂךְ אֲמָרָיו יוֹדֵעַ דָּעַת	Whoever withholds his words knows knowledge
27b	וְקַר־רוּחַ אִישׁ[יוֹדֵעַ] תְּבוּנָה׃	And a man's quiet spirit [knows] discernment
28a	גַּם אֱוִיל מַחֲרִישׁ חָכָם יֵחָשֵׁב	Even a silent fool is reckoned wise
28b	אֹטֵם שְׂפָתָיו נָבוֹן [יֵחָשֵׁב]׃	Whoever shuts his lips [is reckoned] discerning

Both readings are viable for each line, based on analyzing each as a miniature discourse. Even when read together, there is no clear resolution.[26]

Even an ellipsis that cannot be resolved serves a cohesive function, forcing the attentive reader to consider what the poet intended and thus binding two lines together.

VII. PARTICIPANT TRACKING

As we shall see in Psalm 15 (below), keeping track of participants—"participant tracking"—is a cohesive device that a discourse uses to refer to characters when they are brought onto the "stage," referred to (so that readers know who is doing what at any given point), and removed, all without repeating their names every time they do or say something. It is a cohesive device that applies to both prose[27] and poetry. The same paragraph that introduced semantic cohesion (above) illustrates participant cohesion:

> ***My* sister** has a new sweater. It is red—**her** favorite color. **She** wears it nearly every day, so *I* know that **she** likes it. *I* am not all that fond of

26. This sort of conundrum is not uncommon in biblical poetry, where tradition often dictates how a text is rendered in another language and where even reference works have come to support traditional renderings. Discourse analysis may, but often does not, resolve such ambiguities.

27. Hebrew narrative is often careful to mention the actor or speaker every time, but this also serves a discourse function of indicating the relative rank or importance of two or more persons. See Robert E. Longacre, *Joseph: A Story of Divine Providence: A Text Theoretical and Textlinguistic Analysis of Genesis 37 and 39–48*, 2nd ed. (Winona Lake, IN: Eisenbrauns, 2003).

red, so *I*'ll be relieved when **she** stops wearing it. But *I* love ***my*** **sister**, so *I*'m glad it makes **her** happy.

The pronouns ("her," "she") refer to the same person—the speaker's sister, just as "my" and "I" refer to the speaker. The second occurrence of the phrase "my sister" also serves another function. By using the noun phrase a second time rather than another pronoun, the speaker highlights the sister as a person; to use a discourse term, this raises her "prominence." English stories and poems use pronouns ("I," "her") and synonyms (e.g., "her brother" for "James") to keep track of what the characters are saying or doing. Hebrew uses four main cohesive devices to track participant reference: nouns, apposition, pronouns (including pronominal suffixes), and verbal subject affixes (preformatives and sufformatives), which indicate the subject's person, gender, and number.

Looking at now-familiar Psalm 117, we can create a table that tracks of the characters. As with Psalm 15, we list the characters identified in the poem and use two columns for each, one to describe the function of the reference, and the other to list the Hebrew form.

A. PSALM 117

Psalm 117: Participant Tracking

L.	BHS	Characters			
		"you" (plural)		YHWH	
1a	הַלְלוּ אֶת־יהוה כָּל־גּוֹיִם	vbl. sbj.	2mp	name	יהוה
		noun	כָּל־גּוֹיִם		
1b	שַׁבְּחוּהוּ כָּל־הָאֻמִּים׃	vbl. form	2mp	pr. sfx.	־הוּ
		noun	כָּל־הָאֻמִּים		
2a	כִּי גָבַר עָלֵינוּ חַסְדּוֹ			pr. sfx.	־וֹ
2b	וֶאֱמֶת־יהוה לְעוֹלָם			name	יהוה
2c	הַלְלוּ־יָהּ׃	vbl. form	2mp	name	יָהּ

The poem addresses the first "participant," which here is a group—"All nations" (1a) and "all peoples" (1b); the consistently second-person masculine plural imperatives (1a, 1b, 2c) lead readers to expect that the final verb addresses the same participants. The other participant in this poem, YHWH, is referred to in all five lines, three times by name (1a, 2b, 2c) and twice by pronominal suffix (1b, 2a).[28] Since there is no other third masculine singular referent for the suffixes in 1a–2b, these suffixes must refer to him. The person, gender, and number of the imperatives and the gender and number of the suffixes make this poem a cohesive discourse.[29]

Participants can be "tracked" by pronominal forms, verbal affixes (both subjects and objects). Psalm 15, for example, describes two persons: YHWH and the covenantally faithful. First, lineate and gloss the poem.

B. PSALM 15

Psalm 15:1b–5c: Gloss

L.	BHS	Gloss
1b	יהוה מִי־יָגוּר בְּאָהֳלֶךָ	YHWH who he-sojourns in-your-tent
1c	מִי־יִשְׁכֹּן בְּהַר קָדְשֶׁךָ׃	who he-dwells in-mountain-of your-holiness
2a	הוֹלֵךְ תָּמִים	walking-one/m integrity
2b	וּפֹעֵל צֶדֶק	*w*-working-one/m righteousness
2c	וְדֹבֵר אֱמֶת בִּלְבָבוֹ׃	*w*-speaking-one/m truth in-his-heart
3a	לֹא־רָגַל עַל־לְשֹׁנוֹ	not he-walks (slanders) on his-tongue
3b	לֹא־עָשָׂה לְרֵעֵהוּ רָעָה	not he-does to-his-neighbour evil
3c	וְחֶרְפָּה לֹא־נָשָׂא עַל־קְרֹבוֹ׃	*w*-reproach not-he-carries on his-near-one
4a	נִבְזֶה בְּעֵינָיו נִמְאָס	despised-one/m in-his-eyes rejected-one/m
4b	וְאֶת־יִרְאֵי יהוה יְכַבֵּד	*w*-fearing-ones YHWH he-honours
4c	נִשְׁבַּע לְהָרַע	he-swears to-the-evil
4d	וְלֹא יָמִר׃	*w*-not he-changes
5a	כַּסְפּוֹ לֹא־נָתַן בְּנֶשֶׁךְ	his-silver not he-gives with-interest
5b	וְשֹׁחַד עַל־נָקִי לֹא לָקָח	*w*-bribe on innocent-one not he-takes
5c	עֹשֵׂה־אֵלֶּה לֹא יִמּוֹט לְעוֹלָם׃	doing-one/m these not he-slips for-long-time

28. The nouns חֶסֶד and אֱמֶת are not participants because they do not act—they do not *do* anything.

29. This example demonstrates the problem with reading biblical poems as though the verses were original poetic units. If we read line 2a by itself, the pronominal suffix on the verb (שַׁבְּחוּהוּ) seems to be anomalous—it has no referent until the next line when יהוה is named. If, however, we read line 2a as the third line in a poetic composition, its referent is obvious from the preceding two lines because the suffix in 1b also refers to יהוה.

To create a table of participant references, first identify who is mentioned in the poem, and give each person a column (as always, with the columns in the order in which they are mentioned in the poem). There should be two columns for each participant—one of grammatical information about the kind of reference to the participant (noun, proper name, suffix, verbal conjugation, etc.) and one for the actual Hebrew form.

Psalm 15:1b–5c: Participant Reference

L.	BHS	References to			
		"[one] who"		YHWH	
1b	יהוה מִי־יָגוּר בְּאָהֳלֶךָ	מִי	3ms verbal subject	ךָ-	יהוה
1c	מִי־יִשְׁכֹּן בְּהַר קָדְשֶׁךָ׃	מִי	3ms verbal subject	ךָ-	
2a	הוֹלֵךְ תָּמִים		הוֹלֵךְ; ms Ptc		
2b	וּפֹעֵל צֶדֶק		פֹּעֵל; ms Ptc		
2c	וְדֹבֵר אֱמֶת בִּלְבָבוֹ׃	וֹ-	דֹבֵר; ms Ptc		
3a	לֹא־רָגַל עַל־לְשֹׁנוֹ	וֹ-	רָגַל; 3ms verbal subject		
3b	לֹא־עָשָׂה לְרֵעֵהוּ רָעָה	ֵהוּ-	עָשָׂה; 3ms verbal subject		
3c	וְחֶרְפָּה לֹא־נָשָׂא עַל־קְרֹבוֹ׃	וֹ-	נָשָׂא; 3ms verbal subject		
4a	נִבְזֶה בְּעֵינָיו נִמְאָס	ו-	Ptc as subject (but which?)[30]		
4b	וְאֶת־יִרְאֵי יהוה יְכַבֵּד		יְכַבֵּד; 3ms verbal subject		
4c	נִשְׁבַּע לְהָרַע		נִשְׁבַּע; 3ms verbal subject		
4d	וְלֹא יָמִר׃		יָמִר; 3ms verbal subject		
5a	כַּסְפּוֹ לֹא־נָתַן בְּנֶשֶׁךְ		נָתַן; 3ms verbal subject		
5b	וְשֹׁחַד עַל־נָקִי לֹא לָקָח		לָקָח; 3ms verbal subject		
5c	עֹשֵׂה־אֵלֶּה לֹא יִמּוֹט לְעוֹלָם׃		עֹשֵׂה; ms Ptc		
			יִמּוֹט; 3ms verbal subject		

Tracking the participants in Psalm 15 reveals immediately that the human is its main subject; YHWH is a participant only in 1b–c. The "good"

30. This line illustrates the challenge posed by multiple participles: how to tell which participle is the predicate and which the subject? English readers may assume that the first word is the subject (since English is a subject–verb–object [SVO] language), but this is not legitimate for Hebrew poetry. This line could be read as either "Whoever is despised in his eyes is rejected" or "Whoever is rejected is despised in his eyes." Since this behavior

person is referred to primarily by means of verbal forms, whether masculine singular participles (2a–c, 5c) or third person masculine singular verbal forms (3a–c, 4b–5b); the poem signals its own close with one of each (5c). In 4b YHWH is an object of fear, not a participant. Two other patterns also appear: (1) participles and 3ms verbs occur in clumps rather than being interspersed; and (2) the larger pattern of three participles (2a–c) followed by eight 3ms verbs (3a–c, 4b–5b) is replicated in 5c, in which a participle precedes a 3ms verb. Noting the cohesive devices used in a poem is the final step before asking a basic question of poetic exegesis: how each line relates to the immediately preceding line(s).

C. PROVERBS 6:6–11

The sloth and the ant is the second brief poem in Proverbs 6. It has three subjects: the lazy person, the ant, and the personified lack or "want" that is the sluggard's fate.

Proverbs 6:6a–11b: Gloss

6a	לֵךְ־אֶל־נְמָלָה עָצֵל	you/ms-go! to ant sluggard
6b	רְאֵה דְרָכֶיהָ	you/ms-observe her-ways
6c	וַחֲכָם׃	*w*-you/ms-be[come]-wise!
7	אֲשֶׁר אֵין־לָהּ קָצִין שֹׁטֵר מֹשֵׁל׃	which there-is-no for-her chief officer ruler
8a	תָּכִין בַּקַּיִץ לַחְמָהּ	she-prepares in-the-summer her-bread
8b	אָגְרָה בַקָּצִיר מַאֲכָלָהּ׃	she-gathers in-the-harvest her-food
9a	עַד־מָתַי עָצֵל תִּשְׁכָּב	until when sluggard you-lie-down
9b	מָתַי תָּקוּם מִשְּׁנָתֶךָ׃	when you/ms-rise from-your-sleep
10a	מְעַט שֵׁנוֹת מְעַט תְּנוּמוֹת	little-of sleep, little-of slumbers
10b	מְעַט חִבֻּק יָדַיִם לִשְׁכָּב׃	little-of folding-of hands to-lie-down
11a	וּבָא כִמְהַלֵּךְ רֵאשֶׁךָ	*w*-it-comes like-walking-about-one/m your-poverty
11b	וּמַחְסֹרְךָ כְּאִישׁ מָגֵן׃	*w*-your-need/lack like-man-of shield

characterizes a person who is worthy to be in the Lord's presence, we must assume that both rejection and despite are fitting.

Proverbs 6:6a–11b: Participant Tracking

L.	BHS	"you" (masc. sg.)		"ant"		"want"	
6a	לֵךְ־אֶל־נְמָלָה עָצֵל	vbl. sbj.	2ms	noun	נְמָלָה		
		noun	עָצֵל				
6b	רְאֵה דְרָכֶיהָ	vbl. sbj.	2ms	pr. sfx.	־הָ		
6c	וַחֲכָם׃	vbl. sbj.	2ms				
7	אֲשֶׁר אֵין־לָהּ קָצִין שֹׁטֵר מֹשֵׁל׃			rel.	אֲשֶׁר		
				pr. sfx.	לָהּ		
8a	תָּכִין בַּקַּיִץ לַחְמָהּ			vbl. sbj.	3fs		
				pr. sfx.	־ָהּ		
8b	אָגְרָה בַקָּצִיר מַאֲכָלָהּ׃			vbl. sbj.	3fs		
				pr. sfx.	־ָהּ		
9a	עַד־מָתַי עָצֵל תִּשְׁכָּב	noun	עָצֵל				
		vbl. sbj.	2ms				
9b	מָתַי תָּקוּם מִשְּׁנָתֶךָ׃	vbl. sbj.	2ms				
		pr. sfx.	־ךָ				
10a	מְעַט שֵׁנוֹת מְעַט תְּנוּמוֹת						
10b	מְעַט חִבֻּק יָדַיִם לִשְׁכָּב׃						
11a	וּבָא כִמְהַלֵּךְ רֵאשֶׁךָ	pr. sfx.	־ךָ			noun	רֵאשׁ
11b	וּמַחְסֹרְךָ כְּאִישׁ מָגֵן׃	pr. sfx.	־ךָ			noun	מַחְסֹר

Giving each participant a column shows the poem's progression from the sluggard to the ant and back to the sluggard, whose laziness will impoverish him:

1. Three verbal forms refer back to the vocative in line 6a (עָצֵל, "sluggard"): לֵךְ, "Go!" (6a), רְאֵה, "See!" (6b), וַחֲכָם, "And be wise!" (6c).
2. The feminine singular pronominal suffix in 6b (דְרָכֶיהָ, "her ways") refers back to the ant (נְמָלָה, 6a), which is also the referent of the relative אֲשֶׁר (7).
3. Lines 7–8b describe the ant, using pronominal suffixes—־ָהּ, "her" (7–8b)—and verbal forms—תָּכִין, "she prepares" (8a) and אָגְרָה, "she gathers" (8b).

4. The original noun is repeated in 9a and is referred to with two verbal forms—תִּשְׁכָּב, "you lie down" (9a), תָּקוּם, "you arise" (9b)—and three pronomninal suffixes—ךָ-, "you/your" (9b, 11a–b); the repeated noun resumes the original referent after the interruption of the ant.
5. The third participant is called both "poverty" and "lack" (11a–b). The double reference—the only parallel nouns that refer to the same participant[31]—sets off the closing lines, as does their morphosyntax, which forms an incomplete chiasm: a–b–c–c^1–b^1. The pronominal suffixes ("*your* poverty," "*your* need"), however, show that the עָצֵל remains the subject of the poem.

D. PSALM 121

Pronominal forms are cohesive devices because they refer back to something mentioned earlier in the discourse, providing enough information for readers to apply the pronoun to the correct referent. This enforced recall creates cohesion. Some pronominal references, however, lack a textual referent, such as the second-person suffixes in Psalm 121:

Three references to an unknown "I/my" (1a–2) are followed by ten pronominal references to "you/your," all second-person masculine singular (3a–b, 5a–6a, 7a–8), but the text does not identify anyone to whom these refer, which suggests that the second person is intended to draw readers into the text by addressing them directly.

A second aspect of Psalm 121 is the contrast in participant reference. All human references are pronominal, whereas YHWH is referred to by name (יהוה; 2, 5a–b, 7a, 8), by participle (עֹשֵׂה; 2; שֹׁמֵר; 3b, 4b, 5a), or by verbal form (3a–4b, 7a–8), but never by a pronominal suffix. The rule of thumb in discourse is that a participant's importance is highlighted the more fully it is named or defined, or the greater the number of ways it is referred to or described; this analysis demonstrates that YHWH—not the human subject of the poem—is the central figure in Psalm 121 (cf. Psalm 15, above).

31. This assumes that רֵאשׁ and מַחְסֹר are being used synonymously.

Psalm 121: Participant Tracking

L.	BHS	Human beings		יהוה	
1a	שִׁיר לַמַּעֲלוֹת				
1b	אֶשָּׂא עֵינַי אֶל־הֶהָרִים	vbl. sbj.	1cs		
		pr. sfx.	-ַי		
1c	מֵאַיִן יָבֹא עֶזְרִי׃	pr. sfx.	-ִי		
2	עֶזְרִי מֵעִם יהוה עֹשֵׂה שָׁמַיִם וָאָרֶץ׃	pr. sfx.	-ִי	noun	יהוה
				Ptc.	עֹשֵׂה
3a	אַל־יִתֵּן לַמּוֹט רַגְלֶךָ	pr. sfx.	-ךָ	vbl. sbj.	3ms
3b	אַל־יָנוּם שֹׁמְרֶךָ׃			vbl. sbj.	3ms
		pr. sfx.	-ךָ	Ptc.	יהוה
4a	הִנֵּה לֹא־יָנוּם			vbl. sbj.	3ms
4b	וְלֹא־יִישָׁן שׁוֹמֵר יִשְׂרָאֵל׃			vbl. sbj.	3ms
				Ptc.	שֹׁמֵר
5a	יהוה שֹׁמְרֶךָ	pr. sfx.	-ךָ	noun	יהוה
				Ptc.	שֹׁמֵר
5b	יהוה צִלְּךָ עַל־יַד יְמִינֶךָ	pr. sfx.	-ךָ	noun	יהוה
				noun phrase	צִלְּךָ עַל־יַד יְמִינֶךָ
6a	יוֹמָם הַשֶּׁמֶשׁ לֹא־יַכֶּכָּה	pr. sfx.	-כָּה		
6b	וְיָרֵחַ בַּלָּיְלָה׃				
7a	יהוה יִשְׁמָרְךָ מִכָּל־רָע			noun	יהוה
		pr. sfx.	-ךָ	vbl. sbj.	3ms
7b	יִשְׁמֹר אֶת־נַפְשֶׁךָ׃	pr. sfx.	-ךָ	vbl. sbj.	3ms
8	יהוה יִשְׁמָר־צֵאתְךָ וּבוֹאֶךָ מֵעַתָּה וְעַד־עוֹלָם׃			vbl. sbj.	3ms
		pr. sfx.	-ךָ	noun	יהוה

E. PSALM 13

Psalm 13: Participant Tracking

		Characters					
L.	BHS	יהוה		"I"		enemy	
T	לַמְנַצֵּחַ מִזְמוֹר לְדָוִד׃						
2a	עַד־אָנָה יהוה	noun	יהוה				
2b	תִּשְׁכָּחֵנִי נֶצַח	vbl. sbj.	2ms	pr. sfx.	-ֵנִי		
2c	עַד־אָנָה תַּסְתִּיר אֶת־פָּנֶיךָ מִמֶּנִּי	vbl. sbj.	2ms				
		pr. sfx	-ֶךָ	pr. sfx.	-ֶנִּי		
3a	עַד־אָנָה אָשִׁית עֵצוֹת בְּנַפְשִׁי			vbl. sbj.	1cs		
				pr. sfx.	-ִי		
3b	יָגוֹן בִּלְבָבִי יוֹמָם			pr. sfx.	-ִי		
3c	עַד־אָנָה יָרוּם אֹיְבִי עָלָי׃			pr. sfx.	-ִי	vb. sbj.	3ms
				pr. sfx.	-ִי	noun	אֹיְבִי
4a	הַבִּיטָה	vbl. sbj.	2ms				
4b	עֲנֵנִי יהוה אֱלֹהָי			pr. sfx.	-ֵנִי		
				pr. sfx.	-ָי		
4c	הָאִירָה עֵינַי	vbl. sbj.	1cs	pr. sfx.	-ַי		
4d	פֶּן־אִישַׁן הַמָּוֶת׃			vbl. sbj.	1cs		
5a	פֶּן־יֹאמַר אֹיְבִי					vbl. sbj.	3ms
				pr. sfx.	-ִי	noun	אֹיְבִי
5b	יְכָלְתִּיו			pr. sfx.	-ו	vbl. sbj.	1cs
5c	צָרַי יָגִילוּ			pr. sfx.	-ַי	vbl. sbj.	3mp
5d	כִּי אֶמּוֹט׃			vbl. sbj.	1cs		
6a	וַאֲנִי בְּחַסְדְּךָ בָטַחְתִּי	pr. sfx	-ךָ	pronoun	1cs		
				vbl. sbj.	1cs		
6b	יָגֵל לִבִּי בִּישׁוּעָתֶךָ	pr. sfx	-ךָ	vbl. sbj.	3ms		
				pr. sfx.	-ִי		
6c	אָשִׁירָה לַיהוה	noun	יהוה	vbl. sbj.	1cs		
6d	כִּי גָמַל עָלָי׃	vbl. sbj.	3ms	pr. sfx.	-ָי		

This table shows how prominent the "I" of the poem is. Only two lines (2a, 4a) lack a first-person reference. It also shows the relative scarcity of references to the "enemy" and the difference between 5c and other third-person references: in 5c the enemy is plural (צָרַי); the other references are all singular. YHWH is referred to primarily as a verbal subject (2b, 6c): the first time as the subject of the verb of accusation/lament, the second time as the object of the psalmist's song.

VII. SUMMARY

Discourse requires cohesion in order to communicate. It helps readers keep track of participants, follow the flow of thought through a text, and understand the development of a plot. The biblical poets used various cohesive devices, sometimes in isolation, but far more often in combination. Discourse analysis helps us be sure that we do not overlook what these devices contribute to a poetic discourse.

Chapter 8

Logical Cohesion

A poem's logical cohesion—the flow of its argument or thought—depends on its semantic content line by line. In order to study it, we identify each line in two ways: (1) according to the kind of information that it contains; and (2) according to its relationship to the preceding line.

I. KINDS OF INFORMATION

A line of biblical poetry contains one of four basic kinds of information: (1) a *statement*, which may describe someone or something, complain, offer a reason for doing something, or declare the speaker's intent; (2) a *question*; (3) a *command* or *prohibition*; or (4) a *condition*. This is what Psalm 117 looks like when examined this way:

Psalm 117

L.	BHS	Kind of Information
1a	הַלְלוּ אֶת־יהוה כָּל־גּוֹיִם	command
1b	שַׁבְּחוּהוּ כָּל־הָאֻמִּים׃	command
2a	כִּי גָבַר עָלֵינוּ חַסְדּוֹ	statement: reason
2b	וֶאֱמֶת־יהוה לְעוֹלָם	statement: reason
2c	הַלְלוּ־יָהּ׃	command

The above table shows that the structure of Psalm 117 (which we have examined in some detail already) and its content are mutually reinforcing—its cohesive features *and* the kind of information in each line reveals the same three-part structure.

Identifying each line's kind of information can be a separate step, but it can also be combined with the following.

II. INTERLINEAR RELATIONSHIPS

The final stage of discourse analysis for a biblical poem examines the logical relationship between lines based on what has been discovered to this point. There are two basic relationships between consecutive lines—discontinuity and continuity, which always refer to the relationship of each line to the *preceding* line. These two relationships can be signaled by any of the devices discussed above.

The categories here are exemplary and suggestive rather than final or complete:

1. *Discontinuity*. A line may be a seam, signaling a change in subject or topic and opening a new section of the poem.
2. *Continuity*. A line may have one of at least seven continuous relationships to the preceding line or lines:
    a. *similarity* (it is similar to, or overlaps heavily with it, using synonyms or negated antonyms);
    B. *contrast* (it contrasts with it, using synonyms or negated antonyms);
    c. *example/specificity* (it offers a specific example of the general principle in it);
    d. *temporal* (it explicitly or logically precedes or follows the other);
    e. *cause-effect* (it identifies a cause or effect of what is described);
    f. *motive* (it supplies the motive for obeying a command or prohibition);
    g. *explanation* (it explains its meaning).

As a reminder, here is the full analysis of Psalm 117:

Psalm 117: Full Analysis

L.	BHS	Semantics		Syntax		Predicate
1a	הַלְלוּ אֶת־יהוה כָּל־גּוֹיִם	a.b.c	a.b.c	4:1.1.2	P/v—O—S/voc	2mp DV
1b	שַׁבְּחוּהוּ כָּל־הָאֻמִּים׃	$a^1+b^1.c^1$	$a^1+b^1.c^1$	3:1.2	P/v + O—S/voc	2mp DV
2a	כִּי גָבַר עָלֵינוּ חַסְדּוֹ	a.b.c	d.e.f	4:2.1.1	cj—P/v—pp—S	3ms QP
2b	וֶאֱמֶת־יהוה לְעוֹלָם	$c^1.a^1$	$f^1.d^1$	3:2.1	w + S—P/pp	pp
2c	הַלְלוּ־יָהּ׃	a.b	a.b	2:1.1	P/v—O	2mp DV

1. In every way—semantically, syntactically, morphologically—1b is continuous with 1a:
   a. the two lines form a single statement;
   b. the suffix in 1b creates the slightly shorter line without leaving out any syntactical or semantic information. On the contrary, the suffix is a cohesive device that links 1b to 1a since the reader must decide that "him" (1b) refers to YHWH (1a).
   c. These lines form a single unit to the extent that to read them separately would be to misread them.
2. In the same way—semantically and syntactically—2b is continuous with 2a but tied to it by the ellipsis of its predicate, which makes us pause (however briefly) in order to supply either "is," "endures/lasts," or "is strong/mighty." Their chiastic form and the close identity of "his *hesed*" (2a) and "YHWH's faithfulness" (2b), which is reinforced by their immediate juxtaposition at the center of the chiasm, shows that these lines are as much a single unit as 1a–b.
3. Further, the pattern of line lengths (four words followed by three) establishes 1a–b and 2a–b as major sections in this psalm.
4. The pronominal suffix in 2a ("his *hesed*") refers back to "YHWH" (1a) via the pronominal suffix—the verbal object—in 1b, so that we read these two sections as halves of a larger unit (1a–2b), which is reinforced because the "YHWH" of 2b forms a chiasm with the "YHWH" of 1a: "YHWH . . . "him" . . . "his" . . . "YHWH" (a–b–b–a).
5. By reiterating the opening command (הַלְלוּ, "praise!") but using a different form of the divine name ("YH" rather than "YHWH"), 2c rounds out the poem, closes it by returning to its beginning, and invites us to ask why the command is repeated, especially in light of the compression that characterizes poetry.
6. The poetic "seams" or "joints"—indicated by dotted lines—fall between 1b and 2a and between 2b and 2c, as we have seen above; analyzing the relationship of the content shows that both sets of continuous lines are in a relationship of similarity:

Psalm 117: Interlinear Relationships

L.	BHS	Basic Relationship to Preceding Line
1a	הַלְלוּ אֶת־יהוה כָּל־גּוֹיִם	
1b	שַׁבְּחוּהוּ כָּל־הָאֻמִּים׃	continuous
2a	כִּי גָבַר עָלֵינוּ חַסְדּוֹ	discontinuous
2b	וֶאֱמֶת־יהוה לְעוֹלָם	continuous
2c	הַלְלוּ יָהּ	discontinuous

To reinforce the point, the following table combines both diagrams, again showing the interplay of content and form:

Psalm 117: Kinds of Information and Interlinear Relationships

L.	BHS	Kinds of Information	Interlinear Relationships
1a	הַלְלוּ אֶת־יהוה כָּל־גּוֹיִם	command	
1b	שַׁבְּחוּהוּ כָּל־הָאֻמִּים׃	command	continuous: similarity
2a	כִּי גָבַר עָלֵינוּ חַסְדּוֹ	statement: reason	discontinuous
2b	וֶאֱמֶת־יהוה לְעוֹלָם	statement: reason	continuous: similarity
2c	הַלְלוּ יָהּ׃	command	discontinuous

III. CLOSE READINGS

This final section consists of a close reading of three passages in order to demonstrate the kind of information uncovered by discourse analysis. Studying these passages on your own, noting continuities, patterns, etc., before reading the descriptions, will be a good test of what you have been learning.

A. PSALM 103:1–2

The opening lines of Psalm 103 exhibit many of the devices noted above, which both bind these lines together as a unit and set them off somewhat from what follows:

Psalm 103:1a–2b: Gloss

L.	BHS	Gloss
1a	בָּרֲכִי נַפְשִׁי אֶת־יהוה	you/fs-bless! my-soul YHWH
1b	וְכָל־קְרָבַי אֶת־שֵׁם קָדְשׁוֹ׃	*w*-all-of my-inward-parts name-of his-holiness
2a	בָּרֲכִי נַפְשִׁי אֶת־יהוה	you/fs-bless! my-soul YHWH
2b	וְאַל־תִּשְׁכְּחִי כָּל־גְּמוּלָיו׃	*w*-not you/fs-forget all-of his-benefits

Psalm 103:1a–2b: Kinds of Information & Interlinear Relationships

L.	BHS	Semantics		Morphosyntax	
1a	בָּרֲכִי נַפְשִׁי אֶת־יהוה	a.b.c	3:1.1.1	P/v—S—O	2fs DV
1b	וְכָל־קְרָבַי אֶת־שֵׁם קָדְשׁוֹ׃	b'.c'	4:2.2	w + S—O	
2a	בָּרֲכִי נַפְשִׁי אֶת־יהוה	a.b.c	3:1.1.1	P/v—S—O	2fs DV
2b	וְאַל־תִּשְׁכְּחִי כָּל־גְּמוּלָיו׃	a'.d	4:2.2	w + adv—P/v—O	2fs QF

The cohesive devices in Psalm 103:1–2 both bind these lines together as a unit and set them off from what follows. Consider all of the following elements:

1. alternating *line length* (3–4–3–4 words, as in Ps 117:1a–2b) both binds these lines together and separates them from the next six lines, each of which consists of three words (3a–5b);
2. *ellipsis* of the predicate links 1b to 1a;
3. exact *repetition* (בָּרֲכִי נַפְשִׁי) links 2a to 1a;
4. participant tracking:
   a. *pronominal suffixes* (3ms suffixes referring to YHWH (קָדְשׁוֹ, גְּמוּלָיו) link 1b and 2b to 1a and 2a, and 1cs suffixes referring to the psalmist (כָּל־קְרָבַי, נַפְשִׁי) link 2a to 1b to 1a);
   b. *predicate morphology* (the 2fs verbs with the subject נַפְשִׁי [תִּשְׁכְּחִי, בָּרֲכִי], linking 2b to 2a to 1a);
   c. participant tracking separates these lines from the following, five of which have a participial subject/predicate (e.g., הַסֹּלֵחַ, "the one who forgives . . ." [3a; cf. 3b–5a]), a form not used in 1a–2b.

5. More to the point is the *continuity* created by the *contrast* of negating the verbal predicate in 2b (וְאַל־תִּשְׁכְּחִי) so that "do not forget" parallels "bless." Forgetting may not be the opposite of blessing, but remembering is necessary to it—we cannot bless what we have forgotten. Negating an antonym in one line to create a parallel to a "synonym" in another is not uncommon in biblical poems.

Finally, consider a table that summarizes this use of negation to create the oxymoron of a contrasting contininty in these lines.

Psalm 103:1a–2b: Kinds of Information & Interlineaer Relationships

L.	BHS	Kinds of Information	Relationship to Preceding Line
1a	בָּרֲכִי נַפְשִׁי אֶת־יהוה	command	
1b	וְכָל־קְרָבַי אֶת־שֵׁם קָדְשׁוֹ׃	[command]	continuous: similarity
2a	בָּרֲכִי נַפְשִׁי אֶת־יהוה	command	continuous: similarity
2b	וְאַל־תִּשְׁכְּחִי כָּל־גְּמוּלָיו׃	(neg.) command	continuous: contrast

The kind of information contained in the opening lines of Psalm 103 also distinguishes them from verses 3a–5a, all five of which describe YHWH—and there are no commands or prohibitions.

B. PSALM 119:25–28

Psalm 119:25–28: Full Analysis

L.	BHS	Semantics		Morphosyntax	
25a	דָּבְקָה לֶעָפָר נַפְשִׁי	a.b.c	3:1.1.1	P/v—pp—S	3fs QP
25b	חַיֵּנִי כִּדְבָרֶךָ׃	d.e	2:1.1	P/v + O—pp	2ms DV
26a	דְּרָכַי סִפַּרְתִּי	f.g	2:1.1	O—P/v	1cs DP
26b	וַתַּעֲנֵנִי	d¹+c¹	1:1	w + P/v + O	2ms QPr
26c	לַמְּדֵנִי חֻקֶּיךָ׃	d².e¹	2:1.1	P/v + O—O	2ms DV
27a	דֶּרֶךְ־פִּקּוּדֶיךָ הֲבִינֵנִי	e².d³	3:2.1	O—P/v + O	2ms HV
27b	וְאָשִׂיחָה בְּנִפְלְאוֹתֶיךָ׃	g¹.e³	2:1.1	w + P/v—pp	1cs QC
28a	דָּלְפָה נַפְשִׁי מִתּוּגָה	a¹.c.b¹	3:1.1.1	P/v—S—pp	3fs QP
28b	קַיְּמֵנִי כִּדְבָרֶךָ׃	d¹.e¹	2:1.1	P/v + O—pp	2ms DV

The nine lines of Psalm 119 analyzed above and below are structured by the following cohesive devices:

1. *semantic* references;
2. *line length* (none is more than three words long; 29a has four words);
3. *predicate morphology*: both 25a and 28a begin with 3fs *qatal* in *qal* (דָּבְקָה, דָּלְפָה) followed by 2ms *piel* imperative with a 1cs suffix in the next line (חַיֵּנִי, קַיְּמֵנִי) (25b, 28b); neither of these morphologies occurs in the rest of these verses, apart from the middle line of this section (26c), which also has a 2ms *piel* imperative;
4. Lines 25a and 28a have the same subject (נַפְשִׁי);
5. Lines 25b and 28b end with the same prepositional phrase (כִּדְבָרֶךָ);
6. Lines 25b and 28b parallel the semantics and morphology ([3] above) of the middle line ($d^2.e^1$; 26c).
7. Lines 25a-b and 28a-b form a complex semantic, syntactical, and morphological *inclusio* that suggests that these lines are not randomly concatenated but comprise a carefully composed poetic unit within the larger stanza and the entire poem.
8. When we look at these lines in terms of their kinds of information and their interlinear relationships, we find something even more interesting:

Psalm 119:25–28: Kinds of Information & Interlinear Relationships

L.	BHS	Kinds of Information	Relationship to Preceding Line
25a	דָּבְקָה לֶעָפָר נַפְשִׁי	statement: description	
25b	חַיֵּנִי כִּדְבָרֶךָ׃	command	continuous: telic:[1] response
26a	דְּרָכַי סִפַּרְתִּי	statement: description	discontinuous
26b	וַתַּעֲנֵנִי	statement: description	continuous: progress: response

(cont.)

1. The term "telic" (from Greek *telos*, "end, goal") means that a statement shows purpose, gola, or result.

L.	BHS	Kinds of Information	Relationship to Preceding Line
26c	לַמְּדֵנִי חֻקֶּיךָ׃	command	discontinuous
27a	דֶּרֶךְ־פִּקּוּדֶיךָ הֲבִינֵנִי	command	continuous: similar
27b	וְאָשִׂיחָה בְּנִפְלְאוֹתֶיךָ׃	statement: intent	continuous: progress: response
28a	דָּלְפָה נַפְשִׁי מִתּוּגָה	statement: description	discontinuous
28b	קַיְּמֵנִי כִּדְבָרֶךָ׃	command	continuous: telic: response

Describing how each line is related to the preceding line reveals that these lines are even more complex:

1. Unless 25b is read as a response to 25a ("[Therefore] give me life . . ."), it is not connected to the rest of the poem;
2. Line 26a relates primarily to the following lines rather than to 25b;
3. In order to read line 26b as continuous with 26a, it must describe the response to "I recounted my ways" (26a): "I did A, [so] you did B";
4. Line 26c is again discontinuous but closely paralleled by 27a, perhaps implying a causal relationship between "teach me" (לַמְּדֵנִי) and "make me understand" (הֲבִינֵנִי).

Lines 28a–b, as described above, are almost identical to 25a–b, apart from their vocabulary, 28a being another discontinuous line that is followed by an implicit response: "[Therefore], raise me up . . .", and rounding off this unit within the stanza.

C. PROVERBS 6:6–11

Proverbs 6:6–11 offers another brief poem that shows a variety of interlinear relationships. Lineate and gloss these lines.

Proverbs 6:6a–11b: Gloss

L.	BHS	Gloss
6a	לֵךְ־אֶל־נְמָלָה עָצֵל	go/ms! unto ant lazy-one/m
6b	רְאֵה דְרָכֶיהָ	see/ms! her-way
6c	וַחֲכָם׃	w-be-wise/ms!
7	אֲשֶׁר אֵין־לָהּ קָצִין שֹׁטֵר וּמֹשֵׁל׃	which there-is-not to-her chief official ruling-one/m
8a	תָּכִין בַּקַּיִץ לַחְמָהּ	she-prepares in-the-summer her-bread
8b	אָגְרָה בַקָּצִיר מַאֲכָלָהּ׃	she-gathered in-harvest-time her-food
9a	עַד־מָתַי עָצֵל תִּשְׁכָּב	until when? lazy-one/m you/ms-lie-down
9b	מָתַי תָּקוּם מִשְּׁנָתֶךָ׃	when? you/ms-stand from-your/ms-sleep
10a	מְעַט שֵׁנוֹת מְעַט תְּנוּמוֹת	little-of sleep little-of drowsing
10b	מְעַט חִבֻּק יָדַיִם לִשְׁכָּב׃	little-of clasping-of hands to-lie-down
11a	וּבָא כִמְהַלֵּךְ רֵאשֶׁךָ	w-coming-one/m like-walking-about-one/m your/ms-poverty
11b	וּמַחְסֹרְךָ כְּאִישׁ מָגֵן׃	w-your/ms-lack like-man-of shield

And then a full analysis of this poem shows a number of interesting features, which I encourage you to work through and study.

Proverbs 6:6–11: Full Analysis

L.	BHS	Semantics		Morphosyntax	
6a	לֵךְ־אֶל־נְמָלָה עָצֵל	a.b.c	4:1.2.1	P/v—pp—S/voc	2ms QV
6b	רְאֵה דְרָכֶיהָ	$a^1.b^1$	2:1.1	P/v—O	2ms QV
6c	וַחֲכָם׃	d	1:1	w + P/v	2ms QV
7	אֲשֶׁר אֵין־לָהּ קָצִין שֹׁטֵר וּמֹשֵׁל׃	$a.b.c.c^1.c^2$	6:2.1.1.1.1	rel-P/q—pp—Ox3	qv
8a	תָּכִין בַּקַּיִץ לַחְמָהּ	a.b.c	3:1.1.1	P/v—pp—O	3fs QF
8b	אָגְרָה בַקָּצִיר מַאֲכָלָהּ׃	$a^1.b^1.c^1$	3:1.1.1	P/v—pp—O	3fs QP
9a	עַד־מָתַי עָצֵל תִּשְׁכָּב	a.b.c	4:2.1.1	pp—S/voc—P/v	2ms QF
9b	מָתַי תָּקוּם מִשְּׁנָתֶךָ׃	$a^1.c^1.d$	3:1.1.1	adv—P/v—pp	2ms QF

(cont.)

L.	BHS	Semantics		Morphosyntax	
10a	מְעַט שֵׁנוֹת מְעַט תְּנוּמוֹת	$d^1.d^2$	4:2.2	S—P/n	s n
	or			P/n—S	
10b	מְעַט חִבֻּק יָדַיִם לִשְׁכָּב׃	d^3	4:4	adv—P/v	QNC
	or (reading both lines together)				
10	מְעַט שֵׁנוֹת מְעַט תְּנוּמוֹת מְעַט חִבֻּק יָדַיִם לִשְׁכָּב׃	$d^1.d^2.d^3$	8:2.2.4	S—P/n—P/n—P/v	QNC
11a	וּבָא כִמְהַלֵּךְ רֵאשֶׁךָ	a.b.c	3:1.1.1	w + P/v—pp—S	3ms QP
11b	וּמַחְסֹרְךָ כְּאִישׁ מָגֵן׃	$c^1.b^1$	3:1.2	w + S—pp	

Proverbs 6:6a–11b: Kinds of Information & Interlinear Relationships

L.	BHS	Kinds of Information	Interlinear Relationship
6a	לֵךְ־אֶל־נְמָלָה עָצֵל	command	
6b	רְאֵה דְרָכֶיהָ	command	cont.: similarity: progress
6c	וַחֲכָם׃	command	cont.: similarity: progress
7	אֲשֶׁר אֵין־לָהּ קָצִין שֹׁטֵר מֹשֵׁל׃	statement: description	cont.: (6a)
8a	תָּכִין בַּקַּיִץ לַחְמָהּ	statement: description	cont.: contrary-to-expectation
8b	אָגְרָה בַקָּצִיר מַאֲכָלָהּ׃	statement: description	cont.: similarity
9a	עַד־מָתַי עָצֵל תִּשְׁכָּב	question	discontinuous
9b	מָתַי תָּקוּם מִשְּׁנָתֶךָ׃	question	cont.: similarity
10a	מְעַט שֵׁנוֹת מְעַט תְּנוּמוֹת	statement: description	cont.: specificity
10b	מְעַט חִבֻּק יָדַיִם לִשְׁכָּב׃	statement: description	cont.: similarity
11a	וּבָא כִמְהַלֵּךְ רֵאשֶׁךָ	statement: description	cont.: result
11b	וּמַחְסֹרְךָ כְּאִישׁ מָגֵן׃	statement: description	cont.: similarity

Lines 6a–c describe a logical and chronological progress: "Go! . . . See! . . . Become wise!" The action prescribed by each line depends on having done what the preceding line commands: in order to become

wise (6c), the sluggard must study an ant (6b); in order to study an ant, he must find one (6a). The relative אֲשֶׁר in verse 7 refers back to נְמָלָה (6a), and 7 is the longest line in the poem and ends its first section; the next three lines make the point of the illustration (7–8b).[2] Its length highlights the preceding one-word line "Be wise!" (6c), which is (as we might expect in Proverbs) its basic message.

IV. SUMMARY

The ways in which the poet created logical cohesion are discovered by describing the kind of information in each line and the relationship of each line to the preceding, whether discontinuity or continuity in its various forms. This analysis is both anticipated and made possible by describing the poem's semantic cohesion (above). Its primary function is to help us think through the poem step by step, line by line, following the poet's train of thought, which is the goal of exegesis: understanding in order to help others understand.

2. See the further discussion of this poem under "Participant Tracking" (above).

Chapter 9

Conclusion

Answering the questions outlined above—listing nouns and verbs; parsing verbs; glossing the text; determining the length (number of words) and structure (syntax) of each line; analyzing the morphology of predicates; describing the type of each clause and its syntax; and looking for semantic cohesion (semantic analysis, chiasms, ellipses, participant tracking) and logical cohesion (kinds of information and interlinear relationships)—is a lot of work. But it reveals information that would have been obvious to the original readers of biblical poetry—as obvious as changes of mood or tense to native speakers of English when reading poems by William Shakespeare or Robert Frost.

As the process of analyzing biblical poetic discourse demonstrates, the biblical poets crafted their poems with as much care as William Butler Yeats, who revised "The Sorrow of Love" for more than thirty years before he was satisifed. Works written with such attention to detail deserve to be read as carefully as they were composed; noting and enjoying their artistry is an aspect of understanding them, just as ignoring it means that we fail to read them as their composers intended. And recognizing and appreciating—delighting in—the craft and skill entailed in composing any poem is a fitting and proper response to this "other use of language."

Discourse analysis compels us to be attentive, offering us tools to see what is there in the texts that the poets composed by viewing the text from different standpoints. Lineating the text and analyzing the syntax and semantics of each line help us consider what is going on in each line and how it relates to the preceding line(s). Setting out the predicate morphology in an orderly way shows whether or not (and how) a poet used morphology to reinforce a poem's semantic structure.

At the same time, the questions are not magic, nor are they all equally revealing for every poem. Nor are tables and charts the goal—all of these things are merely tools. Used well, they help us outline and describe the poem, but they will not tell us how we should teach or preach or explain it—that is not the purpose of discourse analysis. It does, however, help us see how the poet used his or her linguistic resources and encourages us to think through what the poem says and how it expresses it. And that, after all, *is* the goal.

I. FINALLY: BACK TO PSALM 117

What has all of this work done for our understanding of Psalm 117? First, it reveals how the stems and conjugations of the verbs, the length and structure of the lines, and the vocabulary reinforce the content—all three systems of the language (lexicon, grammar, and syntax) and poetic discourse (i.e., parallelism) together create and reinforce the poem's structure and flow. This interplay allows us to say with a great deal of certainty that Psalm 117 was written as a deliberately three-part poem, with its reason for praise (2a–b) sandwiched between two calls to praise (1a–b, 2c)—that structure is embedded in the nuts and bolts of the poem's language.

And now the effect of the structure becomes more clear. The initial call to praise YHWH lacks context. To paraphrase Pharaoh's response to Moses and Aaron, upon hearing lines 1a–b we might ask "'Who is YHWH" that I should' praise him?" (cf. Exod 5:2). The central section of Psalm 117 explains why its opening summons should be obeyed (2a–b) and thus affects the meaning of 2c, which does not therefore say the same thing as 1a, despite their close parallelism (הַלְלוּ אֶת־יהוה / הַלְלוּ־יָהּ; a.b/a.b^1). Because 2c follows the reasons for praise, it has been provided with a motivation (unlike 1a–b)—we know not only what is being demanded, but why. Examining other psalms of praise, we see that this is normal for biblical worship, which never calls for God to be praised simply because he exists but rather offers reasons, which are either his attributes (as in Psalm 117) or his deeds (as in Psalm 103).

The structure of Psalm 117, including its *inclusio,* is visible even in translation. What is lost in translation, however, is the confluence of factors that make this brief text poetic. Seeing these is the gift of discourse analysis.

— *Chapter 10* —

Examples of Discourse Analysis with Hebrew Poetry

EXAMPLE A: PSALM 13

Below is a full analysis of Psalm 13, including suggested seams between sections. Use this information to determine what sorts of cohesive devices the poem uses to create these seams and whether or not they are valid.

Psalm 13: Full Analysis

L.	BHS	Semantics		Morphosyntax	
T	לַמְנַצֵּחַ מִזְמוֹר לְדָוִד׃	title			
2a	עַד־אָנָה יהוה	a.b.c	3:2.1	pp—S/voc	
2b	תִּשְׁכָּחֵנִי נֶצַח	$d.a^{1}$	2:1.1	P/v + O—adv	2ms QF
2c	עַד־אָנָה תַּסְתִּיר אֶת־פָּנֶיךָ מִמֶּנִּי	$a.c^{1}.d^{1}$	5:2.1.1.1	pp—P/v—O—pp	2ms HF
3a	עַד־אָנָה אָשִׁית עֵצוֹת בְּנַפְשִׁי	$a.e.f.d^{2}$	5:2.1.1.1	pp—P/v—O—pp	1cs QF
3b?	יָגוֹן בִּלְבָבִי יוֹמָם	$f^{1}.d^{3}.a^{2}$	3:1.1.1	O—pp—adv	
3c	עַד־אָנָה יָרוּם אֹיְבִי עָלָי׃	$a.g.h.d^{4}$	5:2.1.1.1	pp—P/v—S—pp	3ms QF
4a	הַבִּיטָה	a	1:1	P/v	2ms HV
4b	עֲנֵנִי יהוה אֱלֹהָי	$a^{1}.b$	1:1.2	P/v + O—S	2ms QV
4c	הָאִירָה עֵינַי	$a^{2}.c$	2:1.1	P/v—O	2ms HV
4d	פֶּן־אִישַׁן הַמָּוֶת׃	d.e	3:2.1	cj—P/v—O?/adv?	1cs QF

L.	BHS	Semantics		Morphosyntax	
5a	פֶּן־יֹאמַר אֹיְבִי	f.g	3:2.1	cj—P/v—S	3ms QF
5b	יְכָלְתִּיו	h	1:1	"P/v + O"	"1cs QP"
5c	צָרַי יָגִילוּ	$g^1.h^1$	2:1.1	S—P/v	3mp QF
5d	כִּי אֶמּוֹט׃	d^1	2:2	cj—P/v	1cs NF
6a	וַאֲנִי בְּחַסְדְּךָ בָטַחְתִּי	a.b.c	3:1.1.1	w + S—pp—P/v	1cs QP
6b	יָגֵל לִבִּי בִּישׁוּעָתֶךָ	$c^1.a^1.b^1$	3:1.1.1	P/v—S—pp	3ms QJ
6c	אָשִׁירָה ליהוה	$c^2.b^2$	2:2	P/v—pp	1cs QC
6d	כִּי גָמַל עָלָי׃	$d.b^2$	3:2.1	cj—P/v—pp	3ms QP

Psalm 13: Predicate Morphology

L.	BHS	Person	Gender	Number	Stem	Conjugation
2a						
2b	תְּשְׁכָּחֵנִי	2	m	s	Q	F
2c	תַּסְתִּיר	2	m	s	H	F
3a	אָשִׁית	1	c	s	Q	F
3b?						
3c	יָרוּם	3	m	s	Q	F
4a	הַבִּיטָה	2	m	s	H	V
4b	עֲנֵנִי	2	m	s	Q	V
4c	הָאִירָה	2	m	s	H	V
4d	אִישַׁן	1	c	s	Q	F
5a	יֹאמַר	3	m	s	Q	F
5b	יְכָלְתִּיו	1	c	s	Q	P
5c	יָגִילוּ	3	m	p	Q	V
5d	אֶמּוֹט	1	c	s	N	V
6a	בָטַחְתִּי	1	c	s	Q	P
6b	יָגֵל	3	m	s	Q	J
6c	אָשִׁירָה	1	c	s	Q	C
6d	גָמַל	3	m	s	Q	P

Psalm 13: Kinds of Information & Interlinear Relationships

L.	BHS	Kinds of Information		Relationship to Preceding Line
T	לַמְנַצֵּחַ מִזְמוֹר לְדָוִד׃			
2a	עַד־אָנָה יהוה	question		
2b	תִּשְׁכָּחֵנִי נֶצַח	question		cont.: similar
2c	עַד־אָנָה תַּסְתִּיר אֶת־פָּנֶיךָ מִמֶּנִּי	question		cont.: similar
3a	עַד־אָנָה אָשִׁית עֵצוֹת בְּנַפְשִׁי	question		cont.: similar
3b?	יָגוֹן בִּלְבָבִי יוֹמָם	question		cont.: similar
3c	עַד־אָנָה יָרוּם אֹיְבִי עָלָי׃	question		cont.: similar
4a	הַבִּיטָה	command		discontinuous
4b	עֲנֵנִי יהוה אֱלֹהָי	command		cont.: similar
4c	הָאִירָה עֵינַי	command		cont.: similar
4d	פֶּן־אִישַׁן הַמָּוֶת׃		statement: telic	discontinuous
5a	פֶּן־יֹאמַר אֹיְבִי		statement: telic	cont.: temporal progress
5b	יְכָלְתִּיו	reason	statement	cont.:
5c	צָרַי יָגִילוּ		statement	cont.: similar (5a)
5d	כִּי אֶמּוֹט׃		statement: reason	cont.: similar (5b)
6a	וַאֲנִי בְּחַסְדְּךָ בָטַחְתִּי	statement (reason?)		discontinuous
6b	יָגֵל לִבִּי בִּישׁוּעָתֶךָ	statement: intent		cont.: result
6c	אָשִׁירָה לַיהוה	statement: intent		cont.: similar
6d	כִּי גָמַל עָלָי׃	statement: reason		discontinuous

EXAMPLE B: PROVERBS 15:31–33

Syntactic analysis is not always easy—when, for example, a line uses participles for both subject and predicate, and we have to allow possibility that it can be read in more than one way. Proverbs 15:32a–b, for example, has so many possible readings that the result is nearly impenetrably complex. Lineate and gloss these lines before going further.

Proverbs 15:31–33: Gloss

L.	BHQ	Gloss
31a	אֹזֶן שֹׁמַעַת תּוֹכַחַת חַיִּים	ear hearing-one rebuke-of life
31b	בְּקֶרֶב חֲכָמִים תָּלִין׃	in-midst-of wise-ones it-lodges
32a	פּוֹרֵעַ מוּסָר מוֹאֵס נַפְשׁוֹ	neglecting-one discipline rejecting-one his-soul
32b	וְשׁוֹמֵעַ תּוֹכַחַת קוֹנֶה לֵּב׃	*w*-hearing-one rebuke acquiring-one heart
33a	יִרְאַת יהוה מוּסַר חָכְמָה	fear-of YHWH discipline-of wisdom
33b	וְלִפְנֵי כָבוֹד עֲנָוָה׃	*w*-before glory humility/affliction

This full analysis simplifies the synactical questions, but we can spell them out in much more detail as in the following table:

Proverbs 15:31a–33b: Full Analysis

L.	BHQ	Semantics		Morphosyntax[1]	
31a	אֹזֶן שֹׁמַעַת תּוֹכַחַת חַיִּים	a.b.c	4:1.1.2	S—P/v—O	fs QPtc
31b	בְּקֶרֶב חֲכָמִים תָּלִין׃	d.e	3:2.1	pp—P/v	3fs QF
32a	פּוֹרֵעַ מוּסָר מוֹאֵס נַפְשׁוֹ	$b^1.c^1$.d.e	4:1.1.1.1	S[S&P/Ptc—O]—P/v—O	ms QPtc
32b	וְשׁוֹמֵעַ תּוֹכַחַת קוֹנֶה לֵּב׃	$a^2.c^1.f.c^2$		w + S[S&P/Ptc—O]—P/v—O	
33a	יִרְאַת יהוה מוּסַר חָכְמָה	a.b	4:2.2	S—P/n	ms n
33b	וְלִפְנֵי כָבוֹד עֲנָוָה׃	$b^1.a^1$	3:2.1	w + P/pp—S	pp

Because some of its lines are highly problematic, this table offers a number of possible renderings (translations in "good" English).

Proverbs 15:31–33: Syntactical Possibilities

L.	BHQ	Valid Syntax[1]	Resultant Gloss
31a	אֹזֶן שֹׁמַעַת תּוֹכַחַת חַיִּים	S—P/v—O	An ear that hears a life-giving rebuke
31b	בְּקֶרֶב חֲכָמִים תָּלִין׃	pp—P/v	lodges among the wise.
32a	פּוֹרֵעַ מוּסָר מוֹאֵס נַפְשׁוֹ	S[S&P/Ptc—O]—P/v—O	Whoever neglects discipline despises his [own] soul
or		S[S&P/Ptc—O]—P/n[S&P/Ptc—O]	Whoever neglects discipline is one who despises . . .
or		P/v—O—S[S&P/Ptc—O]	Whoever despises his [own] soul neglects discipline
or		P/n[S&P/Ptc—O]—S[S&P/Ptc—O]	Whoever despises his [own] soul neglects . . .
32b	וְשׁוֹמֵעַ תּוֹכַחַת קוֹנֶה לֵּב׃	w + S[S&P/Ptc—O]—P/v—O	but whoever listens to rebuke acquires a heart
or		w + S[S&P/Ptc—O]—P/n[S&P/Ptc—O]	but whoever listens to rebuke is one who acquires . . .
or		w + P/v—O—S[S&P/Ptc—O]	but whoever acquires a heart listens to rebuke
or		w + P/n[S&P/Ptc—O]—S[S&P/Ptc—O]	but whoever acquires a heart is one who listens . . .
33a	יִרְאַת יהוה מוּסַר חָכְמָה	S—P/n	The fear of YHWH is the discipline that leads to wisdom
or		P/n—S	The discipline that leads to wisdom is the fear of YHWH
33b	וְלִפְנֵי כָבוֹד עֲנָוָה׃	w + pp—S	And before honor [is] humility.

The syntax of lines 15:32a–b is highly ambiguous; either participle could be subject/topic or comment/predicate; either or both could be substantive or predicate. Does line 32a mean that despising one's own soul leads to neglecting discipline, or does the act of neglecting discipline lead one to despise one's own soul? Or does the line equate the two, so that to despise one's soul is to neglect discipline without implying the

1. The sign "&" means that a participle is functioning as the subject of a larger clause but also as both subject and predicate of its own sub-clause. This is common in biblical poetry.

logical or chronological priority of either, because doing either entails doing both. Does listening to a rebuke (32b) lead to acquiring a heart, or does one need to acquire a heart in order to (truly/genuinely/profitably) hear rebuke, or does this saying also equate two apparently different actions?

In the same way, the nominal clause of 15:33a is ambiguous—is "the fear of YHWH" the subject and the "discipline of wisdom" a predicate nominative, or vice versa, or are they equated ("fear . . . is discipline")? Is "discipline of wisdom" a subjective or objective construct chain, i.e., does it refer to the discipline that comes from wisdom (subjective) or discipline that leads to wisdom (objective)?

The differences are subtle, but real. More to the point, this complexity, which reflects the lines' participial subjects and predicates, sets these lines apart from the straightforward preceding and following (despite the simple alternatives suggested by 15:33a) verses.

In cases like these, English speakers tend to assume that the first substantive is the subject and the second is the predicate, since Subject-Verb-Object (SVO) is normal word order in English, but the patterns of Hebrew and English differ so widely that both readings need to be tested in order to see if one seems more sensible than the other, or if—when multiple readings are valid—the line should be interpreted as deliberately vague or ambiguous.

Appendix 1

The Question of Meter

The idea that there is meter in biblical poetry comes from a syllogism:

Major premise:	classical poetry was metrical
Minor premise:	classical poetry was the highest human poetic achievement
Minor premise:	biblical poems are divinely inspired and therefore the best poetry
Conclusion:	biblical poetry must be metrical

As Gerstenberger says:

> The modern urge to investigate questions of meter and rhythm in Hebrew poetry seems to derive less from the Hebrew scriptures themselves than from our classical forebears. After all, if the Greeks and the Romans knew and used a quantifying and accentuating verse melody, why should the Hebrews not have employed it also?[1]

This conviction has led to many competing attempts to discover and define meter in biblical poetry by, for example, counting the syllables in each line. Gray counted accented (stressed) syllables, Cross and Freedman counted every syllable, and Christensen counted mora. Both forms have some problems. Cross and Freedman count syllables but are undecided whether or not to count half-syllables (syllables with half-vowels). They also base their syllable counts on the "original" form of the text,

1. Erhard S. Gerstenberger, "The Lyrical Literature," in *The Hebrew Bible and Its Modern Interpreters*, ed. Douglas A. Knight and Gene M. Tucker; *The Bible and Its Modern Interpreters*, ed. Douglas A. Knight, 1 (Chico, CA: Scholars Press, 1985), 412–13.

which they reconstruct according to their theory of the development of Hebrew language and orthography.

Gray's approach has dominated studies of biblical poetry and has led critics to emend the text rather freely due to metrical considerations. We do not know what, if anything, the Israelites thought about meter; this is never a legitimate aspect of textual criticism or interpretation.[2]

For example, the poetic portions of *Biblia Hebraica* (*BHK*3) scarcely lacks a page in which one or more words are emended "*m cs*" (*metra causa* = "because of meter"); H. Bardtke, who edited the Psalter in *Biblia Hebraica Stuttgartensia* (BHS), was more conservative but frequently recommends revising the text "*m cs*" (e.g., Ps 4:9[a] "*dl m cs*" = "delete because of meter").[3]

The emerging consensus, however, is that ". . . recent research has concluded that the psalms are not metrical.[4] Even Gerstenberger admits that

> the material condition of our sources [due to oral development and scribal errors—fcp] and the lack of any reliable information make it altogether inadvisable to hope for clear-cut solutions. As Freedman observes, "no magic key has ever been found, or is likely to be."[5]

In sum, it seems appropriate to "delete meter as a category for understanding Hebrew poetry."[6] Text-critical footnotes and comments that appeal or refer to *m cs* ("for the sake of meter") without support from versions or manuscripts may safely be ignored.[7]

---

2. A further factor underlying the assumption that biblical poetry was metrical is the lexical rendering of the root שיר as either "song" or "sing," which leads Western scholars to assume a "singable" meter.

3. The *m cs* notation will not appear in *BHQ*.

4. Tremper Longman III, *How to Read the Psalms*. (Downers Grove, IL: IVP, 1988), 108.

5. Cited in Erhard S. Gerstenberger, "The Lyrical Literature," in *The Hebrew Bible and Its Modern Interpreters*, ed. Douglas A. Knight and Gene M. Tucker; *The Bible and Its Modern Interpreters*, ed. Douglas A. Knight, 1 (Chico, CA: Scholars Press, 1985), 413.

6. David L. Petersen and Kent Harold Richards, *Interpreting Hebrew Poetry* (Minneapolis, MN: Fortress, 1992), 42.

7. The last statement brings up the question of commentaries (articles, monographs, etc.). There is a reason for leaving them until last. If we begin by reading the commentaries, our interpretive agenda—the questions we ask, the answers we expect to find—will be set by their comments rather than by the text. Every commentator has his or her own set of questions, along with particular values, approach, and goals, which you may or may not share or find helpful. Because they represent a great deal of work of the type that we cannot undertake ourselves, use commentaries, but use them wisely. The fundamental rules of commentaries: (1) use them after studying the text yourself; (2) use the most technical commentaries that you find helpful; and (3) always use more than one, preferably at least three.

Appendix 2

Gloss, Meaning, and Translation

A gloss is a form of translation. Glosses listed in lexicons or on databases tend to reflect how words have been translated; they are *not* the word's "basic" or "central" or "real" meaning. Words have ranges of meaning and therefore may have more than one gloss; most of these, however, will be restricted to specific contexts.[1] The more limited a word's range of meaning, the more technical or specialized it is, and the more its content is determined by *what it refers to.* The broader a word's range of meaning, the more its content is determined by *its context.* The word "dog," for example, conveys less information than, or is less specific than, "black Labrador retriever," and so can fit a larger variety of contexts.

In addition to semantic range, words also have what might be called a "load," as in the expression "a *loaded* term." A word's "semantic load" refers to the combination of its *denotation* ("dictionary meaning") and *connotation* (associated emotive or implicit cultural function). In English, for example, "beefy," "chunky," "heavy," "solid," "big-boned," and "fat" could all refer to a person's body, but "solid" tends to be a compliment and "fat" an insult, even though "insult" is not part of the dictionary's definition of "fat."

When we compare languages, the more words' ranges overlap, the more they appear to mean the same thing. Since Biblical Hebrew is a textual language—there are no native speakers of Biblical Hebrew—we

1. The apparent exceptions are narrowly technical terms, whether medical (*pneumococcys*), mathematical (*cosine*), theological (*hypostatic union*), etc.

make educated guesses about the semantic range and connotations of words and phrases, verb tenses, etc., and how they correspond to English.

Consider, for example, this list of Hebrew terms with their usual English glosses, followed by other glosses that suggest a much broader range of meaning:

L.	"Basic" Gloss	Other glosses
אָב	father	ancestor, teacher/master (Elisha on seeing Elijah going up into the sky; 2 Kgs 2.12; cf. 2 Kgs 13.14)
אֹהֶל	tent	home, house
אָח	brother	male relative, someone belonging to the same "people"
אָחוֹת	sister	female relative
אֵם	mother	ancestress
בַּיִת	house	household
בֵּן	son	male descendant; polite address to a younger male ("my son"; 1 Sam 3:16)
בַּת	daughter	female descendant; polite address to a younger female ("my daughter"; Ruth 2:8)
מִשְׁפָּחָה	clan	[extended] family
שֵׁבֶט	tribe	rod, staff (symbol of authority?)

"Father," "son," "daughter," etc. are the usual glosses for these words because these Hebrew and English words usually have the same referent, but each of these Hebrew words may refer to relationships outside the nuclear family, whereas the usual English words almost always refer to parents and their children. The temptation is to think that the first gloss listed for each word is its "real" meaning and that other glosses are "paraphrasing," "extended," or "metaphorical." We may be tempted to think that all male relatives, for example, were considered brothers in our sense of the word,[2] but this is invalid. Nor do we (or can we) know

2. Lot is called Abraham's "brother's son" and David referred to his nephews as "sons of [his sister] Zeruiah," which suggests that Biblical Hebrew lacked a simple lexeme that meant what English means by "nephew." Both Biblical Hebrew and English can refer unambiguously

whether or not this was how they thought about these words. Note the words "son" and "bore" ("gave birth to") in these verses from the brief genealogy in Genesis 46:8–27:

> Now the *son* of Dan was Hushim, and the *sons* of Naphtali were Jazeel, Guni, Jezer, and Shillem; these are the *sons* of Bilhah, whom Laban gave to Rachel his daughter; and she *bore* these to Jacob, all seven lives. (Gen 46:23–25)

Consider the relationships called "son" in these verses ("sons" are in *italics*):

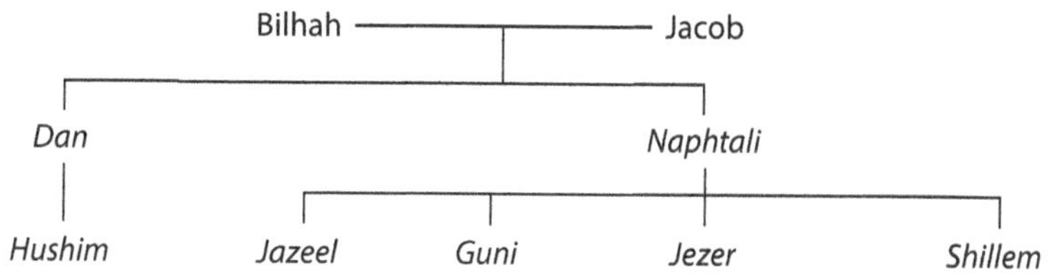

Hushim, Jazeel, Guni, Jezer, and Shillem were Bilhah's *grand*sons, which means that the Hebrew word בֵּן had a broader range of reference than the usual sense of "son." Nor can the function of the verb ילד, glossed "bear/give birth to," correspond to the usual English meaning of "give birth."[3]

Since in this case the semantic range of the usual English glosses is much more restricted than that of the Hebrew terms, the words "son" and "give birth" may be misleading in that they suggest closer genealogical and chronological relationships than the context allows.[4]

This warns us against confusing what Hebrew words refer to with the English words that we use to refer to them. English "son" is usually the most appropriate contextual gloss for Hebrew בֵּן, but this *does not mean* that בֵּן somehow "literally" or "basically" or "fundamentally" means "son,"

---

to a sibling's immediate offspring, but Biblical Hebrew seems to lack single words that have this function.

3. The same pattern describes the descendants of Jacob's other three wives (Gen 46:8–27), some of whom are called "mothers" of great-grandchildren.

4. On the other hand, English does use some of these terms generically—"son" and "daughter" can refer to a younger unrelated male or female, although this is not usual practice.

or even that it means the same thing as "son," but rather that two groups of language speakers have chosen these particular words to refer to what (usually) turns out to be the same thing.

There is another aspect to glossing terms, namely, that many words have connotations that are obvious to native speakers but are invisible to foreigners. Consider, for example, Zephaniah 2:1:

Zephaniah 2:1: Gloss

L.	BHS	Gloss
1a	הִתְקוֹשְׁשׁוּ	Gather yourselves!
1b	וָקוֹשּׁוּ הַגּוֹי לֹא נִכְסָף׃	Gather, unsought nation!

The lexica and versions gloss the root קשׁשׁ as "gather," and so we would be justified in seeing in these lines a call for the people of Judah to assemble, not unlike Moses's calling the Israelites to assemble. The root קשׁשׁ occurs only eight times in Biblical Hebrew, twice describing the Israelites gathering straw for bricks (Exod 5:7, 12),[5] four times someone gathering sticks for a cooking fire (Num 15:32–33; 1 Kgs 17:10, 12); and twice (here) ordering the people of Judah to assemble. Its uses in Biblical Hebrew, along with the contextual references to "chaff" (2a) and God's "hot anger" (2b), suggest that the prophet uses this root to imply that the people are to gather so that they can be burned up in judgment. This meaning, however, is implicit—a connotation—not part of the word's gloss and can only be discovered by studying its biblical occurrences or by referring to a good commentary or lexicon.

5. The verbal root rendered "gather" (קשׁשׁ) is related to the noun קַשׁ, "straw, stubble, chaff," which is almost always a metaphor referring to people who are going to be burned or driven away in judgment.

Scripture Index

Joshua

Judges

Ruth

1 Samuel

2 Samuel

1 Kings

2 Kings

Job

Psalms

Proverbs

Ecclesiastes

Jeremiah

Jonah

Zephaniah

Zechariah

Malachi

Subject Index

Author Index

Basics of Hebrew Discourse Video Lectures

Matthew H. Patton, Frederic Clarke Putnam, and Miles V. Van Pelt

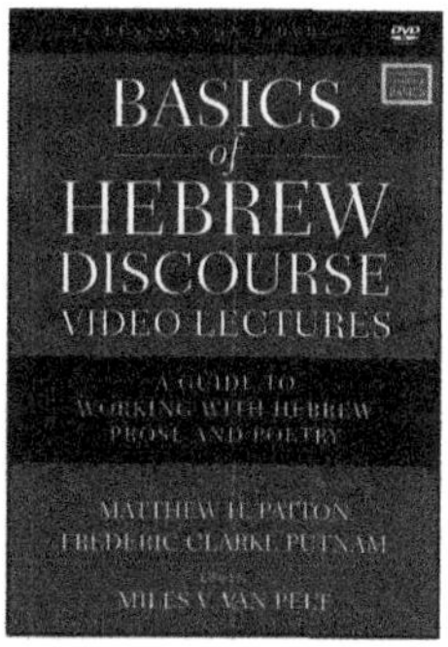

Basics of Hebrew Discourse Video Lectures, presented by Matthew H. Patton, Frederic Clarke Putnam, and Miles V. Van Pelt, is a syntax resource for intermediate Hebrew students. The lectures introduce students to the principles and exegetical benefits of discourse analysis (text linguistics) when applied to biblical Hebrew prose and poetry. Where standard Hebrew reference grammars have traditionally worked to describe the relationship between words and phrases within discrete clauses (micro syntax), discourse analysis works to describe those relationships that exist between clauses and texts (macro syntax).

These lectures fill a needed gap for intermediate Hebrew students and give them the tools to work with Hebrew syntax on the macro level. Professors and pastors working with Hebrew will also find this one-of-a-kind resource highly valuable.

Graded Reader of Biblical Hebrew, Second Edition

Miles V. Van Pelt and Gary D. Pratico

This is a must have resources for second-year Hebrew students, giving them the necessary practice to gain greater proficiency in using the language for exegesis and preaching.

The second edition of the *Graded Reader of Biblical Hebrew: A Guide to Reading the Hebrew Bible* by Miles V. Van Pelt and Gary D. Pratico is a structured introduction to the reading of biblical Hebrew texts. This book is the ideal next-step resource for the student who has completed a year of elementary Hebrew or the pastor or scholar whose language skills need some refreshing.

Through these readings, students will be able to review basic Hebrew grammar, become familiar with issues of intermediate grammar, and gain confidence in handling the Hebrew text. The readings chosen for inclusion, which are arranged generally in order of increasing difficulty, span the whole of the Old Testament and represent some of the most important Old Testament texts from the standpoint of biblical history, theology, and exegesis. Parsing exercises are included with each reading, and there is room for readers to write their own English translation. The many notes that accompany the text include information on:

- Grammar
- Exegetically significant constructions
- Vocabulary words
- Idioms
- Bibliographic information
- and much more.

A vital resource for those wanting to take the next step in learning biblical Hebrew, the *Graded Reader of Biblical Hebrew* guides students as they move beyond the basics and build competency in translating and exegeting the text of the Old Testament.

Biblical Hebrew: A Compact Guide, Second Edition

Miles V. Van Pelt

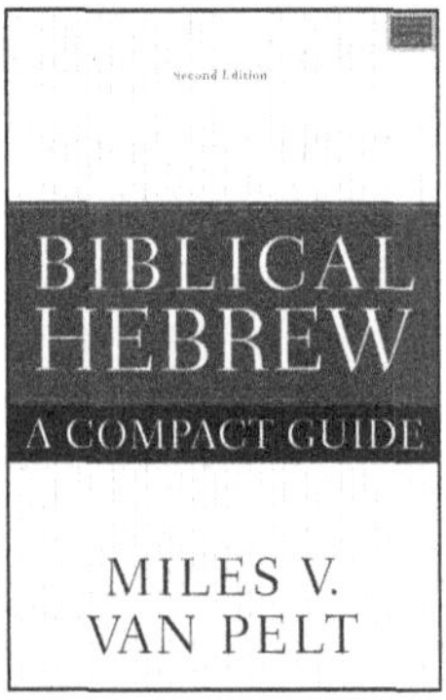

Biblical Hebrew: A Compact Guide, Second Edition by Miles V. Van Pelt is a handy, at-a-glance reference with summaries of Hebrew grammar, paradigms, lexicon, and more. This book is ideal for consulting during translation and exegesis work and aids Hebrew students at all levels by providing key language forms, word usage, and word meanings. This compact guide summarizes the most important information on biblical Hebrew grammar and has been updated to correspond to the third edition of *Basics of Biblical Hebrew Grammar.*

Biblical Hebrew Vocabulary in Context

Miles V. Van Pelt and Gary D. Pratico

Biblical Hebrew Vocabulary in Context by Miles V. Van Pelt and Gary D. Pratico is a biblical Hebrew language resource designed to reinforce a student's basic vocabulary by reading words that occur fifty times or more in the context of the Hebrew Bible. All 642 of these Hebrew words have been collated into 195 key biblical verses and/or verse fragments to help students practice and retain their Hebrew vocabulary. In lieu of rote memorization, *Biblical Hebrew Vocabulary in Context* reinforces essential vocabulary by reading words in the context of the Hebrew Bible. The book includes two primary sections. The first section provides room for students to write their own glosses of the biblical verse and to parse as they feel necessary. An English translation is also provided and any term that appears less than fifty times is glossed. Proper names are identified with gray text. The second section of the book provides the same biblical verses from the first section but with minimal room to write glosses and parse and without an English translation for aid. The end of the book includes a Hebrew-English lexicon of all the words occurring fifty times or more in the Hebrew Bible.

Available in stores and online!

ZONDERVAN®
.com